TARZAN™
ON FILM

SCOTT TRACY GRIFFIN
FOREWORD BY **CASPER VAN DIEN**

Dedicated to Lisa Gordon Wither

TARZAN ON FILM
ISBN 9780857685681

Published by Titan Books
A division of Titan Publishing Group Ltd
144 Southwark Street
London
SE1 0UP
United Kingdom

First edition: August 2016

2 4 6 8 10 9 7 5 3 1

Did you enjoy this book? We love to hear from our readers. Please e-mail us at:
readerfeedback@titanemail.com or write to Reader Feedback at the above address.

To receive advance information, news, competitions, and exclusive offers online,
please sign up for the Titan newsletter on our website: www.titanbooks.com

A CIP catalogue record for this title is available from the British Library.

Printed in China.

TARZAN
ON FILM

SCOTT TRACY GRIFFIN
FOREWORD BY **CASPER VAN DIEN**

TITANBOOKS

CONTENTS

006   **Foreword** - *Casper Van Dien*

008   **Whither the Ape Man?**

010   **1910s**
010   TARZAN OF THE APES (1918)
012   Elmo Lincoln
014   THE ROMANCE OF TARZAN (1918)
015   Enid Markey

016   **1920s**
016   THE REVENGE OF TARZAN (1920)
018   Gene Pollar & Karla Schramm
020   THE SON OF TARZAN (1920)
022   The Cast
024   THE ADVENTURES OF TARZAN (1921)
026   TARZAN AND THE GOLDEN LION (1927)
028   Jim Pierce & Dorothy Dunbar
030   TARZAN THE MIGHTY (1928)
032   Frank Merrill & Natalie Kingston
034   TARZAN THE TIGER (1929)

036   **1930s**
036   TARZAN THE APE MAN (1932)
040   TARZAN THE FEARLESS (1933)
042   Buster Crabbe & Jacqueline Wells
044   TARZAN AND HIS MATE (1934)
048   THE NEW ADVENTURES OF TARZAN (1935)
050   Herman Brix
052   TARZAN ESCAPES (1936)
054   A Cursed Production?
056   TARZAN AND THE GREEN GODDESS (1938)
057   Ula Holt
058   TARZAN'S REVENGE (1938)
060   Glenn Morris & Eleanor Holm

062   TARZAN FINDS A SON! (1939)
064   Tarzan in Florida

066   **1940s**
066   TARZAN'S SECRET TREASURE (1941)
068   Johnny Weissmuller
070   TARZAN'S NEW YORK ADVENTURE (1942)
072   Maureen O'Sullivan
074   TARZAN TRIUMPHS (1943)
076   Frances Gifford
078   TARZAN'S DESERT MYSTERY (1943)
080   Nancy Kelly
082   TARZAN AND THE AMAZONS (1945)
084   Brenda Joyce
086   TARZAN AND THE LEOPARD WOMAN (1946)
088   Acquanetta
090   TARZAN AND THE HUNTRESS (1947)
092   Johnny Sheffield
094   TARZAN AND THE MERMAIDS (1948)
096   Cheeta
098   TARZAN'S MAGIC FOUNTAIN (1949)
100   Lex Barker

102   **1950s**
102   TARZAN AND THE SLAVE GIRL (1950)
104   Vanessa Brown
106   TARZAN'S PERIL (1951)
108   Virginia Huston
110   TARZAN'S SAVAGE FURY (1952)
112   Dorothy Hart
114   TARZAN AND THE SHE-DEVIL (1953)
116   Joyce McKenzie
118   TARZAN'S HIDDEN JUNGLE (1955)
120   Gordon Scott

122 TARZAN AND THE LOST SAFARI (1957)
124   Betta St John
126 TARZAN'S FIGHT FOR LIFE (1958)
128   Eve Brent
130 TARZAN AND THE TRAPPERS (1958)
132 TARZAN'S GREATEST ADVENTURE (1959)
134   Sara Shane
136 TARZAN, THE APE MAN (1959)
138   Denny Miller & Joanna Barnes

140   1960s
140 TARZAN THE MAGNIFICENT (1960)
142 TARZAN GOES TO INDIA (1962)
144   Jock Mahoney
146 TARZAN'S THREE CHALLENGES (1963)
148 TARZAN AND THE VALLEY OF GOLD (1966)
150   Mike Henry & Nancy Kovack
152 TARZAN AND THE GREAT RIVER (1967)
154   Diana Millay
156 TARZAN AND THE JUNGLE BOY (1968)
156   Alizia Gur
158 TARZAN (1966-68)
160   Ron Ely

162   1970s
162 TARZAN'S DEADLY SILENCE (1970)
164 TARZAN'S JUNGLE REBELLION (1970)
166 TARZAN, LORD OF THE JUNGLE (1976-84)
168   Robert Ridgely

170   1980s
170 TARZAN, THE APE MAN (1981)
172   Miles O'Keeffe & Bo Derek
174 GREYSTOKE: THE LEGEND OF TARZAN,
    LORD OF THE APES (1983)

177   Christopher Lambert
179   Andie MacDowell
180 TARZAN IN MANHATTAN (1989)
182   Joe Lara & Kim Crosby

184   1990s
184 TARZAN (1991-94)
186   Wolf Larson & Lydie Denier
188 TARZAN: THE EPIC ADVENTURES (1996-97)
190   La of Opar
192 TARZAN AND THE LOST CITY (1998)
194   Casper Van Dien & Jane March
196 TARZAN (1999)
198   Tony Goldwyn & Minnie Driver

200   2000s
200 THE LEGEND OF TARZAN (2001-2003)
202   Michael T. Weiss
204 TARZAN & JANE (2002)
204   Olivia d'Abo
206 TARZAN (2003)
208   Travis Fimmel & Sarah Wayne Callies
210 TARZAN II (2005)

212   2010s
212 TARZAN (2013)
214   Kellan Lutz & Spencer Locke
216 THE LEGEND OF TARZAN (2016)
218   Alexander Skarsgård & Margot Robbie
220 TARZAN AND JANE (2016)

222   The Works of Edgar Rice Burroughs
223   Further Reading
224   Acknowledgements

FOREWORD *CASPER VAN DIEN*

I was thrilled and honored when my friend, Tarzan expert historian and author Scott Tracy Griffin, asked me to write the foreword to *Tarzan on Film*, his follow-up book to *Tarzan: The Centennial Celebration*. Tarzan has always meant a great deal to me, and the men of my family and Scott thought it would be nice to have a Tarzan write about his experience. So here are some of my memories of my time as the Lord of the Apes ...

My first experience as Tarzan was post-hernia operation at 12 years old. My parents told me that when I was coming out of anaesthesia the nurses had to strap me down because I tried to rip the drip out of my arm, proclaiming I was Tarzan, Lord of the Apes, King of the Jungle, and pounding my chest. Little did I know in this moment that I was having a premonition of what was to come when, years later, I was cast as the 20th Tarzan.

I am the only Tarzan who can say he rode on an actual African elephant in a Tarzan film (*Tarzan and the Lost City*). When we rode in during the scene, the extras who were playing the natives were supposed to run in terror, which they had no trouble doing since they were, in fact, terrified of the massive beast! The camera operator was on a cushion that had a strap underneath the belly of the elephant, stabilizing him and the camera, so he could get an over-the-shoulder shot of the natives running. During the first take, the strap got loose under the elephant's legs. This made the animal uncomfortable and it began to kick from side to side. The slipping cameraman started shouting, "I'm falling!" I had a good grip around the elephant with my legs, so I reached back with my right arm, grabbed the camera, and said, "Hold on to me," which he did, for dear life! The animal trainer came in, cut the strap, and calmed the elephant. By now, the natives had scattered in fear. The director said, "Thank God you saved the camera," to which the camera operator replied, "Forget *that*! You saved *me*. You will always be Tarzan to me."

On another rather interesting day, the second unit assistant director came to my trailer early one morning and said "Mr. Tarzan," (which was what most called me throughout filming) "Come quickly. We really need to get this shot." We drove up to a big fence with barbed wire on top. It looked like the chain to the lock had been cut but we drove through anyway. When we stopped and got out they pointed down to an area and said, "You're gonna run down there for about 100 yards through waist-high, yellow grass, past the cameras." I had on my loincloth and was carrying my bow and knife ... nothing else. When they called action, I started running. I was totally in character, full Tarzan mode, when I suddenly stepped into a hole, falling down and landing chest-deep, catching myself at my shoulders. I did a quick assessment, realizing nothing was broken, just some cuts and slight bleeding. I popped back up and finished my run. The show must go on. The camera guys were laughing and said, "That was so funny, you fell. We saw you go down and pop back up." I said, "Funny?" I walked over to the hole and said, "Look, I didn't just trip. I fell in a hole." I took my bow and showed them how deep it was and pointed out that there were five more holes in the clearing. One of the crew members yelled, "Tarzan, come back. Those are hyena dens. It's a good thing they weren't home." No one had warned me or even checked the clearing before asking talent to set. I later found out that production had cut the fence illegally and we had snuck into and were stealing the shot from Kruger National Park, home of not only the hyenas that were conveniently not at home, but also *lions*! The real kings of the jungle. I saw *The Lion King* and I know that lions sneak up on their prey in tall grass. Just like the grass I was running through. Needless to say, we only got one take of that scene.

Another moment I will never forget was during a scene with Jane and two elephants. They were supposed to walk off together, the big elephant followed by the little elephant (the size of a VW Bug), and we were to wave goodbye. The little elephant walked by and rubbed its head against me during the shot. I pushed its head to encourage it to follow the big elephant and this is when the elephant turned. Its ears went out and it made a loud trumpet huff. It backed up four steps and I yelled, "Jane, *run!*" She took off and the elephant charged and rammed me with its tusks in my stomach. I grabbed ahold of both its tusks, and it lifted me over its head like the *Dirty Dancing* scene, with the elephant playing the role of Johnny. It then slammed me down and backed up, preparing to charge again. At this point, I had had enough and climbed a boulder to safety as the animal trainer ran in to calm the elephant down. Later they explained to me that if you push a baby elephant's head, it will want to play. They love to butt heads. I have a big head, but ... if I hadn't grabbed the tusks they told me it would have run right over me.

I said, "Thanks for the heads up. Would have been nice to know beforehand. Now Mr. Tarzan will go change his loincloth!"

One final favorite memory I carry of this film occurred at the end of a long day of shooting, with me swimming in the muddy river waters where it was rumored that, the day before, someone had been eaten by a crocodile just one mile north of us. The crew was packing up and I was walking back to the trailers, in my loincloth. Wet, sweaty, dirty, bloody, and alone. This is when I saw them, five Harley guys next to their bikes, drinking beers. They were all taller, meaner, and tougher-looking than me. One had a shotgun on his bike and another one had a pistol in his belt. They were all staring me down. I heard one yell to me, "Hey you!" I tried to pretend it wasn't directed at me, until he clearly said, "Hey you, in the loincloth." I turned, filled with dread, imagining the headline: "Tarzan

Found Dead In Africa". The leader said, deadpan, "You the guy playing Tarzan?" Normally this is where I throw in something sarcastic like, "I'm in a loincloth, carrying a knife, what do you think?" but something instinctually came over me and I just said, "Yeah ..." as my voice cracked. He grabbed my hand, shaking it, so excited. He said, "Oh man, you make a great Tarzan. You are all cut up! Could I get an autograph for my son?" I was looking for the hidden cameras. Nope, this was real. I said, "Sure," and signed my first autograph as Tarzan.

I hope you enjoyed these stories. I loved being the 20th Tarzan. As a child, my playground was the jungle and, as Tarzan, the African jungle was my playground. Such a dream come true. It was the role of a lifetime. I'm excited to turn this page and continue the journey with Scott Tracy Griffin's *Tarzan on Film*.

WHITHER THE APE MAN?

Ask almost anyone the world over, "Who is Tarzan?" and they will probably be able to give you some sort of capsule biography of one of the planet's most famous fictional heroes: a child raised by apes to become a jungle superman, who later rescued (and romanced, after a fashion) the city-bred Jane; the author of a mighty cry that summons animals and strikes terror into the hearts of evildoers.

This isn't far off the mark of the pulp fiction hero who appeared in the October 1912 magazine *The All-Story* story *Tarzan of the Apes*, penned by Edgar Rice Burroughs. The literary Tarzan was an English lord, orphaned in the jungles of West Africa and raised to manhood by the great ape tribe that adopted him, whose first encounter with civilized men included a beautiful young woman who became his wife. Here, the story diverges from public perception, as Tarzan's love for Jane Porter lures him out of the jungle, into the world of men, which he also conquers on his own terms. No grunting, monosyllabic,

unwashed Tarzan this! The Tarzan of the novels taught himself to read from books in his parents' log cabin, learned to speak numerous languages, including French, English, German, Arabic, Dutch and a host of African dialects, and reclaimed his hereditary title as Lord Greystoke over the span of 24 novels. After a decade in the House of Lords, he returned to Africa, but it was as an even more powerful force—a man who could now read Latin and take his coffee black while battling lions and crocodiles with just a knife and his teeth.

* * * *

Tarzan's fortunes have ebbed and flowed over the past century. Just when a jaded public is ready to cast off the ape man as a product of a previous age, he springs back to life in a new incarnation, usually cinematic, as a Western-style vigilante hero, a sophisticated world traveler and troubleshooter, a British drawing-room tragedy, or an animated blockbuster from Walt Disney Studios.

With both the release of the 52nd film *and* seventh television series in 2016, the ape man shows he's just as relevant as ever—a primal force that taps into the zeitgeist of any age. Even when he's bad, he's good—Tarzan films that were critically excoriated, like 1918's *The Romance of Tarzan* or the 1981 *Tarzan the Ape Man* remake, still set financial standards. During the deadly influenza epidemic of 1918, excited picture house owners and exhibitors wrote glowing testimonials to the drawing power of the quickie sequel to *Tarzan of the Apes*, which set house records across the land. Metro-Goldwyn-Mayer executives laughed all the way to the bank when the Dereks' derided film starting breaking records for the venerable studio.

* * * *

Tarzan reigned for decades as the most profitable film franchise in history, a juggernaut whose financial windfall would not be surpassed until *Greystoke*, in its early stages, became mired in development hell and James Bond took over in the 1970s as the new champ—only to be dethroned a few years later by Jedi knights and boy wizards and superheroes in spandex. Yet how soon they forget. Tarzan isn't even acknowledged on modern lists of the most successful franchises in history.

In some measure, this is because independent producer Sol Lesser held the financial records tightly to his chest during his 25-year reign that led to 16 films. The canny Lesser loved to leak tidbits to the press that circled him and Burroughs, begging for a snippet of information about their successful operation. Lesser noted that 75 percent of his films' gross came from overseas, where Tarzan was even more popular than the

U.S., eagerly anticipated by Bedouins and Bushmen, and avidly watched by gauchos wherever they could hang a sheet and crank up a projector. But with no stockholders to appease, Lesser could keep his books to himself.

In 1944, the *New York Times* revealed that author Burroughs was earning $150–175,000 on his 20 percent royalties for the one-page synopses he provided to Lesser, making him the highest-paid author in Hollywood—a town that even the esteemed William Faulkner and F. Scott Fitzgerald couldn't conquer in such decisive fashion.

From Tarzan's appearance on the big screen in 1918 until his temporary retreat in the 1970s, there were 40 Tarzan films released in 50 years, with the longest gap between films six years (1921–27). Edgar Rice Burroughs suggested that a Tarzan film should be an annual event, just like the circus, and producers like Lesser delivered. In 1958, producer Sy Weintraub noted that no Tarzan film had ever lost money (as he teased the rights from Lesser's hands for $3 million). Weintraub went on to break more franchise records with films like *Tarzan Goes to India* and *Tarzan's Three Challenges*, each more profitable than the last.

When Tarzan left the cinemas, it wasn't because attendance at his films was lacking. Like an athlete retiring at his peak, the ape man went out on a high note, still drawing theater goers . . . before springing back into action with the box-office success of *Tarzan the Ape Man* in 1981 and the critical acclaim (and Academy Award nominations) of *Greystoke: The Legend of Tarzan, Lord of the Apes*, and Disney's *Tarzan*.

Tarzan hasn't gone anywhere. He's still there. Watching. Waiting. Ready to pounce on an unsuspecting public and delight them.

In the meantime, enjoy his previous 50-plus incarnations on the big and small screen, or the 24 novels. They're all there on DVD, in print, online, or on whatever 21ˢᵗ century platform you like. Then try to withhold that ape cry after watching a few of these.

I dare you.

Opposite: Author Edgar Rice Burroughs (1875–1950) as a young man.

Top left: Tarzan's first appearance in the October 1912 *All-Story* magazine, cover art by Clinton Pettee.

Top right: Director W.S. "Woody" Van Dyke confers with Burroughs and leading man Johnny Weissmuller on the set of MGM's *Tarzan the Ape Man* in 1931.

Middle: 1966 Tarzan screen actor reunion at Churubusco Studios, Mexico: Jock Mahoney (1962–63), Johnny Weissmuller (1932–48), Ron Ely (1966–68), and Jim Pierce (1927).

Bottom: Tarzan and Jane screen actor reunion at the 1975 centennial of Burroughs' birth. Front row: Louise Lorraine (1921), Joyce MacKenzie (1953), Eve Brent (1958), Karla Schramm (1920), and Vanessa Brown (1950). Back row: Jim Pierce (1927), Jock Mahoney (1962–63), Johnny Weissmuller (1932–48), and Denny Miller (1959).

TARZAN OF THE APES *1918*

Lord and Lady Greystoke (True Boardman and Kathleen Kirkham) are stranded in the jungle with their baby son, until attacking apes kill them and adopt their child. As Tarzan (Gordon Griffith) reaches childhood, sailor Binns (George B. French) takes refuge in the Greystoke cabin, teaching him basic English. Binns carries word to England, where Lord Greystoke's dissipated brother's child Cecil (Colin Kenny), has assumed Tarzan's hereditary title. Binns finally musters a search party, which includes Jane (Enid Markey) and her father (Thomas Jefferson). It is love at first sight for Tarzan (Elmo Lincoln), now a man, who must rescue Jane from lions and an abducting native (Rex Ingram).

Tarzan of the Apes' film debut was an auspicious event, with the novel's adaptation becoming one of the first six silent films to earn more than $1 million, selling out theaters across the nation.

On June 16, 1916, Edgar Rice Burroughs sold a film option for his popular 1912 story *Tarzan of the Apes* to William "Smiling Bill" Parsons of the National Film Corporation of America for $5,000 in cash as an advance against royalties, $50,000 in stock and five percent of the gross receipts.

Parsons claimed that this was a record price paid "for film rights on any story" and that this was only possible due to the advance publicity of the nine printings of the Tarzan novels, which had sold 600,000 copies and had been serialized in newspapers nationwide. Burroughs had been pitching the film to producers for two years, but most shied away from it, concerned that a leading man battling apes and lions hand-to-fang couldn't be filmed convincingly.

Parsons raised the venture capital from a Wyoming cattlemen's association and settled into the old Oz studios on Gower Street in Hollywood for pre-production. Child actor Gordon Griffith was cast as the young Tarzan, with Stellan Windrow, a Chicago athlete, as the adult ape man.

The film was directed by Scott Sidney, a veteran of Inceville, who had previously worked with ingénue Enid Markey, and recruited her for the Jane role. Journalist William E. Wing's script was discarded in favor of one by Lois Weber and Fred Miller, with Parsons and crew going off-book to improvise some scenes.

In August, cast and crew boarded a train ferrying five boxcars full of equipment to shoot on location for nine weeks outside Morgan City, Louisiana, in the Atchafalaya River Basin, the largest swamp in North America. When leading man Windrow departed the shoot for military service, the burly Elmo Lincoln was hired to replace him.

The shoot was timed before the sugar cane harvest so the idled workers could portray natives for $1.75 per day. The crew battled chiggers, mosquitoes, disease, and Lincoln's body hair, which grew back so quickly he had to be shaved twice a day.

E.M. Jahraus, former head of the Universal Studios property department, designed 30 ape suits, made from brown goat skins prepared at a tannery in the studio. The suits included masks sporting "an ingenious arrangement of wires" so that the actors could grimace realistically. Eight acrobats were hired to portray the apes, supplemented by 20 gymnasts from the New Orleans YMCA.

Upon their return to Hollywood, the crew shot in Griffith Park, on a yacht in San Pedro, at the E & R Jungle Film Company, and at National Film Studios. Lincoln later claimed that he killed the lion Old Charlie with a sharpened bayonet in their battle, but any footage that might prove or disprove his claim has been lost.

The film debuted at the Broadway Theatre in New York City on Sunday evening, January 27, 1918, at $2 per ticket. With half of the house reserved for industry patrons, the premiere turned away hundreds of ticket-seekers. The following day, the admission line was a block long. Box office receipts on Monday were $2,100, and even greater on Wednesday, with the greatest advance-ticket sales in the venue's history. The film ran seven weeks through the April 2 nationwide release.

Despite receiving an engraved invitation from publicity man Harry Reichenbach, Burroughs boycotted the premiere, unhappy in his dealings with Parsons. He sold his $50,000 in stock for $5,000 and never received any promised royalties beyond his advance. When he finally saw the film in June, he liked it "immensely".

The film's 10 reels, running 130 minutes, were cut to eight for national release. Only 61 minutes of the original footage survive today, approximately five reels' worth.

> *"Do you remember how you sat up most of the night to finish your first real adventure story? Well, it's better than that! And do you remember your first love story? Well, it's better than that!"*
>
> – Chicago Tribune, May 15, 1918

NATIONAL FILM
CORP'N OF AMERICA
PRESENTS
The Wonder Story
of the Age
=

TARZAN OF THE APES

BY EDGAR RICE BURROUGHS

1000 PEOPLE 1000

A First National Attraction

ELMO LINCOLN

Elmo Lincoln tried a variety of stage names, earning credits as Lincoln Helt, Otto Elmo Linkenhelt, Otto Lincoln, and Oscar Linkenhelt, before his name was immortalized as Elmo Lincoln, the first film Tarzan.

Lincoln was born Otto Elmo Linkenhelt on February 6, 1889 in Rochester, Indiana, to businessman Louis R. and his wife Eldora. After gaining some stage experience in local theater, Lincoln worked his way west, serving as a deputy sheriff and locomotive engineer on his journey to California. There, he worked as a dockhand, sailor, and boxer, before one of D.W. Griffith's scouts discovered him lifeguarding at the area later famed as Muscle Beach.

Lincoln debuted in Griffith's Western short, *The Battle at Elderbush Gulch* (1913) as a cavalry sergeant, where his 53-inch chest caught the director's eye. He became a member of Griffith's stock company, with roles in *Birth of a Nation* (1915), *Intolerance* (1916), and *The Kaiser, the Beast of Berlin* (1918).

Lincoln tested for the Tarzan role by climbing a telephone pole guy wire. When original hire Stellan Windrow left the project, Lincoln was hired at $100 per day, a raise from his $75 per day salary with Griffith. Concerned that a leopard skin evoked the circus strongman cliché, he chose a wolf skin as his wardrobe.

After reprising the role in *The Romance of Tarzan*, Lincoln wrote to Edgar Rice Burroughs, suggesting they partner to produce more films, but the author declined. When he couldn't persuade Griffith to shoot a Tarzan picture, Lincoln signed a contract with Universal Studios to star in two serials and two features. Afterward, he returned to the ape man role in *The Adventures of Tarzan*.

During filming of the low-budget Rayart serial *King of the Jungle* (1927), Lincoln's friend Gordon Standing was killed by a lion on set, leading a shaken Lincoln to retire from film for a time. He invested in silver mines in Mexico and ran a junkyard salvage operation in Nevada. In 1939, he returned to Hollywood, but only received bit parts, including silent roles in *Tarzan's New York Adventure* and *Tarzan's Magic Fountain*. In 1950, he toured with the Seals Floto Circus, riding an elephant as "The Original Tarzan". Acrobat and Tarzan fan Vernell Coriell stood outside the tent and gave the ape cry to introduce Lincoln, who had never mastered the cry in his silent days.

Lincoln's three wives included Sadie Whited, Edith M. Coules, and Ida Lee Tanchick, with whom he had his only child, daughter Marci'a Eldora Lincoln. He died unexpectedly of a heart attack on the morning of June 27, 1952, in his small rented apartment near the former studio headquarters of *Tarzan of the Apes*.

Top left: The sailor Binns (George B. French) warns Lord and Lady Greystoke (True Boardman and Kathleen Kirkham) that a mutiny is brewing aboard their ship.

Top right: Lincoln's Tarzan learns to read.

Opposite top: Jane (Enid Markey) and Tarzan (Elmo Lincoln) have a jungle idyll.

Opposite middle left: Tarzan confronts the invaders of his parents' cabin.

Opposite bottom left: Esmerelda (Madame Sul-te-wan), Jane (Markey) and Tarzan (Lincoln).

Opposite bottom right: Elmo Lincoln returned to the franchise for *The Romance of Tarzan* (1918) and *The Adventures of Tarzan* (1921).

THE ROMANCE OF TARZAN *1918*

As the Porter party prepares to depart Africa, cannibals attack. Cecil (Colin Kenny), jealous of Tarzan's prowess and hoping to retain the Greystoke inheritance, convinces the castaways that Tarzan (Elmo Lincoln) has been killed in battle. They return to San Francisco, but Tarzan follows them. There, Cecil continues his machinations, inciting the dance-hall queen La Belle Ondine (Cleo Madison) to seduce Tarzan. Jane (Enid Markey) is distraught, and leaves Tarzan, who returns to his jungle. Stricken by conscience, Ondine confesses the plot, and Jane follows Tarzan back to the jungle where they are reunited.

> *"Elmo Lincoln is the Tarzan and makes the figure a powerful one physically as well as giving a likable character study."*
> – Exhibitor's Trade Review, October 26, 1918

On March 31, 1918, *Variety* reported that a sequel to *Tarzan of the Apes*, titled *The Marriage of Tarzan*, would be produced by William Parsons' National Film Corporation. Production began the following month, but Burroughs was not informed until he read it in Kitty Kelly's *Chicago Examiner* column in May.

The film re-teamed Lincoln and Markey and resumed their story as Tarzan pursues Jane to America. Colin Kenny's opposition to their love continues, aided by actress and pioneering filmmaker Cleo Madison in a vamp role, and Monte Blue as the heavy. A prologue recounted the first film's plot, incorporating footage of Lord and Lady Greystoke in Africa and Tarzan's childhood among the apes.

Parsons built nine sets on the National Film stages, including a saloon 138 feet long, with a staircase on which Tarzan fights a band of assailants, and a giant 60' x 20' tank, 12 feet deep, adorned with a waterfall and filled with 40 residents of the Los Angeles Alligator Farm. Outdoor scenes were filmed at Modjeska Ranch in Southern California; coastal and maritime scenes were shot in San Pedro. The film was helmed by actor and director Wilfred Lucas, from a script by his wife Bess Meredyth, an experienced scenarist who later wrote continuity for the silent-film blockbuster *Ben Hur: A Tale of the Christ* (1925).

Burroughs, unhappy that he was not informed of the production, obtained a court injunction against the film's release until Parsons (who cannily claimed that the film was an adaptation of the second half of the novel he had optioned) paid the author $2,500. The movie, running 96 minutes in seven reels, premiered at New York's Strand Theater on October 14, 1918. The film did not achieve the commercial and popular success of its predecessor. Publicist Harry Reichenbach attributed this to Parsons' unwillingness to spend additional money on promotions or publicity; instead, he staged a contest for exhibitors, offering a total of $1,200 in Liberty Bonds for the most creative promotional campaigns.

> *"Tarzan has the jungle idea of right and justice down to a fine degree. It is a joy to watch him put it into practice."*
> – Motion Picture News, October 26, 1918

ENID MARKEY

After debuting the screen role of Jane Porter in *Tarzan of the Apes*, busy ingénue Enid Markey left the film industry and moved to New York to try her luck on Broadway. She became a successful stage actress, perhaps the first to leave cinema for the stage.

Enid Virginia Markey was born on February 22, 1893 in Dillon, Colorado, to mine and livery stable owner John, and his wife Catherine. She began began acting in local stock productions before graduating from East High School. After her father's death, Markey and her mother set out for California. Landing in San Diego, Markey appeared in a pair of short films for Bison: *The Colonel's Ward* and *The Restoration*. When the company folded, she and her mother moved to Los Angeles, where Enid trod the boards in an Oliver Morosco production.

Enid began working for director Thomas Ince at Inceville, appearing as the leading lady for stars like cowboy actor William S. Hart. Among her early directors was Scott Sidney, who decided she would be the perfect Jane when he was hired to direct *Tarzan of the Apes*; she returned to the role for the sequel, *The Romance of Tarzan.*

Markey turned down the offer of a five-term contract to reprise the Jane role, and moved to New York. She preferred the intimacy of the stage, and hearing the laughter and applause as she performed. "I was tired of making faces," she said of the silent film acting technique. "I really wanted to learn how to act."

In New York, she immediately signed with manager Al H. Woods, and won the lead in *Up in Mabel's Room* in 1919. She appeared in numerous Broadway plays, and summer stock in the off-season. Markey returned to the big screen to reprise her stage role as Aunt Emily in *Snafu* (1945) for Columbia. Her final film appearances include *Take One False Step* (1949) and *The Boston Strangler* (1968).

Markey married George Watson "Ty" Cobb, Jr., an executive with the American Can Company, on October 15, 1942. The two resided at the Algonquin Hotel until his death on March 14, 1948.

Markey guest-starred on radio and in television, and co-starred on the show *Bringing Up Buddy* (1960–61). She also had memorable turns as Barney Fife's landlady, Mrs. Mendelbright, on *The Andy Griffith Show* and as Gomer's Grandma Pyle on *Gomer Pyle, U.S.M.C.*

Markey died on November 15, 1981 in Long Island, New York, after a series of heart attacks. Despite a six-decade career on stage, and in television and film, she is still best remembered today by many as Jane.

THE REVENGE OF TARZAN *1920*

In France, Tarzan (Gene Pollar) befriends the Count De Coude (George Romain) and his wife the Countess (Estelle Taylor), while exposing the villainous cardsharp Rokoff (Armand Cortez) and his henchman Polawitch (Walter Miller). Tarzan foils their plot to kill him, and accepts a diplomatic assignment to Algeria from his friend Paul D'Arnot (Franklin B. Coates). After some adventures there, where he rescues a young woman menaced by a lion, he pursues Rokoff's henchman, bound for South Africa. Tossed overboard his ship off the African coast, Tarzan swims ashore and resumes his wild life. Later, he is reunited with a shipwrecked Jane (Karla Schramm), whom he saves from a lion.

In an August 5, 1918 letter, Edgar Rice Burroughs opened negotiations with producer Pliny P. Craft on an option on the second Tarzan novel, *The Return of Tarzan*, signing a contract with terms similar to those of his deal with William Parsons. Burroughs described his ideal Tarzan in a letter to Craft, and suggested the film be titled *Tarzan of the Jungle*, sub-titled *The Return of Tarzan*.

Craft was furious when Parsons' impromptu sequel, *The Romance of Tarzan*, was released, fearing it infringed his storyline of Tarzan's venture into civilization. Craft sent an angry letter to Parsons at National Film, who paid him $3,000—then cheekily asked Burroughs to reimburse him.

Meanwhile, Elmo Lincoln wrote to Burroughs in 1918, suggesting that they partner to produce more Tarzan films. Burroughs declined; Elmo was not *his* conception of the ape man. Lincoln's Tarzan aspirations were further disrupted when Universal offered him a contract for two features and two serials.

With Lincoln now under contract to Universal, a new Tarzan was needed. Craft sold his contract to the Weiss Brothers of New York, who formed Numa Pictures Corporation and cast local fireman, Joseph C. Pohler, as Tarzan, with concert pianist Karla Schramm as Jane. Harry Revier directed from a script by Robert Saxmar, with George M. Merrick producing. Franklin B. Coates, who had accompanied the 1913–15 Captain J. Campbell Besley expeditions to shoot documentaries in the Amazon jungle, was retained as a technical advisor, and played D'Arnot. The film shot in a Yonkers studio and a palatial home in Lakewood, New York, in late 1919, with exteriors shot in Florida and California. Fifty tons of palms, banana plants, and other tropical verdure were hauled into place in Balboa, by Charley the elephant. "Aeroplane photography" was incorporated to capture the desert vistas and Pollar's travel high through the treetops.

Pollar wrestled a lion trained to play dead after being "killed" by the actor's bare hands. Co-stars included Vivendi the lion, Joe Martin the ape, and Charley, from the Universal menagerie. Additional animals included 50 white horses, two camels, and "five determined old mules who caused directorial upset".

Ten days were devoted to filming the scenes with the ocean liner, yacht, and lifeboat. Co-star Armand Cortez, who had taken his violin along for accompaniment, was too seasick to play for the cast and crew. A poor swimmer, he nearly drowned when the lifeboat capsized, until Revier noticed him and directed a cameraman to pull him out of the ocean.

The film, with full orchestral accompaniment, was previewed for Burroughs and an audience of 900, at the Superba Theatre in Los Angeles on March 5. "You have given my story a remarkable production, and what pleases me most is the faithfulness with which you have followed the original narrative," commented the author in *The Moving Picture World*. "I have no criticism, and am very proud to be identified with the offering."

The film previewed on May 30, 1920 at the Broadway Theatre, opening for the general public the following day, three weeks before general release. It ran in a sell-out engagement for four weeks.

Harry Reichenbach, who had successfully ballyhooed Parsons' *Tarzan of the Apes* into a blockbuster, handled publicity by registering as timber magnate Mr. T.R. Zann at the Belleclaire Hotel on May 23, a week before the opening of the film. He had a large piano case delivered to his room, and ordered 15 pounds of raw meat from the bellboy. When the bellboy questioned the request, Reichenbach showed him Jim, a caged lion, which caused a ruckus (the hotel owner, a friend, assisted in the stunt). At popular demand, Mr. Zann appeared at the Broadway Theatre with Jim as a pre-show prologue, with the cat devouring several pounds of meat for the audience's edification. Trainer Walter Beckwith, whom Burroughs had referred to the film, provided the lion for the stunt.

On April 28, 1920, the Weiss Brothers sold worldwide rights to Samuel Goldwyn for a $100,000 advance and a percentage of the box office. Goldwyn released a 16-page pressbook with a color cover of Tarzan grappling a lion, a rare investment in those days. Two elephants paraded through the streets of downtown Los Angeles promoting the film's debut at the California Theatre. Goldwyn reported record-breaking advances for overseas distribution rights to the picture.

In July, Goldwyn cut the nine reels to seven and retitled the film *The Revenge of Tarzan*, concerned over reports that exhibitors were confusing the title with a re-release of the Lincoln pictures. Burroughs was unhappy with the name change, since he wanted to drive book sales of *Return*.

017

GENE POLLAR

Today, fireman Gene Pollar might seem an unusual choice to play Tarzan, but he was renowned in New York City for his athletic prowess in local events, and was game to wrestle lions for $100 per week, which made him an ideal candidate.

Joseph Charles Pohler was born to second-generation German immigrants on September 16, 1892, and reared in the Yorkville area of Manhattan. After graduating from high school, he worked as an auto mechanic before passing exams for both the city police and fire departments. He chose the fire department because it offered retirement after 20 years of service, versus 25 for the police force. He served two years in the army during World War I before resuming his career with Hook and Ladder Company 20.

Pollar was an excellent athlete, playing on the fire department's handball and basketball teams, and winning the 100-yard dash at the annual city police–fireman competition. He was also a member of the Hudson Boat Club's championship rowing team.

Lounging in his station-house bunk one day, he was called into the office, where he was asked to screen test for Tarzan; he thought he was being hoaxed, but traveled to the Yonkers studio anyway. There he tossed about other actors and wooed actresses, while his wife Ottilie took a studio tour. *The Moving Picture World* noted, "He is a New York boy, and is a remarkable specimen of manhood. In recent tests of physical endurance and qualifications, he passed 100 per cent."

When he was offered the role, he took a leave of absence from his job (which paid $1,000 per year) to accept. He adopted Gene as a stage name, after his only son Eugene, who died at age five of a spinal ailment.

Pollar stood 6'2½", weighed 215 pounds, and was a non-smoker and non-drinker. He wrestled a lion on set for two scenes, supervised by trainer Charles Gay with his .38 pistol. Director Harry Revier noted, "He is a big, unspoiled boy. Doesn't think he's great, enjoys his work; and my—how he can fight! He wades in and does every fight up to the finish." In one scene, Pollar had to make a 25-foot dive fully clothed, then shed his formal clothing and shoes in the water. While filming at sea, cameraman James Hutchison was swept from the deck of the ship, and Pollar dived in and retrieved him.

Perhaps hoping to repeat the success they'd had casting Elmo Lincoln in serials, Universal offered Pollar a two-year contract for $350 a week to make more Tarzan pictures. Pollar eagerly acceded, but the Weiss brothers refused to release him from his contract. As a compromise, they offered him to Universal for $800 a week, $700 of which they would pocket. Disgusted, Pollar left the film industry for good, returning to the fire department.

He took his retirement from the department in 1944 and began working as a purchasing agent for two Manhattan retail chains for the next 15 years. In 1959, he and Ottilie retired to Hollywood, Florida, for the climate. Pollar died October 20, 1971, one month after his 79th birthday, when he suffered a heart attack following surgery. He was survived by second wife Kate.

KARLA SCHRAMM

Karla Schramm portrayed Jane twice, opposite Gene Pollar in *The Revenge of Tarzan* and P. Dempsey Tabler in the serial *The Son of Tarzan*. Schramm was discovered by director D.W. Griffith while appearing in a crowd scene, and cast in a small role in *Broken Blossoms* (1919), starring Lillian Gish. She also had an uncredited role in *His Majesty, the American* (1919), starring Douglas Fairbanks. Following her Tarzan film roles, she returned to her first love, music.

Schramm was born February 1, 1891 in the Los Angeles suburbs to Carl F.W. Schramm and his wife Helene. Around this time the Schramms gifted their oldest daughter, Paloma, aged four, with a piano, soon discovering that she was a child prodigy who wrote her own compositions. Both girls were given private lessons, and became proficient enough to embark on a five-year tour throughout the U.S., landing in Chicago to complete their formal education.

Bitten by the acting bug, Karla returned to Hollywood, but soon left acting and spent the rest of her life studying, performing, and teaching piano, as an associate with the Thilo Becker School in Los Angeles. She avoided the limelight until she resurfaced in 1975 at a reunion of Tarzan and Jane film actors.

Schramm died on January 17, 1980, just short of her 89th birthday. She was cremated and her remains were strewn over the garden of her Los Angeles-area home.

Opposite left: Gene Pollar and Karla Schramm as Tarzan and Jane.

Opposite right: *Tarzan's Revenge* was fireman Gene Pollar's only film.

Top right: Real-life adventurer Franklin B. Coates provided technical assistance on the film's jungle sequences and played Tarzan's friend D'Arnot.

Top left: Pollar leads an unenthusiastic Joe Martin in an ape-call singalong.

Bottom right: Overwhelmed by her near-death-by-lion experience, Jane swoons.

THE SON OF TARZAN *1920*

Tarzan (P. Dempsey Tabler) and Jane (Karla Schramm) have left the jungle to live in England as Lord and Lady Greystoke. Their son Jack (Gordon Griffith) befriends the ape Akut, Tarzan's former companion, now a music-hall attraction. The two flee to Africa, where Jack rescues a young girl (Mae Giraci) from a cruel Arab sheik. With Akut, the pair grow to maturity in the jungle as Korak the Killer (Kamuela Searle) and Meriem (Manilla Martan). When Tarzan's old enemy Paulovitch (Eugene Burr) arrives, the couple's budding love and lives are endangered—but the ape man and his mate haven't given up on their son, and have committed their lives to finding him.

Upon William Parsons' untimely death from kidney failure at age 41 on September 28, 1919, Harry M. Rubey assumed control of National Film Corporation and immediately began negotiating for rights to Burroughs' fourth ape-man novel, *The Son of Tarzan*. The author signed a contract for a 15-chapter serial on November 14, 1919, for $20,000 against his royalty.

Western star Jack Hoxie of the "Lighting Bryce" films, and Rubey's wife Lucille were announced as leads. House Peters, Sr. was initially announced to play Tarzan, with Kenneth Nordyke as Korak at age 15. The serial was to be shot on a South Seas island for atmosphere, with natives furnishing "local color" and transport via the fast yacht *The Star of the East.*

Director Harry Revier from *The Revenge of Tarzan* returned, with Arthur J. Flaven also helming, from a script by Roy Somerville which followed Burroughs' novel more faithfully than most of the Tarzan film adaptations.

Plans to film in the South Pacific were scrapped, with a different cast eventually taking the principal roles. The company had difficulty casting the adult role of Meriem, requiring a beautiful woman with a good figure who was athletic and comfortable in the abbreviated costume of animal skins. After the first two chapters had been filmed and screened, unknown Manilla Martan was cast.

National Film acquired three vacant acres next to the studio to construct a "gigantic jungle set". Scenes were also shot at Burroughs' home on Tarzana Ranch, in the San Bernardino Mountains, and on the Pico Rivera river bottom (now Woodland Park). The San Francisco Embacadero passed for London's waterfront.

Two boats were purchased for the film; Rodgers Bros built the *Lady Alice*, a replica of their yacht *Comfort* (a popular film prop), to be dynamited, burned, and sunk. Before the scene was filmed, real-life pirates slipped aboard both ships and stripped them of their valuables.

Kamuela Searle was injured by an elephant when it dropped a tree trunk to which he was tied; according to Burroughs, the tree trunk broke and Searle was hospitalized, but he did not die from his injuries as was later reported. Tabler and Burr did not escape unscathed, either; both cracked ribs in a fight scene on set.

While Burroughs and daughter Joan were observing the production, a young, nervous lion jumped out of its enclosure, stalked past them as they froze, then jumped back into the enclosure and scrambled underneath a camera on a tripod as the operator gingerly lifted it out of the beast's way. Another lion escaped and roamed a wooded area for several hours. As the company searched for the cat, a small child cried that he'd found the lion. Tabler saw the cat stalking the boy and charged it with "a war whoop that would have put Tarzan himself to shame," scaring the lion off, Burroughs later recalled. When Rubey presented Burroughs' sons with lion cubs for Christmas in 1920, Burroughs wisely re-gifted them to a trainer.

The serial filmed from June 1920 to January 1921, releasing the first chapter in December 1921. By Revier's estimate, the serial cost $106,000 and grossed $176,000 in three months. Howells Sales Company agreed to release it as a feature, so Burroughs spent four weeks in his Tarzana ballroom theater editing the 1923 film *Jungle Trail of the Son of Tarzan* from the serial. Following the release of *Son*, National Film Corporation's assets were seized by the government for "tax difficulties", and the company went out of business.

> **"The Son of Tarzan constitutes the best animal novelty picture ever offered exhibitors."**
> *- Exhibitors Trade Review*, November 13, 1920

THE CAST

The *Son of Tarzan* offered an unconventional scenario for a Tarzan film, since it followed the ape man's son, Jack Clayton, from boyhood to manhood. Author Edgar Rice Burroughs recalled it as a "hectic experience for all concerned", and the casting reflected this, with several actors announced for roles before the final cast was hired. Karla Schramm (*Revenge of Tarzan*) reprised the role of Jane. She and other principals are largely forgotten today, except by Tarzan film aficionados.

Perce Dempsey Tabler (Tarzan) was born on November 23, 1876 near Nashville, Tennessee, to Confederate veteran Major John Henry Tabler and wife Mary. "Percy" attended military school in Nashville, where he excelled in track and field and football, and was an amateur boxing champion. He later studied opera in Leipzig, Germany, migrating to Los Angeles to appear in Thomas H. Ince's Triangle Productions. Following his appearance in *Son*, Tabler fell on hard times, and asked his good friend Edgar Rice Burroughs for a loan to start anew. He and his wife, the former Olive Blanche Trafton, relocated to the San Francisco area, where he became Division Manager with A.M. Byers Co., wrought iron manufacturers. Tabler died June 7, 1956, in San Francisco, age 79.

Samuel Cooper Searle (Korak the Killer) was born on August 29, 1890 at Waichinu, Kauai, Hawaii, the second of nine children of the islands' former sheriff, John Cooper, and Sarah Yates Searle. A popular local athlete, Searle was discovered on the Waikiki beach by Cecil B. DeMille, who encouraged him to pursue acting in Hollywood. Following service in World War I, Searle changed his name to Kamuela for a few film appearances before committing to his true love, painting and sculpture. Though not fatally injured on the *Son* set, as was long rumored, he died an untimely death from cancer on February 14, 1924, age 33.

Manilla Martan's (Meriem) stage name was inspired by Admiral Dewey's Spanish American War victory in the Battle of Manila Bay (she added an extra "l"). She was born Angela M. Martin on July 4, 1898 in Colorado to Salvador and Sarah Martin. After three films with director Harry Revier, he cast her in *Son*. She then departed Hollywood for Broadway, where she appeared onstage as Nita Martan, and returned to the screen in 1927. After leaving the film industry, she married Ernest Klapholz in Arkansas on January 14, 1932, and died June 1, 1986 in Riverside, California, age 88.

Gordon Griffith (Korak the child) was born in Chicago, Illinois, on July 4, 1907, to actors Harry and Katherine Griffith. He began performing at age four with Universal and worked for Vitagraph, Keystone, Metro, and Monogram. Following his acting career, Griffith worked as an assistant director and production manager, before becoming a Columbia production executive under Harry Cohn. Married to Clara Ophüls, daughter of Dr. William Ophüls, former dean of Stanford Medical School, Griffith died of a heart attack in Los Angeles, California, on October 12, 1958, age 51.

Mae Georgia Giraci (Meriem the child) was born in Los Angeles on January 22, 1910 to Italian barber Santo Giraci and his wife Anna De Nubila. Mae was discovered playing in the front yard of her Little Italy home by a casting director and began appearing onscreen under the name Tina Rossi and several variations of her birthname. Despite offers for adult roles, she retired from acting to play the part of wife and mother when she married Herman C. Platz in May 1931 and bore three children. She died January 10, 2006, age 95, in Los Angeles.

Left: P. Dempsey Tabler as Tarzan of the Apes.

Opposite top left: Kamuela Searle as Jack Clayton, Korak the Killer.

Opposite top right: Akut and Meriem (Mae Giraci) find the wounded Jack (Gordon Griffith).

Opposite right middle: Korak (Searle) defends Meriem (Manilla Martan).

Opposite bottom: Tabler's Tarzan throttles the wicked Ivan Paulovich (Eugene Burr) with one hand, at Jane's (Karla Schramm) reproach. Marks from the bandages wrapping Tabler's broken ribs are clearly visible on his torso.

THE ADVENTURES OF TARZAN *1921*

Jane (Louise Lorraine), Clayton (Percy Pembrooke), and the villainous Nicholas Rokoff (Frank Whitson) are stranded in the jungle when their yacht capsizes. Jane and Rokoff are kidnapped for human sacrifice by the sun-worshipping Oparians, led by Queen La (Lillian Worth). Tarzan (Elmo Lincoln) arrives to save Jane and a series of adventures follows, as Rokoff and his lieutenants Gernot (George Monberg) and the Arab slaver Sheik Ben-Ali (Charles Gay) try to recapture Jane to obtain a map to the Oparian treasure that Rokoff scratched onto her back.

Following the successful release of *The Revenge of Tarzan*, the Weiss Brothers' Numa Pictures Corporation decided to film a serial based on the latter half of the novel *The Return of Tarzan* and partnered with the Great Western Producing Company, owned by Oscar and Louis Jacobs, and Louis Stern, Carl Laemmle's nephew.

Since Great Western held Elmo Lincoln under contract for the serials *Elmo the Mighty* (1919) and *Elmo the Fearless* (1920), he was selected to reprise the role of Tarzan, with his *Fearless* ingénue Louise Lorraine in the part of Jane.

Lillian Valentine scripted with titles by Bert Ennis. A one-reel prologue was edited from Lincoln's *Tarzan of the Apes* to provide the ape man's origin story. The film offered the screen debut of La of Opar, a femme fatale from Burroughs' novels, played by blonde Lillian Worth.

Robert F. Hill, an innovative veteran director helmed, with the action captured by a battery of four cameras. Hill's temperament clashed with Lincoln's; when the actor balked at returning to set one day, Hill threatened to have a witch doctor's spell change Tarzan into a different actor. The contrite Lincoln resumed filming.

Lion tamer Charles Gay assumed the role of Sheik Ben-Ali to monitor his charges, which ran rampant through the film, which includes numerous "how'd-they-do-that" lion attacks that remain impressive to modern viewers. There was one accident on set when three spooked lions mauled actors garbed as Arabs. Five actors were hospitalized with their injuries, while three others were badly scratched. Three cameras were destroyed in the melee, but Lincoln and Lorraine escaped unharmed, as did Hill and cameraman Joe Mayer.

Burroughs was a regular visitor to the set, and Hill noted that the author's knowledge was invaluable in injecting the proper atmosphere and suspense into the proceedings. Burroughs was able to capitalize on his first-hand experience with Gay's lion-training methods the following year when he wrote *Tarzan and the Golden Lion*, in which Tarzan adopts an orphaned lion cub and raises it by hand to become his faithful companion.

The serial shot in Hollywood at Great Western's home,

L-Ko Studios, which was nearly ignited during a fire sequence. The city of Sagarone was a Universal City studios backlot set; the Arizona landscape served for desert sequences. Press materials claimed several hundred extras were cast as "Arabs, Oparian warriors, sun-worshippers, headhunters, Zulus, Algerians, and other picturesque types."

Louis Weiss was so pleased with the serial that he screened all 15 two-reel chapters for exhibitors and critics, to show that the production maintained its quality throughout (buyers often purchased a serial after viewing the first few chapters, on the faith that the production quality would remain high for the entire run).

Adventures filmed from January 1 to August 13, 1921, and was released on December 1. Lincoln embarked on a 10-city promotional tour (his first ever), launched in Philadelphia on January 16, 1922, accompanied by publicist and intertitle-writer Bert Ennis in an automobile driven by a leopard-skin-clad chauffeur. The tour included theaters throughout Pittsburgh, Cleveland and Cincinnati, and proved so popular that it was extended two weeks into Kentucky and Tennessee. Further promotion was provided with a script serialization by Maude Robinson Toombs, which was syndicated in newspapers.

The serial was re-released by Weiss Brothers Artclass in 1928, edited to 10 chapters. In 1938, it was re-released again with sound effects and narration by comedian and voiceover performer Bert "The Mad Russian" Gordon.

> **"Some of the actresses are particularly courageous ... I have seen a whole bevy of lionesses pass directly over [Louise Lorraine's] half naked body"**
> - Edgar Rice Burroughs, *Screenland*, June 1922

"ADVENTURES OF TARZAN"

The Wild Animal Serial Supreme
STARRING
Elmo Lincoln
IN
15 Electrifying Episodes

PRODUCED BY
GREAT WESTERN PRODUCING CO.
FOR WEISS BROTHERS'
NUMA PICTURES CORP.

PICTURIZED FROM THE CONCLUDING CHAPTERS OF
"THE RETURN OF TARZAN"
By
Edgar Rice Burroughs

LIONS, ELEPHANTS, CROCODILES, LEOPARDS, APES, MONKEYS AND A HOST OF OTHER JUNGLE DENIZENS. SCENE AFTER SCENE OF THRILL AND EXCITEMENT IN EACH EPISODE OF "ADVENTURES OF TARZAN." THE HEROIC LINCOLN AS TARZAN, THE APE-MAN, IS THE CENTRAL FIGURE IN A SERIES OF HAIR-BREADTH ESCAPES AND WONDERFUL STUNTS WHICH WILL KEEP YOU ON THE EDGE OF YOUR CHAIR THROUGHOUT THE ENTIRE SERIAL.

"THE TARZAN OF TARZANS"

RITCHEY LITHO. CORP. N.Y.

TARZAN AND THE GOLDEN LION *1927*

As Jane (Dorothy Dunbar) and "Tarzan's favorite sister" Betty Greystoke (Edna Murphy) trek home through the jungle, their party is attacked by the evil Esteban Miranda (Frederick Peters) and his allies, including the renegade Wazari defector Awaza (Boris Karloff). Tarzan (James Pierce), accompanied by Jab the lion, leads the Wazari to the rescue. Tarzan later saves John Gordon (D'Arcy Corrigan), who has escaped after years of privation in the diamond mines of the Tangani. Miranda overhears Gordon spin his tale at the Greystoke bungalow, and the race is on to loot the lost tribe's wealth; during the chase, Betty is kidnapped by the Oparians for sacrifice to their lion god in the Temple of Diamonds. Will Tarzan and Jab arrive in time?

On February 15, 1926, Burroughs signed a contract with Joseph Schnitzer, vice president of Film Booking Offices of America (FBO) to film his ninth ape man novel, *Tarzan and the Golden Lion* after two years of negotiations. The picture was produced by Robertson-Cole (R-C) Pictures of FBO, executive produced by Joseph P. Kennedy. R-C had previously handled worldwide distribution of *Romance* for National Film Corporation. The author received $10,000 against royalties for the novel.

Former newspaperman William E. Wing scripted for veteran director J.P. McGowan. Wing had previously written the first draft of *Tarzan of the Apes* for William Parsons, and while Burroughs liked Wing "immensely", he disagreed with the adapter's assertion that endings to popular stories sometimes must be changed for the screen.

James Pierce was hired as Tarzan upon Burroughs' recommendation. Other notables in the cast included Boris Karloff, in blackface as the renegade Wazari Awaza, who casts his lot with the villains, and Lui Yu-Ching ("Long Duck"), the Chinese giant, who stood 7'10"—though some sideshow ballyhoo cited him as 8'6" and even 9'6"—who played Cadj the High Priest. He weighed 350 pounds, wore size 18 shoes, and spoke limited English.

Golden Lion filmed in Sherwood Forest, northwest of Los Angeles, a locale named after the silent Douglas Fairbanks *Robin Hood* movie that previously shot there. *Golden Lion* also filmed at Santa Ana Canyon and Chatsworth and on massive, elaborate sets on the FBO lot from September to December 1926.

In his autobiography, *The Battle for Hollywood*, Pierce noted several incidents on set, including the time he nearly fell from a rope while crossing a canyon hand-over-hand (Pierce later had aerialists' hooks taped to his wrists for security). Another time, after a long, trying day, Pierce instinctively moved his legs to block Numa the lion, when the recalcitrant beast tried to wander off camera during the shot. Stymied, Numa began snarling at Pierce, but trainer Charles Gay quickly intervened and calmed the feline.

On January 3, 1927, ERB wrote to Schnitzer to apprise him that Grosset and Dunlap would produce a photoplay edition of the novel, asking him to forward a set of stills to the publisher. Burroughs noted that he would be sending pages for autograph by the film's principals and others for a 25-copy autographed edition that is today a highly sought collectible.

Burroughs also recommended his friend Louis F. Gottschalk, a former director of the Metropolitan Opera of New York, to compose the score, but James C. Bradford

"I suggest you not miss the new Tarzan picture just being completed by FBO here. I have seen some of the work during the making and also some of the rushes, and am convinced that it is going to be the greatest Tarzan picture ever made. We have found a man who really is Tarzan, and whom I believe will be raised to the heights of stardom." - Edgar Rice Burroughs, in a letter to friend Herbert Weston, December 8, 1926

Together they sat -- ready to face their Doom!

compiled the music from previously published works in a cost-cutting measure.

Released in February 1927, the film earned $198,000 by August. Burroughs, upset at the lack of royalties, complained to Schnitzer, who responded that the film had only earned $4,755 against the author's advance. The disgruntled Burroughs terminated his relationship with FBO.

Long believed lost, a copy of the film was located in France in 1995 and translated into English for DVD release. The modern version is only 57 minutes long and lacks the opening credits and final few minutes of the film. Some of the characters were renamed for the French version. Jane's niece Ruth was reimagined as Tarzan's sister Betty Greystoke, while her love interest, Burton Bradney, Tarzan's ranch foreman, is changed to Jack Bradley in the credits, but later called Burton on the intertitle cards. Cadj the High Priest was renamed as well, and is called Raisoul the giant "high priest and sorcerer".

JIM PIERCE

Jim Pierce is the only ape man actor discovered by author Edgar Rice Burroughs, who spied the 6'4", 225-pound All American football player at a Tarzana pool party and said to friends, "There's my Tarzan!"

Burroughs referred Pierce to FBO Studios for a successful screen test, where he won the role over 92 other aspirants. He was contracted for $75 per week, with a raise to $350 if the film proved a hit.

James Hubert Pierce was born on August 8, 1900 in Freedom, Indiana (population 500), to a young farmer, James, and his wife Henny. His only sibling, sister Joanna, was born during his senior year of high school.

A high-school gridiron standout, Pierce attended Indiana University where he played football. When the entire team enlisted in the military for World War I, Pierce served as an army infantry drill instructor. Following the war, Pierce resumed sports, nicknamed "Babe" and "Big Jumbo" by sportswriters for his size, and earning All American honors at center.

After graduation, Pierce served as an assistant football coach at Arizona University in Tucson and coached the track and basketball teams to conference championships. He travelled to Los Angeles in the summer to do film extra work, receiving a bit part on *The Yosemite Trail*, starring Dustin Farnum and Irene Rich, as his film debut.

Moving to Los Angeles at a girlfriend's behest, he coached football at Glendale High School and attended USC law school at night. After meeting the Burroughs family at their pool party, he began dating Joan Burroughs, 18.

While filming *Golden Lion*, Pierce had a serious car wreck during a driving rain, returning home from a date with Joan. The accident resulted in broken ribs and a punctured lung, and held up the production, which had to shoot long shots and scenes without Pierce while he healed.

Concerned about the eight-year age difference, Pierce and Joan briefly separated, and he dated *Golden Lion* co-star Edna Murphy. After reconciling, he and Joan were married on his birthday, August 8, 1928, at the Burroughs' Mecca Avenue home in Tarzana. They remained happily married for 44 years until her death, with two children, Joanne born Christmas Eve, 1929 (author Burroughs' first grandchild), and son Mike, born in 1934.

Pierce and Joan voiced Tarzan and Jane on the popular 1932 *Tarzan of the Apes* radio show, and its sequel *The Return of Tarzan*, but departed the program after Mike's birth.

Burroughs gave Pierce a contract for the future lead in a Tarzan picture as a wedding present, but Pierce eventually sold his rights to Sol Lesser for $5,000 and was replaced by Buster Crabbe in *Tarzan the Fearless*. Pierce later co-starred as King Thun the Lion Man opposite Crabbe in the 1936 *Flash Gordon* serial.

Pierce continued to appear onscreen, usually in bit parts as tough cops or other imposing types. As his acting career wound down, he opened a flight school, training fliers during World War II, and went into real estate.

Joan had a heart attack and died at midnight, December 31, 1972; Pierce survived her until his death on December 11, 1983. Both are buried in his family plot in Forest Hills Cemetery in Shelbyville, Indiana, near his parents. Their headstones say "Tarzan" and "Jane".

Left: Tarzan (Jim Pierce) and Jab depose the Tangani sun god.

Opposite top: Numa the lion, who played Jab, was a magnificent specimen.

Opposite middle: Tarzan (Pierce) returns Betty (Edna Murphy) to her fiancé Jack (Harold Goodwin) as John Gordon (D'Arcy Corrigan) and several unnamed Wazari observe.

Opposite bottom: Tarzan (Pierce) defends Betty Greystoke (Edna Murphy).

DOROTHY DUNBAR

Dorothy Dunbar's brief career as a film star was eclipsed by her later status as a society dame, with multiple marriages to prominent husbands from a variety of fields.

Edith Augusta Dunbar was born in Cripple Creek, Colorado, on May 28, 1902, and studied nursing, but decided to become an actress, to her mother's dismay. Upon arriving in Hollywood, she signed up for drama classes with Joan Blondell and Betty Davis and attended polo matches with Spencer Tracy and Will Rogers. After eight films, including three Tom Tyler Westerns, she was cast as Jane in *Tarzan and the Golden Lion*.

Dunbar left Hollywood when she married Minneapolis millionaire Tommy Bucklin-Wells II, whom she later named as the love of her life. Bucklin-Wells succumbed to malaria after a trip to inspect their African rubber plantations and died in Dunbar's arms on the ship back to the U.S. Dunbar later married Tino Costa, a Hollywood portrait painter, followed by Spanish diplomat Jaime S. De Gerson y Baretto.

Max Baer met Dunbar while he was ascending the heavyweight prizefighter ranks, and the couple married in Reno in 1931. Sportswriters dubbed their tempestuous union "the battling Baers" prior to their inevitable divorce two years later, before Baer won the 1934 heavyweight title.

Dunbar and her final husband, flight pioneer Russell Lawson, moved to Seattle where they had two sons and avoided the limelight. Dunbar died on October 23, 1992, in Seattle, age 90, preceded in death by Lawson, who died in 1965.

TARZAN THE MIGHTY *1928*

Mary (Natalie Kingston) and Bobby Trevor (Bobby Nelson), a pair of shipwrecked castaways, struggle to survive in the Lost Village of the African coast. The group, descended from stranded pirates and other outcasts, is led by the merciless Black John (Al Ferguson), who seeks to force Mary's hand in marriage. The siblings' plight brings the attention of Black John's hated enemy, Tarzan (Frank Merrill), who rescues them from a series of perils, both human and animal, while Black John plots the ape man's death.

Following the success of *The Adventures of Tarzan* serial, Edgar Rice Burroughs sold screen rights to his fifth and sixth Tarzan novels, *Tarzan and the Jewels of Opar* and *Jungle Tales of Tarzan* to Oscar and Louis Jacobs and Julius Stern in 1922; they paid him $20,000 outright for each novel, with no further royalties due.

On April 14, 1928, Stern, then vice president and general manager of Universal Studios, announced that *Jungle Tales of Tarzan* was in preparation. Filming began May 15 on the Universal backlot.

In his 1973 autobiography *The Strongman*, actor and stuntman Joe Bonomo recounted that he was originally cast in the Tarzan role but bowed out after he broke his leg in a vine-swinging fall on the third day of production. Gymnastics champion Frank Merrill, "the Hercules of the Screen" was then tapped to star by director Jack Nelson, who had previously worked with Merrill on the 1927 Weiss Brothers Artclass serial *Perils of the Jungle*. Nelson's small son Bobby had also appeared in *Peril* and was featured in *Mighty* as Bobby Trevor, a castaway, whose older sister Mary (Natalie Kingston) is Tarzan's love interest and target of the villainous Black John's (Al Ferguson) unwanted attentions. The characters Bob and Mary Trevor also appeared in Rex Maxon's Tarzan Sunday newpaper comic strip continuity in 1931.

Merrill wore a modest over-the-shoulder leopard skin, with his knife in a thong around his neck, his feet decked in furry booties. His vine-swinging and rope-climbing skills enhanced the ape man's arboreal tendencies.

On June 14, 1928, Burroughs saw rushes shown on the Universal lot, and met Merrill and Kingston, but still wasn't happy with the production, which owed him no further payment. The finished serial bore little resemblance to the novel; despite this, the author insisted that the film be subtitled, "Adapted from the famous novel *Jungle Tales of Tarzan* by Edgar Rice Burroughs", showing a close-up of the book's title page. It was the first time on film that Tarzan's love interest was not his wife Jane, another sticking point with the author. The movie did incorporate Tarzan's Greystoke heritage as a plot device, as his uncle journeys to Africa seeking his nephew's fate.

Conceived as a 12-reel serial, *Mighty*'s immediate commercial success merited an extension, so 15 two-reel chapters were produced; production wrapped on October 28, 1928. The serial chapters were released from August 13 to November 19, 1928.

Two prose adaptations by Arthur B. Reeve were released: a 6,000-word adaptation of the first three chapters as a herald, and a 25,000-word newspaper serialization in 15 chapters. Burroughs was paid $1,000 for the newspaper serialization.

Universal head Carl Laemmle ordered most of the studio's silent films, including *Mighty*, burned after sound film technology became the industry standard, but film buffs remain hopeful that a copy of this lost serial will surface.

"In serial form the Edgar Rice Burroughs story, 'Jungle Tales of Tarzan,' will be known as 'Tarzan the Mighty.' It will be Universal's lead-off serial and there is a great rush on amongst the mighty men of Los Angeles to play Tarzan." – Universal Weekly, April 28, 1928

TARZAN *the* MIGHTY

with **FRANK MERRILL** *and* **NATALIE KINGSTON**

AN ORIGINAL SERIAL PRODUCED BY UNIVERSAL PICTURES CORPN.
BY SPECIAL ARRANGEMENT WITH

EDGAR RICE BURROUGHS

AUTHOR OF "TARZAN OF THE APES" AND "THE CAVE GIRL"

Directed by JACK NELSON

"Frank Merrill, the splendidly muscled athlete is ideally cast as Tarzan" - Motion Pictures News, July 21, 1928

FRANK MERRILL

Frank Merrill worked patiently in the background, portraying Arab antagonists in *The Son of Tarzan* and *The Adventures of Tarzan* before earning the lead in two Universal serials.

Merrill was born Otto Adolph Poll in Newark, New Jersey, on March 21, 1893. A 6', allegedly 108-pound "stripling" he joined the National Turners gymnasium and dedicated himself to his sport. A few years later, a friend submitted Merrill's photo (without his knowledge) to an English contest seeking "The World's Most Perfectly Developed Man", and Merrill came in second.

In 1916, Merrill joined the Newark Police Department, and served the Sixth Precinct with distinction for three years, carrying an elderly woman out of her burning third-floor apartment and breaking up an armed robbery, marching the perpetrators to jail at gunpoint.

While working as a patrolman, Merrill's gymnastics ascendance began. He won 55 national, metropolitan, and Southern California championships, plus YMCA and city championships in rope climbing, the Roman rings, and parallel bars. He won the U.S. national gym championship in the Roman Rings five consecutive years and the metropolitan championship for eight straight years while residing in New Jersey. He set 27 world records during his tenure.

In 1919, Merrill obtained a 90-day leave of absence from the Newark Police Department so he could compete in a gymnastics meet in California. He didn't return to New Jersey until 1930.

Merrill assimilated quickly into Southern California life, joining the Los Angeles Athletic Club to continue his training and working as a stuntman and bit player. He attempted to change his name to Frank Merriwell, after the popular hero of athletic novels, but Street & Smith, owners of the copyright, obtained an injunction, so he settled for Frank Merrill as his stage name.

His athletic skills were highlighted in a series of action pictures for Bud Barsky's Hercules Films in 1924–28. Stunt work in filmmaking's infancy wasn't easy—Merrill nearly died when the brakes on a car he was driving failed and he plowed through a house at 75 miles per hour, crawling out of the wreckage with only minor injuries.

Merrill's Tarzan was the first to vocalize the ape cry when his second serial, *Tarzan the Tiger*, was dubbed for sound. After *Tiger* wrapped, Merrill went on a promotional tour for the films, challenging the audience to surpass his feats of strength. Reportedly, none could.

Production of a third Universal serial, based on *Tarzan the Terrible*, was contemplated, but ultimately did not happen. *Tiger* was Merrill's final film.

Merrill became Los Angeles Park Commissioner in 1933, and recreation director for the city of Los Angeles. He was active in community affairs and local politics as a candidate and campaign manager. After retiring from civil service in 1963, he volunteered at the YMCA as a gym instructor. Merrill died at home on February 12, 1966 in Hollywood, preceded in death the previous year by his wife of 51 years, Elsie. He is interred in the Hollywood Forever Cemetery, Abbey of the Psalms.

Left: Frank Merrill's Tarzan made good use of his rope, a carryover from the Tarzan novels.

Opposite top left: Tarzan (Merrill) battles Taug the ape (Charles Gemora).

Opposite top right: Black John (Al Ferguson) tries to coerce Mary (Natalie Kingston) to marry him.

Opposite middle: Frank Merrill as Tarzan the Mighty.

Opposite bottom: Natalie Kingston as Mary Trevor.

NATALIE KINGSTON

Along with Lydie Denier and Glenn Close (if one counts voiceover work), Natalie Kingston is one of the few actresses to play both a Jane and a non-Jane character in the Tarzan films.

A beautiful brown-eyed brunette, Kingston was born in Vallejo, California, on May 19, 1905 to Sigurd Adolph Ringstrom and Natalie Vallejo Heraszthy Ringstrom. A descendent of some of California's most prominent early settlers, Kingston's lineage included paternal grandfather Count Agoston Heraszthy of Hungary, dubbed the "father of viticulture" in California after he arrived in 1849 and began cultivating grapes, and her maternal great-grandfather, General Mariano Guadalupe Vallejo, California's first governor.

Educated at the Dominican convent at San Rafael, Kingston enjoyed her music studies, often composing words and stories and interpretive dance steps to accompany the tunes. At 13 she ran away and returned home. She resumed high school in San Francisco and began dancing on the local stage a year later, after convincing the brother–sister stage producing team of Fanchon and Marco to hire her.

A skilled acrobatic and ballroom dancer, she was soon performing in Los Angeles, where producer Rufus LeMaire of the Winter Garden on Broadway saw her act, and hired her for the *Broadway Brevities* 1920 revue at the Winter Garden Theater.

She later returned to Los Angeles to dance for Fanchon and Marco, where she was discovered by F. Richard Jones, Mack Sennett's supervising director, who began casting her in comic two-reelers in 1923 as one of Sennett's bathing beauties. After 18 months, Kingston asked to be released from her contract so she could appear in dramas. Kingston's busy film career continued, as she was selected as one of 13 Wampas Baby Stars in 1927.

Kingston eloped to Tijuana, Mexico, on June 19, 1928 with George Andersch, a Los Angeles broker. Columnist Wade Werner claimed she was the first screen star to elope to Mexico by airliner. She retired from acting in 1933, and the pair remained married until Andersch's death in 1960. Kingston died February 2, 1991 in West Hills, California.

TARZAN THE TIGER *1929*

Tarzan (Frank Merrill) returns to the lost city of Opar to replenish his fortune with Oparian gold, trailed by Albert Werper (Al Ferguson), who is in league with the slaver Achmet Zek (Sheldon Lewis). In Tarzan's absence, Zek raids the ape man's estate and kidnaps Jane (Natalie Kingston) to sell her into slavery. Stricken with amnesia during an accident, Tarzan must rescue Jane from Zek and Werper, as the jealous high priestess La of Opar (Mademoiselle Kithnou), whose love Tarzan once renounced for Jane, schemes to kill Jane and claim Tarzan.

Tarzan the Mighty was a hit for Universal Studios, so the studio purchased the film rights to *Tarzan and the Jewels of Opar* from Oscar and Louis Jacobs and Julius Stern for $10,000 in March 1929, with no further payments to author Burroughs.

The studio sought to duplicate *Mighty*'s successful formula, so Frank Merrill, Natalie Kingston, and Al Ferguson continued as principals, with Kingston now playing Jane, Lady Greystoke, and Ferguson as the soldier-of-fortune Albert Werper. This time, Universal's storyline followed Burroughs' novel, with the Eurasian Mademoiselle Kithnou portraying La of Opar, and Sheldon Lewis as the brigand chief and slaver Achmet Zek.

Henry McRae, dubbed the "King of the Serial Makers" and an action specialist, was retained to direct from Ian McCloskey Heath's scenario, which was titled by Ford Beebe. The 15-chapter serial began filming on June 17, 1929 on the Universal Studios backlot. The set portraying the city of Sagarone in *Adventures* hosted an Arab slave mart in this incarnation.

The serial offered plenty of thrills to viewers, with Merrill's athletic prowess again highlighted, as he scrambled up ropes and swung on vines. In one scene, he leaped off a charging elephant and grabbed a vine to swing and knock a camel-rider off his mount. Three times during filming, Merrill had accidental falls of nearly 20 feet from the trees, but his tumbling ability saved him from serious injury. Trainer Melvin Koontz and his wrestling lion Jackie doubled for Merrill in cat combat scenes. Kingston's allure was employed in a tasteful nude scene, obscured by bushes, with her perhaps wearing a body stocking.

The serial was released in December 1929. A sound version, with sound effects, music and the first Tarzan yell, was later released, but no dialogue was recorded, so the title cards remained.

Unlike *Mighty*, which was heralded with an elaborate promotional campaign, very little supporting material was produced for the serial, which wasn't reviewed by the contemporary trades. Merrill embarked on an 18-month tour to support the serials, performing athletic feats in his Tarzan wardrobe.

Universal debated continuing the series with a serial adaptation of *Tarzan the Terrible*, but ultimately declined to remain in the Tarzan business, rather than deal with an incensed Burroughs.

TARZAN THE TIGER

By
Edgar Rice
Burroughs

with
Frank
Merrill
and
Natalie
Kingston

NEW
Adventures
Hazards
Thrills

PRINTED IN U.S.A.

TARZAN THE APE MAN *1932*

Jane Parker (Maureen O'Sullivan) *arrives at the African trading post of her father James* (C. Aubrey Smith) *as he and his partner Harry Holt* (Neil Hamilton) *prepare a safari up the perilous Mutia Escarpment in search of the fabled elephant graveyard. During their dangerous journey they encounter Tarzan* (Johnny Weissmuller), *a wild man, who abducts Jane. Taken with his innate bravery, nobility, and innocence, she falls in love with him during their jungle interlude. When Jane returns to her father's party, they are taken captive by savage dwarves and sentenced to die in a pit with a ferocious gorilla. It's up to Cheeta, Tarzan's ape companion, to call Tarzan and his elephants to the rescue.*

"This is a real Tarzan picture. It breathes the grim mystery of the jungle; the endless, relentless strife for survival; the virility, the cruelty, and the grandeur of Nature in the raw." – Edgar Rice Burroughs, in a letter to director Woody Van Dyke, February 19, 1932

Following the critical and commercial success of the Academy Award-nominated hit *Trader Horn* (1931), Metro-Goldwyn-Mayer (MGM) production head Irving Thalberg sought another jungle property to be filmed as a follow-up. Director W.S. "Woody" Van Dyke shot more than a million feet of film for *Horn* on his 1929 African safari, and Thalberg wanted to use the stock footage of animals, tribesmen, and scenery in a new picture.

Negotiations with author Burroughs began in March 1931, as *Horn* continued to drive box office profits. On April 15, a deal was reached, paying Burroughs $20,000 plus $1,000 per week for five weeks for his services. Rather than optioning an existing novel, as the silent films had done, MGM crafted an original scenario for the ape man.

Horn scripter Cyril Hume's first draft was a direct sequel to that film, with Horn leading a scientific expedition into the African interior in search of a lost city of moon worshippers. A female scientist with the expedition is abducted by Tarzan, who later saves the party from sacrifice to a giant gorilla god. The script was retooled, replacing Horn with African trader James Parker, whose daughter Jane accompanies his expedition to the elephants' graveyard. C. Aubrey Smith, who had portrayed Horn's friend in the original film, was cast as Parker.

The successful *Horn* production team of Van Dyke, cinematographer Clyde De Vinna, editor Ben Lewis, and

recording director Douglas Shearer were retained to film the first talkie Tarzan. British actor Ivor Novello was hired to script dialogue, which did not include the famous "Me Tarzan! You Jane!" line, as the ape man made introductions simply by thumping his chest, then Jane's, and speaking their names.

MGM tested most of the actors in its stable, including Charles Bickford, John Mack Brown, Tom Tyler, Joel McCrea and Clark Gable. Olympian Buster Crabbe also read for the role. The studio had decided to cast Olympic shot-putter Herman Brix (whom Douglas Fairbanks had referred), until he was sidelined after injuring his shoulder in the football picture *Touchdown* (1931).

Hume met Johnny Weissmuller, in town for a BVD promotion, at the Hollywood Athletic Club, and referred him to Van Dyke and producer Bernard Hyman. They recognized Weissmuller as the ideal candidate, signing him on October 16 for $250 per week. On October 30, Maureen O'Sullivan was contracted to play Jane for $300 per week, and production began the following day.

The film shot entirely in Southern California, on the MGM Backlot 2 jungle set, at Iverson Movie Ranch, and by Lake Sherwood in Ventura County. The feature made extensive use of matte paintings, rear-projection and other cutting-edge photographic tricks to create the illusion of danger in darkest Africa.

Several touches from *Trader Horn* remained, such as the use of Swahili words, and naming Tarzan's domain the Mutia Escarpment, after Mutia Omoolu, the African who had portrayed Horn's gunbearer and later travelled to Hollywood for re-shoots of that picture. Tarzan's origin, and his Greystoke lineage, is never addressed in the MGM films.

Bert Nelson of the A.G. Barnes Circus was hired to wrangle the animals, as was George Emerson, who also doubled as Weissmuller when wrestling lions. The cast included 23 Indian elephants (fitted with prosthetic ears and tusks to appear African), 12 zebras, nine hippopotami, eight hyenas, eight antelope, seven lions, one gnu, 100 baboons and monkeys, and Emma the chimp.

Circus aerialist Alfredo Codona of the Flying Codonas did the vine-swinging trapeze work in Sherwood Forest, with brother Lalo donning an ape suit to perform as his catcher; the shots were re-used in subsequent MGM Tarzan pictures. Weissmuller did many of his other stunts, including swimming and diving, climbing trees, fighting, and riding the elephants.

Tarzan's signature cry was created by sound engineer Shearer. Studio publicity claimed that he mixed a hyena's yowl played backwards, a camel's bleat, the pluck of a violin string, and a soprano's high-C note, but it was actually a palindrome of a human yell, the same forward as backwards, with a high note (perhaps from a clarinet) in the middle. Weissmuller learned to emulate the electronically sweetened sound, which he did for the later RKO Tarzan films.

There was no score to the film; the song "Voodoo Dance" by George Richelavie, arranged by Fritz Stahlberg and P.A. Marquardt, played over the main titles, while Tchaikovsky's "Overture to Romeo and Juliet" was used in the final scene.

The eight-week shoot wrapped on December 28 at a cost of $652,675. The film's opening was postponed to March 25, 1932, due to the Lindbergh baby kidnapping, which monopolized media coverage.

The film was among MGM's top money-makers of 1932, and was one of the 15 most profitable films of the year. Burroughs noted in a May 9, 1932 letter to his friend Bert Weston that Los Angeles theaters scheduled seven shows on Saturday and Sunday to meet the public demand.

Burroughs sent Van Dyke a congratulatory letter of effusive praise on February 19 after viewing the picture. On May 31, he wrote to producer Bernard Hyman, suggesting an annual spring Tarzan film, to be anticipated like the circus "to which the Tarzan picture is analogous". Tarzan's place in film history was now secure.

"The thrills come so thick and fast that one breathless moment follows another with exciting rapidity."
- Louella O. Parsons, *Los Angeles Examiner*, May 9, 1932

Opposite: Johnny Weissmuller and Maureen O'Sullivan: one of cinema's all-time great romantic pairings.

Top left: Legendary photographer George Hurrell shot Weissmuller in a variety of poses.

Top right: O'Sullivan takes aim during the river crossing sequence at Lake Sherwood.

Bottom left: Acrobats and little people portrayed the primates in *Ape Man*, as they would in *Greystoke* five decades later.

Bottom right: MGM staple Cheeta the chimpanzee made her debut in *Ape Man*, played by Emma and trained by Bud Barsky.

TARZAN THE FEARLESS *1933*

Mary Brooks (Jacqueline Wells) and her boyfriend Bob Hall (Eddie Woods) are seeking Dr. Brooks (E. Alyn Warren), Mary's scientist father. They are led by the scheming safari guides Jeff Herbert (Philo McCollough) and Nick Moran (Matthew Betz), who plot to kill Tarzan (Buster Crabbe) for a reward and loot the hidden city of Zar's riches. Tarzan rescues Mary, as the men are captured and prepared for sacrifice by the high priest, Eltar (Mischa Auer). A series of chases and escapes ensues as Tarzan fights to reunite Mary and her father and foil the looters' scheme.

In January 1929, Edgar Rice Burroughs sold an option to produce a film or serial, titled *Tarzan the Fearless*, to G. Walter Shumway and Jack C. Nelson. The contract stipulated that the film must be made within seven years, and Burroughs would receive $10,000 upfront upon production and 10 percent of the gross. Jim Pierce contracted with them to play Tarzan, against Burroughs' advice.

As MGM began pre-production on *Ape Man*, Irving Thalberg, excited with the commercial potential of the film, began negotiating with Burroughs for rights to further pictures, suggesting one per year for three years—provided the rights were exclusive.

Hearing of this, Shumway and his attorney showed up at Burroughs' Malibu home, to pay their $10,000 advance, insisting that their option had not expired. As they handed Burroughs 10 $1,000 bills, he tossed them back, with comedic results as the two scrambled to chase down the windblown bills.

Independent producer Sol Lesser bought Shumway and Nelson's option, and cannily agreed to allow MGM to release their big-budget picture first if his could follow, signing an agreement on March 26, 1932 which granted him rights to make additional Tarzan pictures. In January 1933, with *Ape Man* a hit and *Mate* in the scripting phase, Lesser submitted his screenplay to Burroughs for approval; the author's only suggestion was that Lesser tone down the sexual suggestiveness.

Lesser's next task was to find a leading man. Pierce, now married and a father, was no longer in physical condition for the role, and lacked the fame to be a marquee draw. He balked at giving up his option, and worked out furiously to get in shape. In response, Lesser threatened to hire popular satirist Corey Ford to pen a Tarzan burlesque, with scenes including Jane boosting Tarzan into a tree. Pierce accepted a $5,000 buyout to walk away from the role.

Hoping to repeat MGM's success with Weissmuller, Lesser hired 1932 Olympic swimming gold medalist Larry "Buster" Crabbe, currently appearing onscreen in Paramount's *King of the Jungle*, based on the C.T. Stoneham story about a feral man raised by lions. Jeanette Loff and Frances Rich were announced to play the female lead before Jacqueline Wells (who later changed her name to Julie Bishop) was eventually hired to play Mary Brooks.

Robert F. Hill (*The Adventures of Tarzan*) returned to the series to direct from an original script by Basil Dickey, George Plympton, and Walter Anthony, which featured a monosyllabic wild man in the MGM mold. The picture shot at Iverson's Movie Ranch and in the Lake Sherwood area.

The film featured lion wrestling, a crocodile fight, and high-flying vine acrobatics, the latter recycled in Lesser's later RKO Tarzan films. The ape man's yell was crafted by Crabbe's father-in-law, sound engineer Tom Held, as a high-pitched "Ah-Ahhhh-Ah!" that was re-used in Lesser's next film, *Tarzan's Revenge* (1938). Unlike the MGM films, *Fearless* included a complete musical score, supervised by Abe Meyer.

Fearless was filmed as a 12-chapter serial, but Lesser decided upon a novel distribution strategy, which didn't produce the intended results. The first four chapters were released together as a feature film, with the intention that theaters follow it with the weekly serial installments; however, some theaters aired only the feature, which left viewers dissatisfied with the unresolved ending. The feature was released in Britain with footage from the later serial chapters added to conclude the story. This 85-minute feature version survives and is available on DVD.

"That one-tenth of a second changed my life. It was then that [Hollywood producers] discovered latent histrionic abilities in me."
– Buster Crabbe, on winning the gold medal

Left: Tarzan (Buster Crabbe) confronts the High Priestess of Zar (Carlotta Monti).

Opposite bottom left: Aerialist Alfredo Codona did vine work for *Fearless*.

Opposite top right: Author Edgar Rice Burroughs chats with leading lady Jacqueline Wells and an affectionate Jiggs.

Opposite bottom right: A lady's wardrobe is always the first casualty when she's lost in the jungle.

BUSTER CRABBE

Like Johnny Weissmuller, Buster Crabbe earned the Tarzan role on the reputation of his Olympic gold medal in swimming—he broke the retired Weissmuller's record in the 400-meter event in the 1932 Games. Unlike Weissmuller, Crabbe appeared in a single Tarzan film, later earning fame in the role of space hero Flash Gordon.

Clarence Linden Crabbe was born on February 7, 1908 in Oakland, California, to Edward and Agnes Crabbe. He was named for his grandfather, and nicknamed "Buster". The following year, brother Edward Clinton Simmons Crabbe, Jr., nicknamed "Buddy", was born.

In 1913, the family moved to Hawaii, where Edward managed a pineapple plantation and later worked in real estate. Buster and Buddy attended the Honolulu Military Academy, which merged with Punahoa, the oldest school in Hawaii, in 1925. Crabbe won 16 letters in football, basketball, track, and swimming and five ROTC gold medals for best soldier.

Like most Hawaiians, Buster reveled in an aquatic existence; his swimming prowess brought him an offer to join the Outrigger Canoe Club swim team. Buster idolized local hero Duke Kahanamoku, and became a distance swimmer. Although the older Weissmuller was a sprinter, he defeated Crabbe in their competitions.

Crabbe qualified for the 1928 Olympics, winning the 400-meter and 1,500-meter U.S. championships, but he caught the flu on the ocean voyage to Amsterdam, and his only success was a bronze medal in the 800-meter relay.

Upon returning to the U.S., Crabbe accepted a swimming scholarship to USC. He took classes by morning, worked as a department store stockboy in the afternoons, and swam during the evenings, training for the 1932 Olympics. He graduated in 1931 with a degree in political science, hoping to attend law school.

Crabbe won the 400-meter event by one-tenth of a second, in 4:48.4, beating Johnny Weissmuller's record of 4:52. He was the only U.S. medalist in the men's swimming competition, with Japan winning the rest of the events.

On April 13, 1933, Crabbe married Adah Virginia Held, whom he had met when she vacationed in Hawaii as a schoolgirl, and resumed courting while at USC. They had two daughters and a son.

Crabbe began working in films as an extra and stuntman during his college years. In 1931, he unsuccessfully auditioned for the lead in MGM's *Tarzan the Ape Man*. Following his Olympic victory, he signed a Paramount contract and appeared in the movie *King of the Jungle* (1933), as Kaspa, a feral man raised by lions. This led to an offer from Sol Lesser to play the jungle lord in *Tarzan the Fearless*.

Crabbe won cinematic immortality on loan to Universal as the lead in the science fiction serial *Flash Gordon* (1936), based on the Alex Raymond comic strip. The serial's popularity generated two sequels *Flash Gordon's Trip to Mars* (1938) and *Flash Gordon Conquers the Universe* (1940). He also played the title role in the science fiction serial *Buck Rogers* (1939) which helped cement his sobriquet, "King of the Serials".

Crabbe appeared in scores of B-movies, including the long-running Billy the Kid Western series for Producers Releasing Corporation. After a successful stint opposite Eleanor Holm in Billy Rose's Aquacade, Crabbe formed his own touring swimming exhibition, Buster Crabbe's Aquacade, to tour Europe.

In the 1950s, Crabbe began appearing on television in a fitness program, hosted clips of his old Westerns, and played lead opposite son Cuffy in the series *Captain Gallant of the Foreign Legion*. He also founded a boys' camp in the Catskills, worked as a water sports director for the Hotel Concord in the Catskills, and founded Buster Crabbe Swimming Pools.

He retired to Arizona with Virginia, where he continued to lecture on fitness, appear in commercials and endorsements, and compete in AAU National Masters swimming events. The science fiction revival of the 1970s brought him new fame and acclaim, with roles on television, interviews, and convention appearances.

Crabbe died of a heart attack at his Scottsdale home on April 23, 1983, age 75, and was buried in Scottsdale's Green Acres cemetery.

JACQUELINE WELLS

Jacqueline Wells began her prolific career as a child star, acting in numerous B-movies for two decades before changing her stage name to Julie Bishop to sign a Warner Brothers contract and appear onscreen with many of the era's top leading men.

She was born Jacqueline Brown in Denver, Colorado, on August 30, 1914, to William Wells Brown, a prominent banker and oil executive, and wife Blanche. Wells spent her early years in Wichita Falls, Texas, moving to Los Angeles with her mother at age five after her parents separated.

When she expressed an interest in acting, her mother enrolled her in Theodore Kosloff's dance class. After debuting onscreen in *Children of Jazz* (1923), she appeared in numerous films before taking a hiatus to attend Hollywood High School. After her graduation, Wells won leads onstage at the Pasadena Playhouse, where she was re-discovered and signed to a contract by producer B.P Shulberg, later contracting with Columbia and Paramount, and appearing opposite Buster Crabbe as Mary in *Tarzan the Fearless*.

Concerned that she was becoming typecast as a B-movie actress, she did a tour onstage in stock to hone her craft. Upon her return to California, she signed a contract with Warner Brothers and changed her name to Julie Bishop to begin anew in Hollywood.

Among her roles as Julie Bishop were *International Squadron* (1941) with Ronald Reagan; *Northern Pursuit* (1943) with Errol Flynn; *Action in the North Atlantic* (1943) with Humphrey Bogart; *Sands of Iwo Jima* (1949) and *The High and the Mighty* (1954) with John Wayne; *Rhapsody in Blue* (1945) with Robert Alda; *The Last of the Redmen*, with Buster Crabbe as the villainous Magua; and *The Big Land* (1957), her final film, with Alan Ladd.

Wells was married three times, first to Walter Booth Brooks III; followed by Colonel Clarence Adelbert "Shoopy" Shoop, a test pilot and Hughes Aircraft vice president with whom she had a son and daughter; and, following Shoop's death from cancer, Beverly Hills surgeon William Bergin. Daughter Pamela Shoop followed her mother's career as an actress and became a popular television guest star with more than 60 credits, while son Stephen graduated from medical school.

Wells died of pneumonia on her 87th birthday, on August 30, 2001, at home. She was survived by Bergin, her son, her daughter, and one grandchild.

TARZAN AND HIS MATE *1934*

Still hoping to claim the fortune in ivory at the elephants' graveyard, Harry Holt (Neil Hamilton) enlists his friend Martin Arlington (Paul Cavanagh) to return to the Mutia Escarpment. He also hopes to convince Jane (Maureen O'Sullivan) to leave Tarzan (Johnny Weissmuller) and return to civilization with him. Once there, Arlington takes matters into his own hands—with disastrous results.

"There hasn't been anything like this one since the days of the Circus Maximus" *- New York American, per Hollywood Reporter, April 25, 1934*

With *Tarzan the Ape Man* a certified hit, MGM immediately contracted with Burroughs for a sequel, with options for two more films, paying him $45,000.

In June 1932 Bud Barsky (a former independent producer and chimp trainer who worked on *Ape Man*) was announced as the sequel's scripter, assisted by R.L. Johnson and Arthur S. Hyman. As pre-production progressed, other staff writers— including Leon Gordon, C. Gardner Sullivan, Oliver H.P. Garrett, and Howard Emmett Rogers—contributed to the project. James Kevin McGuinness eventually received credit.

African locations were considered for the picture, with a huge forest fire planned to threaten the safari party. Studio executives later cancelled the fire sequence and African travel, probably influenced by the hardship, privation, and expense of *Trader Horn*'s shoot. It would be years before another major Hollywood motion picture mounted an African expedition of such vast scope.

Shooting on *Tarzan and His Mate* began August 2, 1933, with MGM art director Cedric Gibbons helming in his first and last directorial effort (Van Dyke was unavailable) and Clyde De Vinna back on the lead camera. Weissmuller and O'Sullivan reprised their roles, as did Neil Hamilton. Southern California filming locations included Lake Sherwood and Sherwood Forest, Big Tujunga, China Flats, and the swamps of Woodland Park, near Pico-Rivera in Whittier.

Production halted three-and-a-half weeks later; when it resumed shortly thereafter, Paul Cavanagh had replaced silent screen idol Rod La Roque in the role of Arlington. Then production was shuttered again, and reconvened with Jack Conway in the director's chair (though Gibbons retained directorial credit, and served as inspiration for the name of the hostile tribe, the Gibonis).

Murray Kinnell and Frank Reicher, playing the smaller, uncredited roles of greedy hunters Tom Pierce and Henry Van Ness, were replaced by William Stack and Desmond Roberts for undisclosed reasons. The schedule was reshuffled further when O'Sullivan had to bow out for 45 days for an appendectomy.

Realizing that they had to compete with high expectations generated by blockbusters like *King Kong* (1933), producers

045

used every camera and special effects trick at their disposal. The secretive Newcombe department, headed by Warren Newcombe, provided photographic effects. Matte paintings offered scope to the African setting, rear-projection simulated dangers like threatening beasts, and well-integrated stock footage blended African animals and locations into the storyline. After several days of fruitlessly strategizing the logistics of photographing O'Sullivan topless, but obscured by foliage, the wardrobe department provided her a skimpy two-piece outfit. The film's imagery, dialogue, violence, and suggestiveness pushed the censorship boundaries of the era.

The studio built a huge model crocodile from steel and rubber for Weissmuller to wrestle in an 18-foot-deep tank; when he stabbed it in the neck, nigrosine sacks released dye in the water to simulate blood. The footage was impressive enough to recycle in future films. Josephine McKim, an Olympic champion swimmer and O'Sullivan's stunt double, appeared in the scene, and swam nude in another sequence, an underwater ballet with Weissmuller. (RKO's *Bird of Paradise* had previously included a similar swimming scene between Dolores Del Rio and Joel McCrea.)

Mary the black rhino was purchased from the Hagenbeck Zoo in Germany for $10,000 expressly to appear in the film. She was trained by George Emerson and Volney Phifer, who taught her to lie down, roll over, and allow Emerson (and Weissmuller) to ride her. To photograph her charge, the skittish beast was trained to scurry back to her corral when startled; cameras in pits filmed the ensuing gallop. Mary stormed the camera cage once, but the rattled crew was unharmed. Following the production's wrap, Mary was sold to Ringling Brothers, Barnum & Bailey Circus.

Prosthetic-ear-clad elephants and miniature elephant models were filmed and rear-projected to add numbers to the graveyard's defensive herd. James McKay directed some action sequences, with Errol Taggart and Nick Grinde shooting animal footage.

The flying Codonas portrayed Tarzan, Jane and Big Cheeta swinging through the trees, and the Picchiani troupe of acrobats donned ape suits for the scene where the unconscious Weissmuller is lowered to the ground. Trainer Bert Nelson wrestled a lion on the Olympian's behalf. An adagio team performed Jane's leap from the trees into Tarzan's arms.

Lion trainer Louis Roth supplied 38 lions for the climactic battle, shot in a 300-square-foot enclosure. As dummies of hostile tribesmen were thrown from the trees, the lions attacked meat staked to the ground, to appear as if they were attacking the dummies. Newcombe's department conjured the lion attacks on the elephants.

The film wrapped on March 10, but more shots were staged throughout the month, including Jane's face-off with the lions, during which Betty Roth, Louis's wife, stood in for O'Sullivan. The final cost was $1,279,142.

"Voodoo Dance" again played over the main titles, with Dr. William Axt's "My Tender One" (previously used in MGM's *Eskimo*) at the film's end. "Soldier on the Shelf", by Sherman Myers, a contemporary piece, plays on the phonograph as the hunters try to woo Jane back to civilization.

The film was submitted to the Production Code Administration (PCA) office to preview for objectionable content on April 5. It was rejected, but MGM released it with three versions of the swimming sequence anyway: with the fully nude scene intact, with Jane topless, and with the sequence omitted (to accommodate the local obscenity laws of each community). Incensed, the Code office demanded the scene's removal from all future prints. Media mogul Ted Turner restored the film to its original state in 1986 when he acquired the MGM film library.

Reviews in *Variety* and the *Hollywood Reporter* criticized the film's length after its April 9 Los Angeles release, so nearly 15 minutes of violence and suggestive dialogue were cut, reducing it from 11 reels to 9. On April 20, the edited film was released in New York.

The picture is one of the high points in the franchise's history, regarded by many fans and film historians as the best of the Tarzan films, due to the high production value and action sequences. In 2003, the picture was added to the National Film Registry of significant films deserving preservation.

Left: In the MGM films, Tarzan called elephants "Timba", perhaps a variant of the Swahili word "Tembo".

Opposite top left: Harry Holt (Neil Hamilton) and Martin Arlington (Paul Cavanagh) try to convince Tarzan and Jane to guide them to the elephant graveyard.

Opposite top right: First-time director Cedric Gibbons confers with Weissmuller.

Opposite bottom left: Behind the scenes with O'Sullivan, Cavanagh, Hamilton, and Weissmuller.

Opposite bottom right: Maureen O'Sullivan's abbreviated wardrobe was eliminated from future Tarzan films after censors refused to approve *Mate* for its nude scenes, dialogue, and sexual undertones.

"**There are thrills and thrills galore in the new Tarzan picture which opened before an almost hysterical audience at the Capitol Theatre yesterday.**"
– *New York News*, per *Hollywood Reporter*, April 25, 1934

THE NEW ADVENTURES OF TARZAN *1935*

Major Francis Martling (Frank Baker), his daughter Alice (Dale Walsh), and her fiancé Gordon Hamilton (Harry Ernest) organize a safari to Guatemala to recover the Green Goddess—a Mayan idol that contains the secret to a powerful explosive—and recruit Tarzan (Herman Brix) to act as their guide. They are trailed by Raglan (Don Castello), a criminal who hopes to steal the idol from them, and Ula Vale (Ula Holt), a mystery woman bent on stopping Raglan. Upon reaching the Dead City, the party finds that its Mayan inhabitants have no intention of sharing the idol.

The New Adventures of Tarzan holds a special place in the hearts of Edgar Rice Burroughs fans as the only Tarzan film footage actually produced by the author.

In May 1934, Ashton Dearholt, a former actor and Burroughs family friend, convinced the author to invest in a production company founded expressly to film the author's literary works. Burroughs-Tarzan Enterprises (BTE) was thus established, headquartered at 8476 Sunset Boulevard, with George W. Stout, Ben S. Cohen, and Dearholt as promoters and Burroughs as owner; he had 40 percent of the stock to their 20 percent apiece. Burroughs licensed the fledgling company to produce a 12-chapter serial with no more than 25 reels for $20,000, and delegated all film matters to his partners.

Olympic shot-put silver medalist Herman Brix was cast as Tarzan, at a salary of $75 per week. Jiggs the chimp, who played MGM's Cheeta, was cast as Nkima; trainers Tony and Jackie Gentry received $2,000 for the shoot (Jackie pulled double duty as the Mayan queen).

New Adventures offered Tarzan no Jane or opportunity for romance; instead, Dearholt cast his real-life paramour Ula Holt as the female lead, who enjoys only a bit of mild flirting with the ape man in the final scene. Dearholt played the villain Raglan, under the pseudonym Don Castello, which he adopted from his mother's maiden name.

Edward Kull directed the serial from a script by Charles Royal and Edwin Blum. The production filmed for three days at the former Selig Zoo, where trainer Melvin Koontz—doubling for Brix—wrestled Jackie the lion.

On December 1, 1934, Dearholt and a crew of 28 sailed for Guatemala with their equipment aboard the *Seattle*. The difficulties began as soon as the ship anchored.

There was no deep-water port, so the trucks and equipment were unloaded into small boats three miles at sea during a storm, with everything subjected to intense customs inspection. To reach the filming location the crew had to drive the filled-to-capacity trucks over narrow, treacherous mountain roads through lashing rain. The company ran out of funds and

Dearholt wired Burroughs for more, forcing the author to take out a $50,000 bank loan to finish the picture.

The crew filmed in Chichicastenango, the old Spanish capital Antigua, and the Mayan ruins at Tikal. For the jungle scenes, they took a boat upriver on the Rio Dulce and shot footage in the trees along the riverbank, just a few feet from the boat.

Native extras were paid a nickel a day; those who volunteered to battle Brix were given 20 cents. Brix later noted in a personal interview that they nearly killed him in their zeal to earn the extra 15 cents.

Back in Hollywood, two versions of the footage were prepared: the 12-chapter serial and a film that incorporated the first two serial episodes with a bit of original material added to make a seven-reel, 75-minute feature. Stock photography of African animals, including elephants, rhinos, giraffes, lions, and wildebeest was inexplicably cut into the storyline, which was set in Guatemala.

By the time the serial and feature were ready for theaters MGM was back in the Tarzan business and didn't want any competitors. The studio threatened to withhold future ape man movies from theaters that booked the BTE film, so larger chains shunned *New Adventures*. The domestic box office suffered from MGM's tactics, but the project did well financially overseas.

In December 1935, the company was renamed Burroughs-Tarzan Pictures (BTP). Jesse Goldburg was hired to coordinate exploitation and publicity; with the company floundering financially, Goldburg was offered a 50 percent commission to book the film into theaters.

Through his aggressive salesmanship, Goldburg was able to pay off Burroughs' bank note by June 28, 1940. Burroughs was so grateful that he granted Goldburg sole rights to the two films on an ongoing fifty-fifty basis. Goldburg continued to schedule the films in limited releases for years thereafter.

Despite Dearholt's high aspirations, his hopes to produce additional pictures ran aground when Burroughs declined to continue financing the company. The company released three non-Burroughs pictures in 1936 *The Drag-Net*, *Tundra*, and *The Phantom of Santa Fe* and closed shop in 1937.

DEARHOLT-STOUT AND COHEN present

The NEW ADVENTURES OF TARZAN

featuring
HERMAN BRIX
WORLD FAMOUS ATHLETE
and OLYMPIC GAMES CHAMPION

ULA HOLT · FRANK BAKER
LEWIS SARGENT AND A TREMENDOUS SUPPORTING CAST

From the thrilling story by
EDGAR RICE BURROUGHS

A BURROUGHS-TARZAN ENTERPRISE

FILMED IN GUATEMALA BY THE ASHTON DEARHOLT EXPEDITION

HERMAN BRIX

Herman Brix was the third of four Olympians cast as Tarzan, and bears the distinction of author Edgar Rice Burroughs' personal approval in the role.

Harold Herman Brix was born in Tacoma, Washington, on May 19, 1906, one of five children of prosperous lumberman Anton Henry Brix and his wife Minna. After a growth spurt at age 12, Brix began working in the lumber camps, building a sturdy physique. He followed his older brother Egbert to the University of Washington, where both competed on the football and track teams, and Herman also took up the shot-put.

Brix won the 1927 NCAA shot-put championship his junior year, and went undefeated his senior year, winning the 1928 Olympic trials and a trip to Amsterdam. There, third-ranked John Kuck won the gold medal for the USA, leaving Brix to take the silver medal. It was the only time Brix lost to Kuck.

Despite his business administration degree, Brix was unlucky in his search for employment after his return from the Netherlands, until he received an invitation to join the Los Angeles Athletic Club. There, his prowess caught Douglas Fairbanks' attention; the leading man referred Brix for the role of Tarzan in MGM's *Tarzan the Ape Man*, but a broken shoulder suffered during the filming of the football picture *Touchdown* (1931) cost Brix the role.

Still recuperating from the injury, and exhausted after driving from Los Angeles to San Francisco for the trials in Harold Lloyd's borrowed car, Brix failed to qualify for the 1932 Los Angeles Olympics, ending his athletic aspirations. He met Jeanette Braddock, daughter of *Los Angeles Times* city editor Ralph Braddock, at an Amateur Athletic Union speaking

engagement, and began dating her. They eloped to Santa Barbara on January 31, 1933, and later had two children.

Brix won the role of Tarzan for Burroughs-Tarzan Enterprises' serial *The New Adventures of Tarzan* and two features cut from the footage, his casting personally approved by Burroughs; his audition consisted of athletic feats like rope climbing, alongside numerous other candidates.

While on location in Guatemala, a cut on his knee became infected, swelling up like a cantaloupe; when he was evacuated downriver, a fruit plantation doctor lanced the infection. He carried the scar—as well as one on his scalp from Cheeta's teeth—for the rest of his life. The 6'2" Brix returned to Los Angeles weighing 168 pounds, having lost 30 pounds after contracting amoebic dysentery and suffering other privations.

Resuming his Hollywood career, he was relegated to low-paid roles in memorable Republic serials like *The Lone Ranger* (1938) *Hawk of the Wilderness* (1938), *The Fighting Devil Dogs* (1938), and *Daredevils of the Red Circle* (1939). Realizing that he was typecast, he changed his name to Bruce Bennett, redoubled his commitment to his craft, and began winning roles in memorable films like *Sahara* (1943), *Mildred Pierce* (1945), *The Treasure of Sierra Madre* (1948), and his favorite, *The Man I Love* (1946), opposite Ida Lupino.

After the Bill of Divorcement forced studios to shed many of their contract players including Brix, he went into sales, desiring stable employment to support his family, and eventually became a successful Beverly Hills realtor. He and his wife enjoyed world travel, and visited 86 countries.

Brix passed away on February 24, 2007, age 100; he was preceded in death by wife Jeanette on June 30, 2000. He was cremated and his ashes scattered at sea.

TARZAN ESCAPES *1936*

Rita and Eric Parker (Benita Hume and William Henry) journey to Africa to convince their cousin Jane (Maureen O'Sullivan) to return to England to help them claim an inheritance. However, their treacherous safari guide Captain Fry (John Buckler) has other ideas: capture Tarzan (Johnny Weissmuller) for display on the carnival circuit, and barter Jane and her cousins to the hostile Hymandi tribe in return for safe passage through their country. Unfortunately for Fry and his captives, the Hymandi aren't known for accommodating outsiders.

"New 'Tarzan' Excellent"

– Hollywood Reporter headline, October 24, 1936

In 1934, MGM committed to make a third Tarzan film, a troubled shoot which would gain the reputation of being jinxed following re-writes, re-shoots, and the untimely deaths of some involved.

By January 1935, a treatment for *Tarzan Returns* had been completed by cameraman, director, and writer Karl Brown. Louis Mosher, Wyndham Gittens, Otis Garrett, and John Farrow (who married Maureen O'Sullivan following the production's wrap), all subsequently worked on the story, which initially cast Jane's cousins in a more negative light, as Jane must be declared dead for them to claim their inheritance. Rita Parker was conceived as a seductress who flirts with Tarzan and collaborates with Captain Fry.

MGM hoped to re-purpose its plentiful supply of artificial bats (crafted for *Mark of the Vampire*) for a gruesome scene in the tentatively titled *Tarzan and the Vampires*. Filming began in late July 1935, directed by James McKay, who had shot animal sequences for *Trader Horn* and the preceding Tarzan films. Retitled *The Capture of Tarzan*, the production lensed for 95 days, with William Wellman and George B. Seitz also shooting footage. When the film wrapped, a series of internal conferences were held from November 10 through the end of the year to troubleshoot the picture. MGM executives were dissatisfied with the finished project, believing it lacked a central plot menace, among other flaws, and the story was retooled, toning down the romantic tension between Rita and Tarzan, altering the characters' motivations, and adding comic relief with Rawlins (played by Herbert Mundin). This time, the changes resulted from internal decisions, not pressure from the PCA.

Cyril Hume was assigned to rewrite the script, and contributed the treehouse (the earlier version had Tarzan and Jane living in a cave furnished with jungle amenities). The pair's jungle aerie was a six-room bungalow high in a cottonwood tree, with wraparound porch, elephant-powered elevator, chimp-powered fan, turtle shell sink, and dried mud oven built entirely without nails or fastenings. All-natural materials included logs, bamboo, wicker, rattan, thatch and split bamboo blinds. Weissmuller helped lay the flooring and O'Sullivan wove mats to give them firsthand experience in the construction. Kitchen implements included earthenware utensils, gourd dishes, bamboo forks, and flint knives. The treehouse was created at Brent's Mountain Crags (Crater Camp) in the Santa Monica Mountains, on the 20th Century Fox Ranch. A matching replica was built on an MGM soundstage, with interiors on another stage.

The film resumed production from July 13 through September 4, 1936, with the same cast and cinematographer, Leonard Smith, but with Richard Thorpe directing. Studio publicity claimed the production was using notes from the University of California, compiled by anthropologists who taught Ishi the Yahi Indian to speak English, and these lessons would be applied to Tarzan's instruction in the film (formerly, his speech had been either grunts or imitative). According to the press kit, Ernest Wilson, MD, an African physician born near Victoria Falls and a native Swahili speaker, tutored Weissmuller in the language on set. HRH Crown Prince Modupe of Nigeria served as a technical advisor because of his "first-hand knowledge of Africa". The Hymandi tribe, in keeping with tradition, was not based on historical lore, but on producer Bernard Hyman's name.

The climactic elephant stampede, Weissmuller's crocodile and wildebeest battles, Codona's aerial work, and the safari's Mutia Escarpment climb were recycled from previous MGM Tarzan pictures, along with *Trader Horn* location footage and Jane's adagio jump into Tarzan's arms. After the Hays office crackdown on the nudity in *Mate*, Maureen O'Sullivan was clothed in a modest leather shift, and the treehouse was given twin beds.

The film was re-cut with the new material, and previewed. After scenes with the vampire bats swooping onto the swamp-mired safari terrified children, the bats were nixed. The resulting picture was far more family-friendly than previous MGM efforts, and marked a change in direction for the series, which would be geared to juveniles for the next two decades.

The *Trader Horn* main title music, "Cannibal Carnival" by Sol Levy replaced "Voodoo Dance" as the opening number, with Dr. Axt's "My Tender One" at the closing. The film's final cost was $1,058,430.

The picture was released on November 6, 1936, nearly a year late, to positive reviews. However, the production troubles gave MGM executives pause in renewing the option, and Sol Lesser, waiting in the wings, saw his second chance to make a Tarzan picture.

053

A CURSED PRODUCTION?

Tarzan film production has always involved an element of danger, due to the challenging locations, inclement weather, uncooperative animals, and cast injuries. The mishaps on *Tarzan Escapes* were so numerous that even the *Hollywood Reporter* took notice of the "jinxed" production.

Perhaps the first omen was when a canoe bearing Maureen O'Sullivan, William Henry, director James McKay, assistant director Art Smith, and art director Elmer Sheeley capsized, dumping them and their equipment into the studio lake (fortunately all were good swimmers who didn't require rescue). Then, birds delivered C.O.D. for a scene at Brent's Crags in Malibu proved to be homing pigeons; when their cage was opened, they promptly flew away, delaying production.

The misfortunes began to intensify. Actor John Buckler broke his right arm during a fall on set, and had to wear a special cast and use his left hand. O'Sullivan spent 30 minutes treed by lions released for exercise during the lunch break. A wardrobe lady, returning from lunch, finally summoned help.

On another occasion, sharpshooter Fred Lee shot a lion that was menacing O'Sullivan. The production retained the top marksman in the industry; meanwhile, across town, Charles Bickford was mauled by a lion on the set of *East of Java* and nearly died from his injuries.

The *Los Angeles Sentinel* reported that 75 native extras went on strike, which ended in a stalemate when they were released from duty. Trouble began when the actors, hired to play safari porters, were re-assigned to portray savage tribesmen—without the usual upgrade in pay for having their hands and faces painted (the paint was an irritant, and difficult to remove).

Ten days after production wrapped, MGM's beloved production head Irving Thalberg died at his Santa Monica home from pneumonia. One week before the film's release, co-star John Buckler, just 30, died tragically with his actor father Hugh Buckler, 55. While traveling to their Malibu Lake house for a Halloween Eve party, John lost control of his car in a downpour and skidded and flipped into the lake, where both drowned; the wreckage wasn't discovered until the following day. A Broadway veteran, Buckler appeared in only six films. Less than three years later, co-star Herbert Mundin, 40, was also killed in a car wreck. The amount of misfortune surrounding the troubled production would not be equaled until producer Sy Weintraub assumed control of the franchise, and determined to imbue his films with realism—at a high cost to those involved.

Above: Giant devil bats were re-purposed from MGM's *Mark of the Vampire* (1935) for *Tarzan Escapes*, in a scene that proved so terrifying to youngsters that it was cut from the re-edited film.

Opposite top left: Pygmies (portrayed by local children) rescue Tarzan's party from the swamp.

Opposite top right: Captain Fry, Rita, and Eric admire Tarzan and Jane's steeds.

Opposite middle left: Jane (Maureen O'Sullivan) fist-bumps her appreciation for their succor while cousins Eric and Rita (William Henry and Benita Hume), Tarzan (Weissmuller) and Captain Fry (John Buckler) watch.

Opposite bottom: Tarzan chained—in a scene from *The Capture of Tarzan* that was cut from the re-edited *Tarzan Escapes*.

TARZAN AND THE GREEN GODDESS *1938*

As Tarzan (Herman Brix) and the Martling party prepare to return to civilization with the Green Goddess and its powerful secret, Raglan (Don Castello) steals the idol and the chase is on! The ape man, Major Martling (Frank Baker), George (Lew Sargent), and Ula Vale (Ula Holt) pursue Raglan through the jungle, where they are waylaid by the vengeful Mayans, furious at the theft of their icon.

Billed as "the amazing sequel to *The New Adventures of Tarzan*", this 72-minute film was compiled from material in episodes 3–12 of *The New Adventures of Tarzan* serial, with previously unreleased footage added to enhance the storyline.

Burroughs-Tarzan Enterprises' successor, Burroughs-Tarzan Pictures, had been shuttered in 1937, making *Goddess* the final film released under Burroughs' personal imprint.

> *"Herman Brix, who still gets billing as an Olympic champ, is at home in the Tarzan role . . ."*
> – *Weekly Variety*, January 1, 1938

Above: Tarzan (Herman Brix) saves Ula Vale (Ula Holt) from a marauding leopard.

ULA HOLT

Ula Holt played the mysterious Ula Vale in the BTE Tarzan productions, and remained an enigmatic part of Tarzan film lore for many years after her brief career and abrupt retirement.

Holt was born Florence Eugene Watson on May 18, 1915 in Los Angeles, California. A competitive swimmer, she was portraying a Mayan princess in the RKO film *Adventure Girl* (1934), shot in Guatemala, when she met Lee Ashton Dearholt, Jr., a studio staffer who was reorganizing the company's Guatemala operation.

Upon their return to the States, Ashton divorced his wife, former actress Florence Gilbert, to marry Watson, to whom he gave the stage name Ula Holt (he had formerly acted under

the stage name Richard Holt). Gilbert later married author Edgar Rice Burroughs.

After forming Burroughs-Tarzan Enterprises, Dearholt cast Holt as the *The New Adventures of Tarzan*'s leading lady and returned to Guatemala to shoot the film; it was Ula's only credited role. Following the picture's release, the couple left the film industry. Dearholt died on April 27, 1942, at age 48. Holt later married William Anderson Gleason, taking the name Jewel Watson Gleason, and bore a son and daughter.

Holt died in Clay County, Florida, on January 18, 1982 and is buried in Oakwood Cemetery in Charlottesville City, Virginia, alongside her second husband, who died in 1986.

TARZAN'S REVENGE *1938*

Eleanor Reed (Eleanor Holm) accompanies her parents Roger and Penny (George Barbier and Hedda Hopper) and her milquetoast fiancé Nevin Potter (George Meeker) on an African expedition to capture animals for zoos. On the riverboat, Eleanor catches the eye of Sultan Ben Aley Bey (C. Henry Gordon), who bribes their guide Olaf (Joe Sawyer) to abduct the girl for his harem. When Eleanor falls into a mud hole, Tarzan (Glenn Morris) rescues her, and later liberates the party's trapped animals, taking Eleanor away for an idyllic jungle romp, including a spate of synchronized swimming. When Bey finally springs his trap, Tarzan springs into action to rescue Eleanor.

After the tribulations of producing *Tarzan Escapes*, MGM declined to renew their option; in 1936, Sol Lesser optioned all of Burroughs' published works and embarked on the production of his second ape man film, *Tarzan's Revenge*.

World-class athletic prowess was still a requirement for aspirants to the jungle lord's title. Lesser wooed 1936 Olympic decathlon champion Glenn Morris for the role; other candidates included 1936 Olympic discus gold medalist Ken Carpenter, Yale football star Larry Kelly, heavyweight boxing title-holders Max Baer and Jimmy Braddock, and professional wrestlers Sandor Szabo and Dave Levin.

New York Yankees star Lou Gehrig, intrigued by the possibility of a film career, directed his manager to contact Lesser, who requested photos of the slugger's physique. Gehrig complied, posing for a series of photos wearing a leopard skin and toting a club, but he was unable to unseat Morris, whom Lesser contracted for 10 Tarzan pictures.

Olympic swimming champion Eleanor Holm was cast as Tarzan's love interest Eleanor—due to her notoriety, Lesser didn't believe audiences would accept her as anyone *but* Eleanor, though the character was originally named Cynthia in the script. Both leads were acting neophytes.

Scripted by Robert Lee Johnson and Jay Van, *Revenge*'s plot followed MGM's *Ape Man* template, but with more humor and less bloodshed. Morris's Tarzan is offstage for much of the film, and only has two battles, with a lion and against natives on a rope bridge.

Despite early predictions of a Guadalajara, Mexico,

location shoot, director D. Ross Lederman filmed riverboat dock and trading post scenes on the 20th Century Fox backlot in Century City and jungle and swimming scenes at the 20th Century Ranch (later Malibu Creek State Park).

Actress Nana Bryant was originally cast as Holm's mother; when she was recalled to MGM for another picture, she was replaced by Hedda Hopper. Actor George Barbier was seriously injured when he fell through the suspension bridge. He was admitted to Hollywood Hospital, where Edward T. Fogel, MD, diagnosed fractured ribs and possible internal injuries. Barbier recovered and resumed his busy dramatic career.

Completed on November 1, 1937, *Tarzan's Revenge* was released January 7, 1938 by Paramount Pictures, and garnered poor reviews, suffering by comparison to MGM's big-budget efforts.

Although a sequel, *Tarzan and His Woman*, was announced by Lesser on November 24, to star Morris and be scripted by Carroll Young for Paramount, the film was never made. Young later worked on five Tarzan film scripts for Lesser. In the meantime, Lesser decided to accept a $500,000 offer from MGM for three of his Tarzan picture options.

After flying back to New York with Billy Rose, a tired-looking Holm noted she'd lost 15 pounds on the shoot and weighed only 98 pounds. She was bruised and suffering from a bad cold, having spent the final week of filming being roughly tossed into the mud by Morris. Smarting from the bad reviews, both Olympians retired from acting.

> *"Two races with an alligator are enough for my lifetime. I outswam him twice, but I figured the alligator might break my winning streak the third time out. When I made it to shore, I did five things. Put on my robe, got into my car, drove to my hotel, packed my things, and grabbed the first plane to New York."* — Eleanor Holm, *The Nine Lives of Billy Rose*, 1968

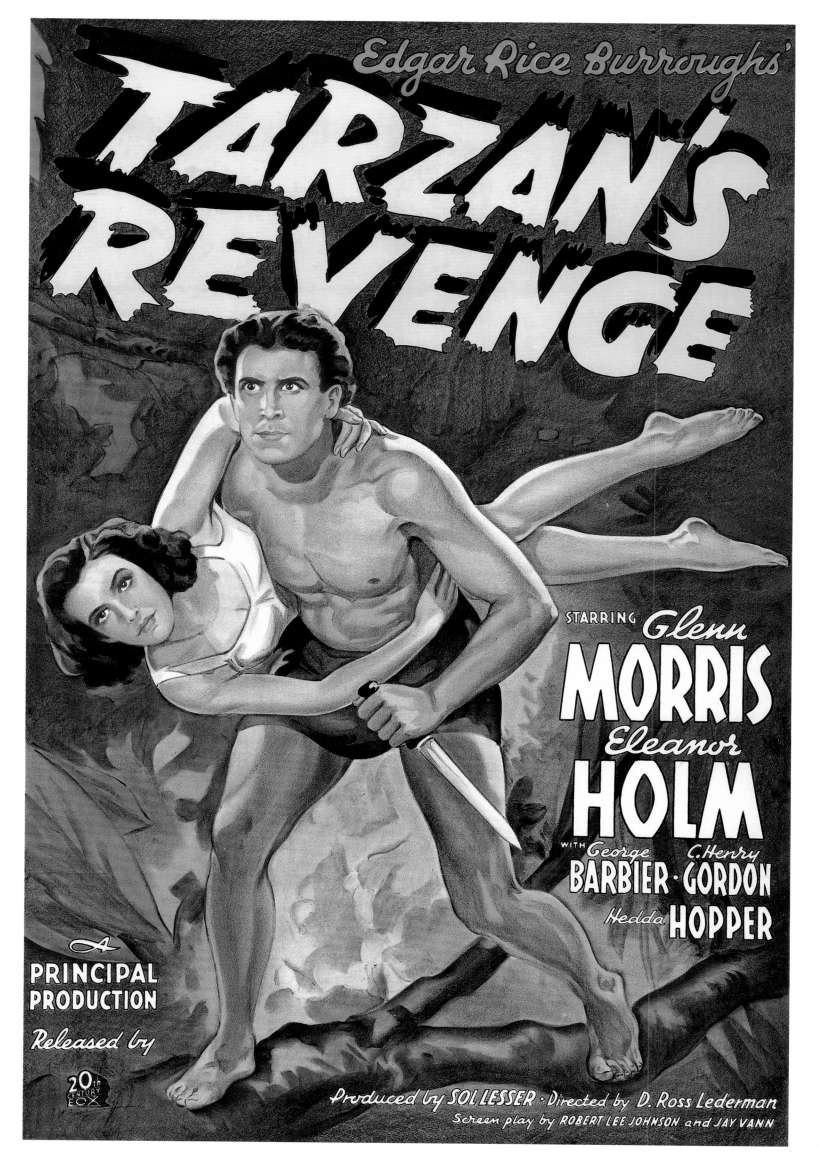

GLENN MORRIS

Glenn Morris won the decathlon at the 1936 Berlin Olympics, in a world-record performance that earned honors and accolades back home, including the year's James E. Sullivan Award as the nation's top amateur athlete. Hollywood beckoned the 6'2", 195-pound athlete, but proved a fickle mistress.

Glenn Edgar Morris grew up running the two miles to and from school from his family's pinto bean farm outside Simla, Colorado, hurdling creeks and fences, as he honed the athletic ability that would later bring fame. One of seven children, he was born on June 18, 1912 in St. Louis, Missouri, to John Francis and Emma Rodett Morris. When Glenn was three, the family relocated to Simla.

Morris excelled at football, basketball, and track in high school, and built hurdles and jump pits to train on the farm. He enrolled at Colorado State College (now Colorado State University) in Fort Collins in the fall of 1930, where he played football, basketball, and track as a freshman, but dropped the basketball after one year to concentrate on football and track.

As a senior, Morris was an All Conference tight end on the football team and set the school record in the intermediate hurdles, while serving as student body president. He graduated June 6, 1934, with a degree in economics and sociology.

Morris worked as a graduate assistant coach the following year and sold cars while he trained on campus for the 1936 Olympics under head coach Harry Hughes. He only competed in the decathlon three times, setting a national record at the Kansas Relays and world records at the Olympic trials and 1936 Berlin Olympics. It was an American medal sweep, with Morris's gold medal followed by Robert Clark's silver and Jack Parker's bronze, in lifetime bests for each in the event.

Returning to Colorado, Morris married his college sweetheart, Charlotte Edwards. When Tarzan producer Sol Lesser requested photos, Morris submitted shots taken by filmmaker Leni Reifenstahl during his Olympics competition, which sealed the role for him. Morris re-settled in Tarzana, California, and appeared in small parts in *She Married an Artist* (1937) and *Hold That Co-Ed* (1938).

When Morris's role as Tarzan didn't generate further film offers, he returned to Colorado, where he sold insurance. There, Charlotte divorced him in 1939, and he signed to play football with the Detroit Lions in 1940. Misfortune followed, and his football career ended when his leg was broken in the first game.

On October 5, 1942, Morris enlisted in the U.S. Navy for World War II. He was accepted to Officer's Candidate School, and commissioned as a lieutenant. Assigned to the *U.S.S. Banner*, he served as an amphibious assault craft beach landing master, tasked with retaking the Pacific Islands from the Japanese, under heavy fire. Morris was discharged on July 1, 1947 with numerous medals and ribbons.

His war experiences left him with post-traumatic stress disorder and the former national hero was never the same. He lived in the San Francisco area and worked in the naval shipyards as a steelworker and construction worker. He also worked intermittently as a security guard and parking lot attendant.

Morris died of heart failure on January 31, 1974, in the Palo Alto, California Veterans Administration hospital, after a long illness, survived by two brothers and two sisters. He was buried at Skylawn Memorial Park in San Mateo, California, and his memorabilia was donated to Simla High School, which instituted an annual Glenn Morris Award, given to a student who excels athletically and academically.

ELEANOR HOLM

Despite her 1932 gold medal and numerous world records in swimming the backstroke, Eleanor Holm was more famous for *not* competing in the 1936 Berlin Olympics when she was dismissed from the Olympic team for drinking and carousing, a penalty that she said "made" her career.

Holm was born on December 6, 1913 in Brooklyn, New York, the youngest of seven children of Franklin Holm, a Fire Department Chief, and wife Charlotte. The family summered in Long Beach, where the Women's Swimming Association of New York trained. At 13, Holm joined the organization and began competing against adults, winning the national title in the backstroke in 1928. She finished fifth in the 100-meter backstroke at the Amsterdam Olympics and resolved to win the next time.

Returning home, she appeared in the Ziegfeld Follies for three months, but departed to concentrate on her Olympics training. Holm easily won the 100-meter backstroke gold medal at the 1932 Los Angeles Olympics in a world-record time of 1:19.4.

Studios wooed her, and she signed a contract with Jack Warner, earning $500 a week and Wampas Baby Star of 1932 honors while taking drama lessons from coach Josephine Dillon (the former Mrs. Clark Gable). A few months later, she resigned, concerned that a swimming role on film would compromise her amateur status and her further Olympic aspirations.

On September 2, 1933, she married bandleader Arthur Jarrett, Jr., a friend from their days at Erasmus Hall High School in Brooklyn. She toured the country with Jarrett, singing nightclub duets with him and training afterward, sleeping all day.

She boasted that her training regimen was champagne and cigarettes, as sportswriters circled her, caught in the gravitational pull of her charisma. She continued to set world records in a seven-year streak of undefeated competition, and became the first woman to earn a place on three Olympic swimming teams in 1936.

On the cruise to Europe aboard the *U.S.S. Manhattan*, she socialized with her journalist and celebrity friends, which angered AAU President Avery Brundage, who expelled her from the team for breaking training by gambling and drinking. Despite protests from her teammates and supporters, Brundage was adamant, and Holm witnessed the Berlin Olympics from the sidelines, while attending fetes arranged by the Nazi regime for foreign celebrities.

Upon returning to the U.S., she signed with Broadway impresario Billy Rose to appear in his Aquacade with Johnny Weissmuller at Cleveland's Great Lakes Exposition. That fall, she flew to Hollywood to film *Tarzan's Revenge*, an experience that soured her on Hollywood.

She divorced Jarrett and married Rose on November 14, 1939, and appeared in his 1939–40 Aquacade at the New York World's Fair opposite Johnny Weissmuller and, later, Buster Crabbe. She and Rose divorced in an acrimonious filing dubbed the War of the Roses, with Holm settling on February 27, 1954 for a large portion of Rose's fortune. Later in life, she dated Tommy Whalen (declining to marry so that she could still receive large alimony checks from Rose), and settled in Miami, where she socialized, did interior decorating, and invested in the stock market. She died of kidney failure on January 31, 2004, age 90.

Opposite: Olympic champions Glenn Morris and Eleanor Holm portrayed Tarzan and Eleanor.

Above: Tarzan rescues Eleanor from Sultan Ben Aley Bey's (C. Henry Gordon) harem, as turncoat safari guide Olaf (Joe Sawyer) watches.

TARZAN FINDS A SON! *1939*

Cheeta finds a baby orphaned in a plane crash and delivers it to Tarzan (Johnny Weissmuller) and Jane (Maureen O'Sullivan), who name the child Boy (Johnny Sheffield) and raise him as their own. Five years later, Sir Thomas Lancing (Henry Stephenson) arrives, searching for the wreckage, led by opportunistic safari guide Mr. Sande (Henry Wilcoxon) and his greedy clients Mr. and Mrs. Austin Lancing (Ian Hunter and Frieda Inescort)—who stand to inherit a fortune if there are no survivors.

"Boy strong. Call Elephant!" – Tarzan
"Elephant? With a little nose like that?" – Jane
"Later call Elephant. Now call—Boy!" – Tarzan

Despite its troubled production *Tarzan Escapes* proved highly profitable, generating $2 million at the box office. MGM decided to continue with the franchise, and in 1937 offered Burroughs $75,000 for three more ape man films. Sol Lesser, having experienced more difficulties than anticipated in *Tarzan's Revenge*, and realizing that more big-budget MGM films were in his long-term best interest, sold his rights for three films to MGM for $500,000.

The agreement was finalized in July 1938, and Cyril Hume was again assigned scripting chores. An early draft had Tarzan and Jane giving birth to a son and returning to England for the jungle lord to assume his Greystoke title; unhappy there, the family returns to Africa. By August 18, the English trip was out, and Hume had the unmarried couple discovering the foundling child in the jungle, to circumvent Production Code restrictions. Hume's script saw Jane killed at the end, and was titled *Tarzan in Exile*.

Richard Thorpe and Leonard Smith returned as director and first cameraman. A jungle set was built onstage at MGM, with interior and exterior treehouse sets; locations included Lake Sherwood and the 20th Century Fox Ranch. MGM's Lot 2 hosted the plane wreckage, river, Tarzan Rocks, exterior camp, and Zambeli village. The dump tank on Lot 1 was used for waterfall scenes. The film also shot at Goebel's Lion Farm in Thousand Oaks, and incorporated aerial animal footage purchased from Martin and Osa Johnson's documentary *Baboona* (1935), along with the usual *Trader Horn* stock shots.

Crown Prince Modupe, an Oxford graduate and the nephew of Chief Babolala of Nigeria's Europa tribe made his screen debut (uncredited) and worked as a technical advisor on tribal customs for the film. The Zambeli tribe's name was an inside joke referencing producer Sam Zimbalist.

Production rolled from January 9 to March 25, with a trip to Florida for exterior shots after studio work was completed. In a January 6, 1939 letter to the studio vice-president Al Lichtman, Burroughs urged MGM to reconsider killing Jane (speared by the Zambeli), noting that he had tried to dispatch Jane in the pulp serialization for *Tarzan the Untamed*, until outcry from readers (and his family) forced him to resurrect her at the novel's end. MGM agreed, and by January 31 an alternate ending with Jane surviving was added to the script. On April 19 the alternate ending was shot, along with other retakes.

O'Sullivan was pregnant during filming, so she was carefully photographed, covering her stomach with props. Her work on re-shoots finished just two weeks before the May 30 delivery of her first child with husband John Farrow, Michael Damien Villiers Farrow. Dickie and Buddy Smith, the six-month-old twins of a studio employee, played Boy as a baby, with Johnny Sheffield making his feature film debut as the older Boy. Sheffield was stunt-doubled by Harry Monty, "The Midget Strongman", who also portrayed a munchkin and flying monkey on *The Wizard of Oz* (1939). Though Boy is a grand-nephew of Lord Greystoke in the storyline, no connection is made between Tarzan and the Greystoke lineage.

The film's original prints were tinted Sepia Platinum to give them a blue-green tone. An extended version of "Cannibal Carnival" played over the credits, with Axt's "My Tender One" at the closing. The final cost was $887,210. The picture previewed at the Carthay Circle Theatre on Friday, May 26, 1939, and saw wide release on June 16, 1939. The film is filled with sublime humor, which sets it apart from previous MGM and silent entries, and makes it an American classic suitable for all ages.

TARZAN
Finds a Son!

WITH *Johnny* **WEISSMULLER**

Maureen **O'SULLIVAN**

JOHN SHEFFIELD ·
IAN HUNTER ·
HENRY STEPHENSON ·
FRIEDA INESCORT ·
HENRY WILCOXON ·
LARAINE DAY ·

SCREEN PLAY BY CYRIL HUME · BASED UPON THE CHARACTERS CREATED BY EDGAR RICE BURROUGHS
DIRECTED BY **RICHARD THORPE** · PRODUCED BY SAM ZIMBALIST

A Metro-*Goldwyn*-Mayer
PICTURE

ALL NEW!
THE FIRST
TARZAN PICTURE
IN 3 YEARS!

063

TARZAN IN FLORIDA

With the addition of Johnny Sheffield to the cast, MGM executives decided a location shoot would enhance the storyline; Florida was chosen because the clear water in Crystal Springs and Silver Springs, near Ocala, was perfect for underwater filming.

The crew traveled 6,000 miles by rail in customized coaches. Included were Johnny Weissmuller, his fiancé Beryl Scott, director Richard Thorpe, and Johnny and Reginald Sheffield. Pregnant Maureen O'Sullivan remained in Hollywood.

"Jungle Larry" Tetzlaff, 19, a protégé of Frank "Bring 'Em Back Alive" Buck and a budding herpetologist, was hired to work with reptiles on the film and doubled for Weissmuller, as did Newt Perry, a popular local swimmer who performed at Silver Springs and could hold his breath underwater for three minutes and 45 seconds.

O'Sullivan was doubled by Elsie Davis, a Chamber of Commerce employee, in long shots, and Mrs. Ralph Slatten (who better resembled her) for close-ups. Newt Perry's sister Eileen doubled Frieda Inescort, while his cousin Newton Fivash doubled Wilcoxon. Forty locals played the safari porters.

Sheffield was also doubled in Silver Springs by Edward "Gooley" Green, 10, a local boy who shot underwater sequences with Weissmuller's double, Perry. Two 300-pound sea turtles, named Johnny and Maureen, were purchased in Florida for use in the underwater swimming sequences.

Baby Bea the elephant made her debut in the film. She was purchased from the Detroit zoo by MGM and named for trainer George Emerson's wife, Bea. She was 16 months old, 3'9", and weighed 650 pounds, reputed to be the smallest baby elephant in America. She made the trip to Florida on the same train as the actors and crew, in a heated baggage car, strapped into a harness to prevent falls when the train went around curves. Emerson and an assistant trainer provided 24-hour companionship in 8-hour shifts. The car featured a complete kitchen, stocked with 100 pounds of rice, 10 bushels of carrots, and 50 bushels of assorted vegetables.

Sheffield named Bea "Buli" onscreen, and would refer to future juvenile elephants by that name, which means "teapot" in Swahili. Baby Bea was a quick study; she watched as Queenie, playing her mother Timba, limped about the set, then quickly adopted a hopping limp into her repertoire of tricks—a stunt which she had to un-learn, since her character wasn't injured in the film!

While in Florida, Weissmuller was inducted as an honorary member of the Cherokee tribe, "Chief Swim Fast". The film crew presented Shorty Davidson, the co-owner of the Silver Springs attraction, with one of Weissmuller's loincloths, signed by the cast and crew; Davidson's descendants still have the loincloth which is occasionally displayed in Ocala.

Opposite: Tarzan (Johnny Weissmuller) and Jane (Maureen O'Sullivan) adopt a forest foundling (twins Dickie and Buddy Smith).

Top left: Weissmuller personally selected Sheffield from 300 applicants.

Top right: Sheffield proved a game addition to the cast.

Near right, second from top: Boy had an elephant of his own, played by Baby Bea.

Second from bottom: Weissmuller and Sheffield filmed on location in the Florida swamps.

Bottom left: In the original storyline Jane died from her wounds.

Far right: Tarzan teaches Boy the swingin' ways of the jungle.

TARZAN'S SECRET TREASURE *1941*

An expedition of scientists arrives in the jungle, led by Professor Elliot (Reginald Owen), seeking a lost tribe. When Boy (Johnny Sheffield) innocently shows Medford (Tom Conway) and Vandermeer (Philip Dorn) his gold nuggets, they take Boy and Jane (Maureen O'Sullivan) hostage, forcing Tarzan (Johnny Weissmuller) to lead them to the ore, then trapping him in a ravine. Their path to escape, guided by Jane, lies through dangerous Joconi country, but, like all baddies, they've underestimated the ape man and his friends, Cheeta, Tumbo (Cordell Hickman) and O'Doul (Barry Fitzgerald).

MGM returned to screenwriter Cyril Hume, who had struck gold with *Ape Man* and *Son!* to script their fifth Tarzan picture. Since he killed Jane in his original script for *Son!*, he had the grieving Tarzan burn down the treehouse, and retire with Boy to live in the jungle.

"Sylvia Starke, International Glamour Girl No. 1" arrives to hunt big game, meets the jungle lord, and romance with a happy ending ensues. Brenda Frazier, a popular American debutante of the Depression era (and November 14, 1938 *Life* magazine cover girl) dubbed "Glamour Girl No. 1" may have been an inspiration for the storyline.

Following Jane's resurrection in the re-edited version of *Son!* Hume's Glamour Girl script was rejected on July 7, 1939. Hume asked to leave the project and Miles Connolly and Paul Gangelin were hired, producing a more conventional storyline wherein members of a scientific expedition discover gold on the Mutia Escarpment, and begin scheming to possess it.

Early plans to shoot exteriors in Africa, with Edgar Rice Burroughs along for the publicity value, were scrapped as wartime travel restrictions began to take effect. A new lake and jungle were constructed on MGM Lot 2 and Lot 3, with the ending farewell sequence shot at Iverson Movie Ranch. The MGM set, covering 80 acres, was the largest engineered for a jungle picture. Richard Thorpe returned to direct, with camerawork by Clyde De Vinna. Shooting took two months, from June 14 to August 18, 1941, with additional pick-up shots in late September and October.

The film relied heavily on recycled footage to cut costs. Seen again were the safari's climb up Mutia Escarpment, Codona's trapeze work, Weissmuller's crocodile battle, the native torture ceremony, and Mary the rhino's charge (with Cordell Hickman's Tumbo dodging in front of the rear-projected footage).

The storyline introduced Hickman's Tumbo, a native playmate for Boy, orphaned when plague strikes his village. His grandmother was played by Mandy Calvin, 102 (reputed to be a former slave), discovered when Thorpe put out a casting call for the oldest black woman in Los Angeles. Calvin's stand-in was the runner-up for the role, age 92. Despite the apparent adoption of Tumbo by the Tarzan family, Hickman did not return to the series, but went on to become the City of Los Angeles high school high-jump champion, later entering the dry-cleaning business in Leimert Park.

Animal trainer George Emerson debuted a new trick, a tightrope-walking lion who follows Boy through the trees on cables dressed as vines. While shooting the scene where Barry Fitzgerald shadow-boxes a lion, the cat, Pasha, ran amok on set, stalking Fitzgerald as crew members scrambled into the trees. Electrician Paul "Shug" Keeler saved the day by toppling a light fixture to distract the nervous cat until Louis Roth could round him up. Menelik, an experienced film lion, was then substituted for Pasha, whose repertoire was more circus-trick-oriented. Twenty circus elephants were hired to stage the climactic battle.

The crew decamped to Florida for more water work, shooting on location in Wakulla Springs. Underwater scenes were shot by Lloyd Knechtel from a diving bell lowered via barge. Local Florida State College for Women co-ed Jean Knapp doubled for O'Sullivan on a three-week contract, insured for $5,000, and Gooley Green again stunt-doubled Sheffield. Animals on site included elephants Sally, Happy, and Queenie, two chimps, and a 500-pound turtle from Key West. The swimming elephant footage was an accident—Happy fell off a raft, and Knechtel kept the cameras rolling in his diving bell. Three hundred locals dressed as Joconi tribesmen (the now-standard inside joke on production manager Joe Cohn), all supervised by Wakulla Springs manager Newt Perry, who also doubled for Weissmuller as needed.

An extended version of "Cannibal Carnival" was re-recorded for the credit sequence, followed by David Snell's "Maisie Was a Lady". Once again, "My Tender One" played at the end. Like in *Son!*, the film prints were tinted Sepia Platinum. The final budget was $978,135.

The film was released on December 24, 1941, shortly after the U.S. entered World War II. Author Burroughs viewed it incognito in a Honolulu theater.

"It's an all-out Tarzaner, this one"
- Edwin Schallert, *Los Angeles Times*, March 27, 1942

JOHNNY WEISSMULLER

Critics and the public alike were captivated by Johnny Weissmuller's performance as Tarzan, enthralled by his chemistry with his leading lady Maureen O'Sullivan and lack of self-consciousness onscreen. The ape man proved the perfect role for the former athlete, who had no pretensions about becoming a serious thespian and reveled in the rewards provided by his hard work and attendant fame.

Janos Weissmuller was born on June 2, 1904 to Petrus and Elizabeth Weissmuller in the village of Freidorf, in the Banat region of the Austro-Hungarian Empire (now part of Romania). His family emigrated to the U.S. shortly afterward. Younger brother Peter was born September 3, 1905 in Windber, Pennsylvania; concerned that his foreign birth would disqualify him from the 1924 Olympics, Johnny switched birth certificates with Peter to secure his passport.

Weissmuller attended St. Michael's parochial school and Manierre public school, but dropped out to help support the family with odd jobs including delivery boy, bellboy, and elevator operator. An avid swimmer from childhood, the gangly 6'3" Weissmuller auditioned for renowned swimming instructor "Big Bill" Bachrach in October 1920, and won a membership to the Illinois Athletic Club, one of the nation's pre-eminent swimming programs.

He made his AAU swimming debut on August 6, 1921, winning the 50-yard freestyle event. Weissmuller competed at numerous distances and remained undefeated until his retirement, compiling a record 36 individual championships and 67 world championships while setting 94 American records and 51 world records, winning five gold medals in the 1924 and 1928 Olympics. Associated Press sportswriters and broadcasters named him "Greatest Swimmer of the Half-Century, 1900–1950".

Following his 1928 Olympic victories, Weissmuller signed an endorsement deal with BVD swimwear. He made a cameo in his first motion picture, *Glorifying the American Girl* (1929) and authored *Swimming the American Crawl* (1930) with Clarence A. Bush.

Tarzan the Ape Man scripter Cyril Hume discovered him working out at the Hollywood Athletic Club, and referred him to director Woody Van Dyke and the MGM producer Bernard Hyman, who had been stymied in their search for the perfect lead for their picture.

Weissmuller's twelve appearances as Tarzan cemented his status as the greatest and most memorable of the film Tarzans. MGM kept him on contract solely for Tarzan pictures, so he spent his considerable free time sailing his yacht, the *Allure*, to Catalina and palling around with celebrity friends like John Wayne. The studio did loan him out for live shows in Billy Rose's summer Aquacades, co-starring with Eleanor Holm and Esther Williams.

During World War II, Weissmuller worked at the Hollywood canteen and made public appearances with other performers; he also taught naval recruits how to swim underwater to escape flaming oil spills. After aging out of the Tarzan role, he donned safari khakis to play Alex Raymond's comic-strip hero Jungle Jim in a series of 16 films and a 1955–56 television series.

Weissmuller's five wives included actresses Bobbe Arnst and Lupe Velez, socialite Beryl Scott, amateur golfer Allene Gates, and German expatriate Maria Bauman. He had three children with Scott: John Scott, Jr., Wendy Anne, and Heidi Elizabeth.

Following his retirement from acting, he founded a swimming pool company, and worked as the curator of the Swimming Hall of Fame in Fort Lauderdale, and as a celebrity greeter at the Caesar's Palace casino in Las Vegas.

After a series of strokes and other health problems, Weissmuller moved to Acapulco, where he died of a pulmonary edema at home on January 20, 1984, age 79, with Maria at his side. He was buried at the Panteón Valle de la Luz. As his casket was lowered, the Tarzan cry sounded.

Opposite: MGM commissioned a series of glamor shots of Weissmuller and O'Sullivan for their fifth film together.

Above: Boy and Jane are taken hostage by Vandermeer (Philip Dorn) and Medford (Tom Conway), who decide crime pays better than scientific inquiry.

Middle right: When O'Doul (Barry Fitzgerald) is stricken ill, Tarzan and Professor Elliot (Reginald Owen) nurse him.

Bottom right: A scientific party arrives just in time to prevent Boy from becoming a native sacrifice.

"With his flowing hair, his magnificently proportioned body, his catlike walk, and his virtuosity on water, you could hardly ask more in the way of perfection."
– Thornton Delehanty, *New York Evening Post*, *Tarzan the Ape Man* review

TARZAN'S NEW YORK ADVENTURE *1942*

Animal trapper Buck Rand (Charles Bickford) and his trainer Manchester Mountford (Chill Wills) arrive in Tarzan's jungle, piloted by nice guy Jimmy Shields (Paul Kelly). Believing Tarzan (Johnny Weissmuller) and Jane (Maureen O'Sullivan) killed in a Joconi attack, they take Boy (Johnny Sheffield) to New York City to serve as a pint-sized animal trainer in their circus. Cheeta saves Tarzan and Jane, who must brave the wilds of civilization to rescue their son.

Almost immediately after wrapping *Tarzan's Secret Treasure* re-shoots in October 1941, MGM put *Tarzan's New York Adventure* into production, lensing in six weeks from December 1941 to February 1942.

Film lore has it that Maureen O'Sullivan, who was tiring of the series, was enticed to return with a promise of a couture wardrobe, designed by Howard Shoup. Weissmuller was also fitted for a natty suit, his first time in civilized clothes for the MGM films.

Originally titled *Tarzan Against the World*, the picture shot on the MGM Lot 2, with second unit shots, *sans* cast, filmed in New York. The film recycled aerialist Alfredo Codona's vine-swinging sequences from *Ape Man*, and the cast's Florida swimming footage from the previous picture.

The Hagenbeck-Wallace Circus, wintering in Southern California, was rented and set up on the MGM lot for the film. Former screen Tarzan Elmo Lincoln played one of the roustabouts tasked with stopping Tarzan. Boy's performance with three juvenile elephants was accomplished by MGM trainer George Emerson, standing off-camera, giving the animals their cues.

Tarzan's Brooklyn Bridge dive was achieved by dropping a dummy from the scenic tower of Lot 3 into the tank underneath. Tarzan's jump was compared to that by Steve Brodie, who became a celebrity following his claim to have jumped from the bridge and lived in 1886; he was accused of using a dummy double in the stunt. "Take a Brodie" became popular slang for a suicidal venture. The strong currents in the river were actually more dangerous than the fall.

The film took full advantage of the comedy potential in the unconventional scenario, with a steady stream of amusing set-ups, as Tarzan and Cheeta sought to make their way through the urban jungle and the strange conventions of civilized men. The picture also utilized the largest supporting cast of MGM contract players of any Tarzan film.

The production was the last of three film options purchased from Sol Lesser in July 1938, and the final MGM film. With the loss of the foreign market to World War II, MGM executives decided to end their decade-long association with the franchise, which reaped greater financial returns overseas than in the U.S.

Shooting was completed on January 27, 1942. On February 3, 1942, MGM announced that they were out of the Tarzan business and Weissmuller and O'Sullivan were released from their contracts.

The film was airlifted to Iceland for the May premiere as entertainment for the U.S. troops stationed there. It was transferred from 35mm to 16mm for easier transport and dropped by parachute onto the military base. This was the first of 1,200 films shown free to U.S. armed forces.

The film was released only six months after the previous MGM film, the fastest turnaround for an MGM Tarzan sequel, and continued the series' profitable reign, making more than $1 million against its $707,166 budget by year's end. At 71 minutes, it was the shortest of the MGM Tarzan films.

Author Edgar Rice Burroughs, touring the South Pacific as a war correspondent, saw the film in Sydney, Australia, on January 5, 1943. The screening, arranged by MGM's Australian executives, was followed with a round of print, radio, and newsreel interviews in which Burroughs expressed confidence in the series' new producer, Sol Lesser.

"I can see the 24-sheets now—the Boy King of the Jungle!"

– Manchester Mountford

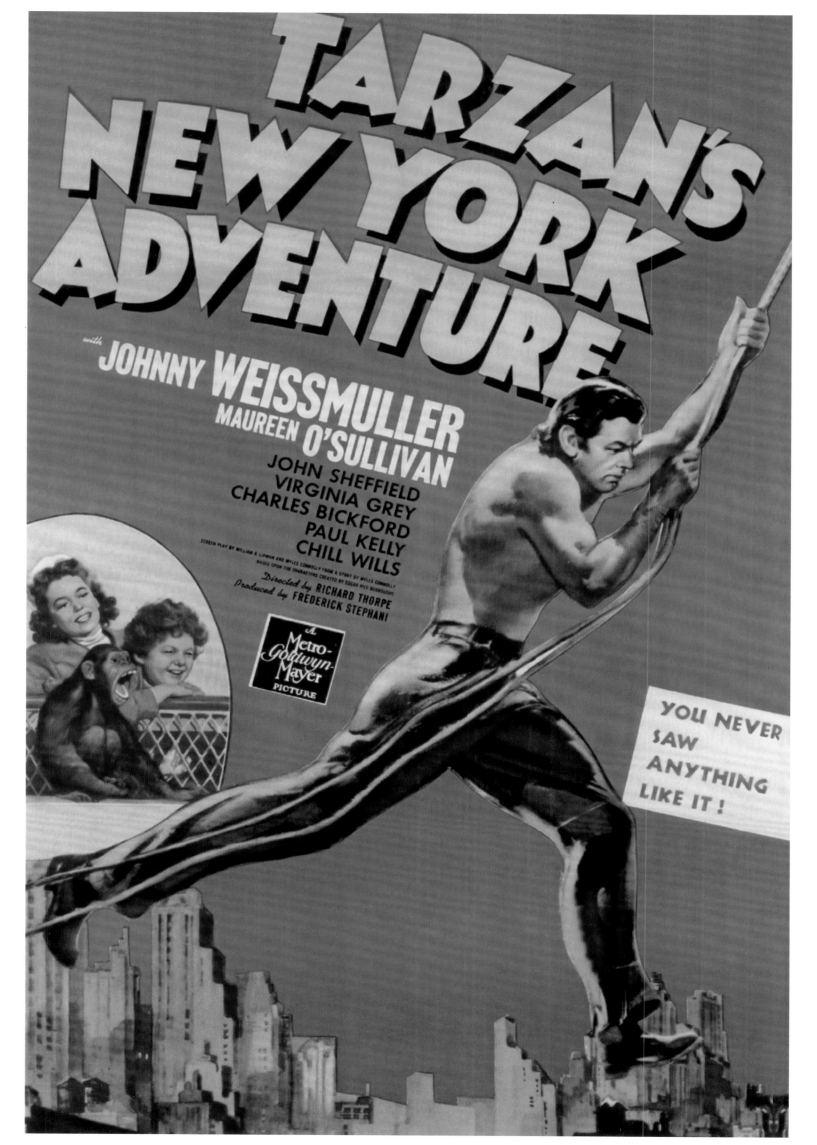

MAUREEN O'SULLIVAN

Maureen O'Sullivan's portrayal of Jane and the chemistry she shared with Johnny Weissmuller were an integral element in the Tarzan films' worldwide popularity. Their performance became one of filmdom's all-time great romantic pairings.

O'Sullivan, who had been released from a 20th Century Fox contract after several films, was down to her last $150 and planning to leave showbusiness and return to Ireland when she decided to invest in new headshots for submission to MGM. She was personally chosen by production head Irving Thalberg to appear opposite Johnny Weissmuller in *Ape Man*, and tendered a studio contract which lasted nine years. Standing at only 5'3", the petite O'Sullivan was a perfect physical complement to Weissmuller's athletic brawn.

The oldest of five children, Maureen Paula O'Sullivan was born on May 17, 1911 in Boyle, County Roscommon, Ireland, to army officer Charles Joseph O'Sullivan and Mary Fraser O'Sullivan, in a tiny apartment above a draper's store. Her father, a member of the elite Connaught Rangers, was stationed at the barracks nearby.

O'Sullivan attended convent school in Dublin, then transferred to the Convent of the Sacred Heart at Roehampton, where she came in second to her friend Vivien Leigh in a vote for most beautiful girl. O'Sullivan completed her formal education at a Parisian finishing school.

She was discovered by director Frank Borzage at the Dublin International Horse Show dance in September 1929. O'Sullivan, now 18, was cast in the role of Eileen O'Brien in *Song O' My Heart*, filming on location. Borzage signed O'Sullivan to a Fox contract, and brought her to Hollywood; she was released from her three-year contract after six pictures underperformed at the box office.

At MGM, she became a popular second lead in numerous films, including *The Thin Man* (1934), *The Barretts of Wimpole Street* (1934), *David Copperfield* (1934), *Anna Karenina* (1935), *A Day at the Races* (1937), and *Pride and Prejudice* (1940). O'Sullivan also played the lead in B-movies, unlike Weissmuller, who was confined to Tarzan pictures by the studio.

On September 12, 1936, O'Sullivan married John Villiers Farrow, an Australian native who worked as a scripter on *Tarzan Escapes* (1936) and went on to author several books and direct films. The couple had seven children, including daughters Maria de Lourdes (Mia) and Theresa (Tisa), who followed Maureen into the acting profession.

After terminating her MGM contract, Maureen and John moved to Canada so Farrow could join the Canadian Royal Navy for World War II service, where he contracted typhus. O'Sullivan temporarily retired from acting to nurse Farrow and rear their children.

O'Sullivan returned to the screen in *The Big Clock* (1948), directed by Farrow, and resumed work in film, television, and stage. Her final film credit was *The River Pirates* (1988), based on the Willie Morris novel *Good Old Boy*, filmed in Natchez, Mississippi.

She had her Broadway debut in *Never Too Late* (1962). Two months after the show's opening, Farrow died of a heart attack on January 28, 1963. After a hiatus to mourn his passing, O'Sullivan returned to the show for a two-year run at her children's urging.

O'Sullivan and longtime friend Robert Ryan began dating after becoming reacquainted at a dinner party, but he died of cancer in July 11, 1973, before they could wed. O'Sullivan maintained a bedside vigil with his family before he passed away.

On August 22, 1983, O'Sullivan married James Cushing, a retired construction executive from New York State. They split their time between a log cabin in Grantham, New Hampshire, the family house in Schenectady, New York, and an Arizona condominium. O'Sullivan died of heart failure on Monday, June 22, 1998 at Scottsdale Memorial Hospital in Arizona.

"Miss O'Sullivan, ideally cast, puts emotional power as well as physical allure into her strenuous part."

– Daily Variety, April 7, 1934, Tarzan and His Mate review

TARZAN TRIUMPHS *1943*

Nazi paratroopers occupy the lost city of Palandrya, enslaving the peaceful inhabitants in an effort to secure tin and petroleum reserves. Princess Zandra (Frances Gifford) escapes and pleads with Tarzan (Johnny Weissmuller) to aid her people. Tarzan resists involvement, until the Nazis kidnap Boy (Johnny Sheffield), leaving the ape man for dead. Tarzan must infiltrate the city, free the inhabitants, and defeat Colonel von Reichart's (Stanley Ridges) troops before the commander radios for reinforcements.

"Now, Tarzan Make War!"

Beset by declining foreign revenues in wartime Europe, Metro-Goldwyn-Mayer Studios sold its interest in Tarzan films to producer Sol Lesser, which included Johnny Weissmuller's and Johnny Sheffield's contracts. Maureen O'Sullivan, then starting a family with spouse John Farrow, declined Lesser's invitation to join the cast.

The MGM treehouse, Tarzan yell, creative personnel, and intellectual property were not included in the agreement, forcing Lesser to reinvent the franchise. He negotiated a deal with the U.S. State Department to shoot the film as war propaganda, hiring Jewish Austrian émigré William (Wilhelm) Thiele to direct from a script by Roy Chanslor and Carroll Young. In the film, Tarzan—serving as a metaphor for isolationist America—refuses to get involved in the Nazi threat, until the menace becomes personal; theaters erupted in cheers when the ape man declared, "Now, Tarzan make war!"

Lesser wooed burlesque-queen-turned-actress Anne Corio to replace O'Sullivan, but when she declined, he decided to hold the role of Jane open and cast Frances Gifford in a non-romantic female lead. The Lucky Baldwin estate in Arcadia (today the Los Angeles County Arboretum) provided jungle locations, as did Lake Sherwood and the RKO studios backlot in Culver City. A new treehouse was designed and built, and a new yell recorded (without post-production sweetening), which Weissmuller was able to emulate. Paul Sawtell scored, with Constantine Bakaleinikoff conducting. The production filmed from mid-August to mid-September, 1942 for a February 19, 1943 release by distributor RKO Radio Pictures, Inc.

Despite the high body count of slaughtered Nazis (and their victims), the film was Lesser's most profitable Tarzan picture; he estimated that it paid Burroughs a quarter of a million dollars in royalties. It was later released on a twin bill with Lesser's follow-up, *Tarzan's Desert Mystery*.

"Tarzan to the Rescue . . . braving the Pit of Pythons and the Stream of Cannibal Fish to Save a Pagan Princess from ruthless Men of Evil!"

FRANCES GIFFORD

Frances Gifford is best remembered for her role as Nyoka Meredith in the Republic serial *Jungle Girl* (1941), which saw a return to the popular silent-film era tradition of female leads, pioneered by women like Pearl White and Ruth Roland. Though based on one of Edgar Rice Burroughs' jungle novels, the chapter-play bore little resemblance to its source material. Audiences didn't mind, as they inhaled their weekly fix of a beautiful woman escaping danger at every turn.

Mary Frances Gifford was born on December 7, 1920, the only child of an electrician father and housewife mother. She

was a popular student at Woodrow Wilson High School in Long Beach, California, where she was a cheerleader, tennis team captain, and valedictorian of her class. She also served as Queen of Long Beach for the 1936 Tournament of Roses Parade in Pasadena.

Gifford, who enrolled at UCLA in pre-law, visited Samuel Goldwyn Studios with a friend and walked out with a contract after a studio executive insisted she take a screen test. The Hollywood Press Photographers Association named her a Flash-lighters Starlet of 1936, and celebrity photographer Clarence Bull declared her to be one of the 10 most beautiful women he'd shot throughout his career.

After her Goldwyn and subsequent RKO contracts elapsed, Gifford eloped with actor James "Jimmy" Dunn on Christmas Day, 1937, but the marriage failed. Gifford secured a Paramount contract, which led to her first major lead as Helen Forbes in the Hopalong Cassidy film *Border Vigilantes* (1941) and loanouts to *Jungle Girl* and *Tarzan Triumphs*.

Her dedication eventually resulted in an MGM contract, and the studio refused to loan her out for a follow-up Tarzan picture, casting her as lead Viola Johnson in *Our Vines Have Tender Grapes* (1945) among other films.

Gifford's career was cut short by a bad automobile accident on New Year's Eve, 1948, resulting in a head injury and lacerations to her face and hands. This, combined with the deaths of her parents, led to severe depression for which she was hospitalized for a time at the Camarillo State Hospital. Upon her release from the facility, she worked for the American Cancer Society, and as a volunteer typist for the Pasadena Public Library. Gifford died of emphysema at a Pasadena convalescent center on January 22, 1994, age 73.

Left: Frances Gifford as Princess Zandra of Palandrya, who enlists Tarzan's aid against invading Nazis.

Opposite top left: When Boy is kidnapped, it becomes personal for Tarzan.

Opposite top right: Zandra, held captive by Colonel von Reichart (Stanley Ridges) and his Sergeant (Sig Rumann).

Opposite middle: Captured by the Nazis—but not for long!

Opposite bottom: Cheeta radios Nazi headquarters.

TARZAN'S DESERT MYSTERY *1943*

Tarzan (Johnny Weissmuller), Boy (Johnny Sheffield), and Cheeta set off across the great desert to procure fever medicine plants for the British war effort. On their trek, they become embroiled in intrigue in the city of Bir-Herari, where the benevolent sheik (Lloyd Corrigan) has ceded control to the merciless merchant Paul Hendrix (Otto Kruger), a Nazi agent working on behalf of the Germans. With the aid of traveling magician Connie Bryce (Nancy Kelly), Tarzan must defeat Hendrix's plot and harvest the needed plants in prehistoric jungles teeming with exotic dangers.

Buoyed by the success of *Tarzan Triumphs*, producer Sol Lesser rushed another wartime propaganda film into production. He retained the successful team of director William Thiele, scripter Carroll Young, and composer Paul Sawtell for the film, tentatively titled *Tarzan Against the Sahara*, and *Tarzan and the Sheik*. Production began in April 1943 and ran through late May. Retitled *Tarzan's Desert Mystery* and released on December 8 in the same year as its predecessor, it was the quickest turnaround for a sequel in the series since *The Romance of Tarzan* in 1918.

Maureen O'Sullivan was still uninterested in returning as Jane, and Gifford was bound by her new MGM contract, so Lesser hired Nancy Kelly as the female-lead-not-named-Jane. In addition to location work at the Arboretum and RKO Encino Ranch, desert sequences were filmed at Olancha Dunes near Lone Pine, California, a popular Western film location. The village of Bir-Herari was shot on the "Street of Miracles" set left from Cecile B. DeMille's *The King of Kings* (1927), so named because the $82,000 set paid for itself many times over after more than 200 productions lensed there. Cheeta, on loan from MGM for $1,000 per week on an eight-week guarantee, was complemented by Pair O' Dice, a paint stallion who portrayed the horse Jaynar. Cowboy actor Ben Johnson doubled Weissmuller in an action sequence requiring a quick mount.

The fever-medicine jungle was a rare instance where a Tarzan film offered a fantastic scenario like those in Burroughs' Tarzan novels, with stock dinosaur footage from *One Million B.C.* (1940) showcasing forced perspective shots of battling monitor lizards and baby alligators sporting prosthetic fins. This angle was eliminated from publicity campaigns for re-releases.

"Turbaned chieftains and desperate enemy agents in a blood-lashing drama of the dunes . . . with Tarzan and a lovely girl condemned to the hangman's noose!"

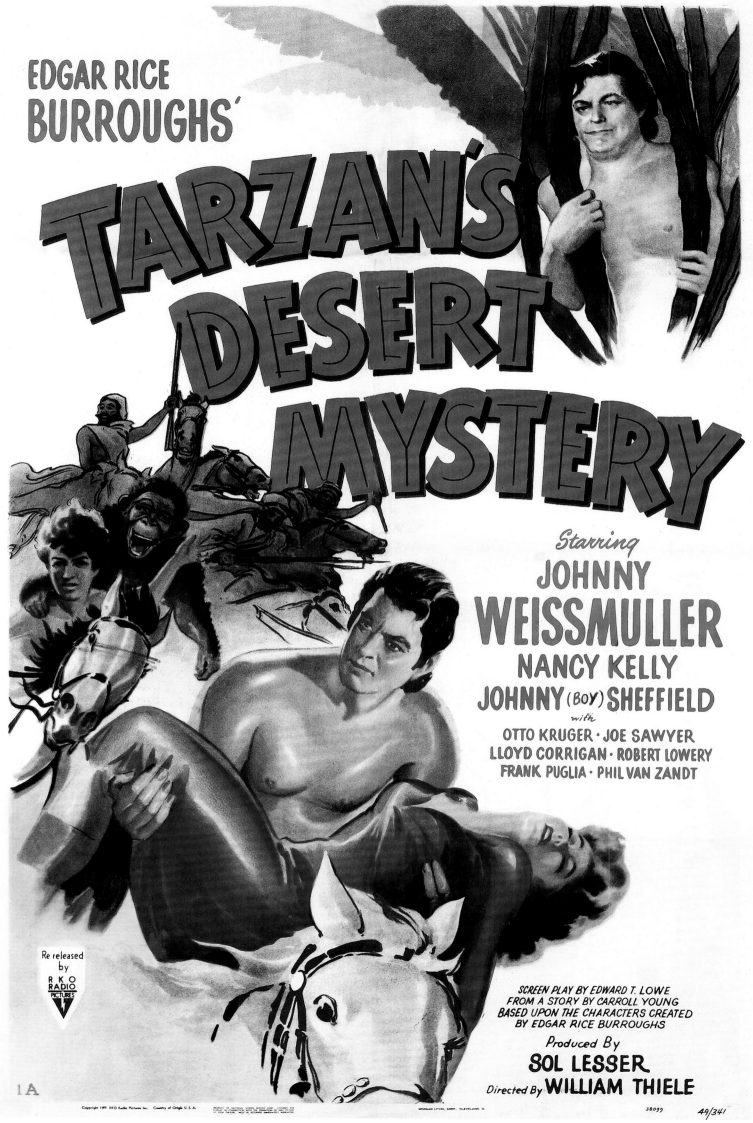

NANCY KELLY

Still hoping to convince Maureen O'Sullivan to return to the jungle as Tarzan's mate, Jane, and desirous of continuing his winning formula for *Tarzan Triumphs*, Sol Lesser sought a "pert, bold, alluring blonde, mettlesome, smart-cracking," female lead for *Tarzan's Desert Mystery*, "a Maisie type" like that played by Anne Sothern in titular films of the era. Nancy Kelly won the role and delivered a winsome, winning performance as a traveling magician who risks her life to avert the Nazi peril in a corner of North Africa.

Born on Good Friday, March 25, 1921 in Lowell, Massachusetts, Kelly entered showbusiness early, as a child model and actress, following in her thespian mother Nan's footsteps (as did younger brother Jack, Jr.) while her father Jack sold tickets to Broadway shows. Kelly appeared in 52 films between ages four and six; her many commercial shoots led to her being dubbed "America's Most Photographed Child" by a group of professional photographers.

Taking a break from film, Nancy attended the Bentley School for Girls, where she continued to act in school plays and on the radio. Her breakout role in *Susan and God* on Broadway in 1937 won a contract with 20th Century Fox, resulting in lead performances in 27 films. Two of her highest-profile roles came in 1939, opposite Tyrone Power in *Jesse James* and Spencer Tracy in *Stanley and Livingstone*.

Her greatest success came as the mother of the title character in the Broadway premiere *The Bad Seed*, for which she won a 1955 Tony Award as Best Dramatic Actress. Reprising the role onscreen, she received an Academy Award nomination for Best Actress the following year. She was also nominated for a prime-time Emmy Award in 1957 for her role in "The Pilot" episode of *Studio One*.

She continued to appear on television and was a top box-office draw of the Los Angeles stage, known as "The First Lady of Los Angeles Theatre" for her formidable talent. Married three times, Kelly died at home in Bel Air, California, on January 2, 1995, survived by her daughter and granddaughters.

Opposite top: Traveling magician Connie Bryce (Nancy Kelly) has a secret message for Prince Selim's (Robert Lowery) father, the Sheik.

Opposite bottom left: Tarzan comes to Connie's rescue—or so he thinks.

Opposite bottom right: Accused of Selim's murder, Connie is captured and sentenced to death.

Top left: Escaping from Bir-Herari, the fugitives plot their next move.

Top right: Paul Hendrix (Otto Kruger), and his henchmen, led by Karl (Joe Sawyer), pursue the trio across the desert.

Middle: Elephants rescue Tarzan from a man-eating plant, one of many dangers in the fever-medicine jungle.

Bottom: Tarzan and Hendrix battle in the spider cave.

TARZAN AND THE AMAZONS *1945*

Jane (Brenda Joyce) returns from civilization with her friend Sir Guy Henderson (Henry Stephenson), who leads a scientific expedition. When Cheeta gives Jane a gold bracelet filched from the Amazon Athena (Shirley O'Hara), the scientists' curiosity is piqued—but Tarzan (Johnny Weissmuller) refuses to betray the Amazons' location. Led by the greedy local trader Ballister (Barton MacLane), the men convince Boy (Johnny Sheffield) to take them to the lost city of Palmyria. There, they are imprisoned, but loot the city and escape in a running battle. Boy is captured by the Amazons and sentenced to death for his role in the affair. It remains for Tarzan to bring peace to Palmyria.

Amazons have appeared in several incarnations in Tarzan, including the Burroughs novel *Tarzan the Magnificent*, Burne Hogarth's newspaper comic stories, and the 1990s *Tarzan* television series starring Wolf Larson. This film's Amazons may owe a debt to history, since their city of Palmyria is reminiscent of Palmyra, the Syrian city ruled by Queen Zenobia during the Roman era.

Following his stint filming re-shoots on *Tarzan's Desert Mystery*, associate producer Kurt Neumann was given a term contract by Sol Lesser. He was assigned directorial duties on *Tarzan and the Amazons*, and dispatched on a cross-country tour seeking 48 tall, athletic "Glamazons", while scouting Utah and the High Sierras for locations to match the African veldt.

Upon Neumann's return, Lesser decided to continue using Baldwin Park and the RKO 40 Acres lot for his jungle opus, which offered a cast of leggy beauties to up the sex appeal quotient. Despite gossip columnist Louella Parsons' premature announcement in December, 1943 that Maureen O'Sullivan

would return for this film, she declined Lesser's employment offer due to her pregnancy with daughter Mia Farrow. Blonde Brenda Joyce was cast to portray Jane and shooting began in September 1944, wrapping the following month.

Lesser's "find" for this film was Shirley O'Hara, who played lead Amazon Athena, with a capable supporting cast that included Henry Stephenson (formerly Sir Guy Lancing in *Tarzan Finds a Son!*) in another uppercrust British role, and Madame Maria Ouspenskaya (who portrayed Maleva the gypsy in *The Wolf Man*) as the Amazon Queen. The Russian-born Ouspenskaya, a noted Hollywood drama coach, was nominated for a Best Supporting Actress Academy Award twice, for *Dodsworth* (1936) and *Love Affair* (1939). Barton MacLane essayed his first villainous role in the series well enough to be invited back for *Tarzan and the Huntress* (1947). Edgar Barrier was originally announced in the role played by Don Douglas; Barrier would join the series for the following installment, *Tarzan and the Leopard Woman*.

Robert E. Lee Brown, a noted leather craftsman, designed the snake and tree logo (perhaps inspired by the Garden of Eden), and crafted leather belts and ornaments to feature the design. Lesser's daughter, Marjorie Lesser Pfaelzer co-scripted with John Jacoby; it was her second assignment after *Three Is a Family* (1944), and her only credited Tarzan script, though she contributed to other films in the series.

Lesser was so pleased with the rough cut that he upped the budget $100,000 dollars to shoot additional footage, recalling Weissmuller, Joyce, O'Hara, Sheffield, Cheeta, and three Amazons in December. The film showcased Weissmuller's swimming prowess in a crocodile chase and battle, which was not as elaborate as the popular MGM sequence, with its giant robot reptile. Released April 29, 1945, *Amazons* was the only Tarzan film shot under Lesser's Champion Productions banner.

"Astounding and spectacular adventure—revealing the secret sect of warrior maidens pitting their primitive weapons against the ruthless assault of brutal and cunning trespassers!"

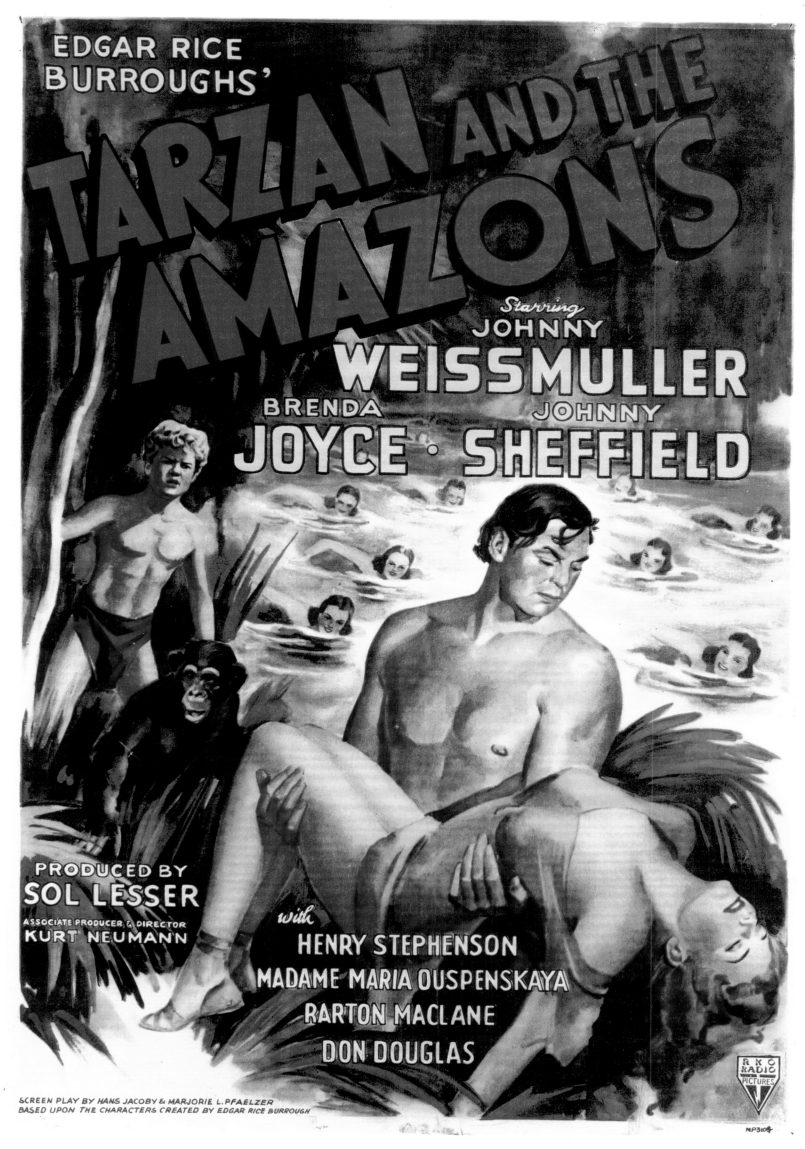

BRENDA JOYCE

Maureen O'Sullivan was such a tough act to follow that producer Sol Lesser delayed recasting the Jane role for two films. He eventually found his ideal replacement in Brenda Joyce, who proved to be a good fit for Johnny Weissmuller's Tarzan and Johnny Sheffield's Boy.

Joyce was born Betty Leabo in Excelsior Springs, Missouri, on February 20, 1917, the only child of Grafton and Rosalie Roberts Leabo. At age five, Joyce moved to California with her mother after her parents separated. A studious bookworm, she won a scholarship to USC, but later transferred to UCLA. She began modelling in 1938, appearing in ads for hosiery, shoes, cars, toothpaste and golf clubs in *Life* magazine and other national periodicals.

Her modelling work caught the attention of executives at 20th Century Fox, where she was assigned to a contract and cast as Fern Simon in *The Rains Came* (1939), the 58th actress screen tested for the part in a $45,000 talent search. She adopted her stage name from actresses Brenda Frazier

and Alice Joyce, and took acting lessons from Madame Maria Ouspenskaya, who would later appear with Joyce in *Amazons*.

After several supporting roles, Joyce won her first lead as "Fredricka Barrett" in the Fox comedy *Marry the Bo$$'$ Daughter* (1941), about a woman who falls in love with her father's efficiency expert. Despite her studio build-up as an attractive, available, single woman, she had no interest in arranged romances. Following a 10-year courtship, she married Owen Ward on January 18, 1941 in a simple ceremony officiated by her uncle, a Methodist minister. She and Ward had begun dating after meeting at Mount Vernon Junior High School in Los Angeles.

After the couple's first daughter was born in November 1942, Joyce chose to forgo her $100,000 annual salary to raise her family and be with Owen, an accountant who had joined the wartime army and was stationed in Florida. In 1944, a son was born, and Brenda Joyce's film career seemed to be a thing of the past.

Tarzan producer Sol Lesser had other ideas, and contracted her for five Tarzan films, with the promise that she would only have to make one film per year. Concerns about fans' acceptance of a blonde screen Jane were allayed when the series continued its profitable ways.

When her contract ended, Joyce retired from acting for good, moving to Laguna Beach, California, to raise her family, which now included another daughter. After her marriage with Ward ended, she spent a decade in Washington, D.C. working for the Department of Immigration, helping recent immigrants find housing and jobs. She later called this "the most rewarding work of my life." In the 1980s, Joyce relocated to Carmel, California, and took a position as the director of the Catholic Resettlement Office in Seaside, California, a job which she held for 10 years.

Joyce died of pneumonia on July 4, 2009 in a Santa Monica, California, nursing home. She was survived by her son, two daughters, and three grandchildren.

Left: Brenda Joyce joined the series as Jane for five films.

Opposite top left: Boy (Johnny Sheffield) and Tarzan (Johnny Weissmuller) journey to Randini to welcome Jane back to the jungle.

Opposite top right: Tarzan, with Basov (Lionel Royce) and Sir Guy Henderson (Henry Stephenson), realizes Jane's present from Cheeta will cause trouble.

Opposite middle: After breaking the law by leaving the Amazons' hidden valley, Athena (Shirley O'Hara) pleads with the queen (Maria Ouspenskaya) for forgiveness.

Opposite bottom left: Tarzan (Weissmuller, with Don Douglas, Barton MacLane, J.M. Kerrigan, and Henry Stephenson) does not trust the safari party's motives.

Opposite bottom right: Tarzan returns the purloined artifacts to the Amazon queen.

TARZAN AND THE LEOPARD WOMAN *1946*

While visiting the settlement of Zambesi, Tarzan (Johnny Weissmuller) and his family learn that the colonial government has expanded its jurisdiction to cover the Bagandi territory, but the locals are having none of this! Led by the evil Dr. Lazar (Edgar Barrier) and his paramour Lea (Acquanetta), they have formed a cult of Leopard Men to stop the progress of civilization into their domain. Lea's young brother Kimba (Tommy Cook), a budding psychopath, is dispatched to spy on Jane (Brenda Joyce) and Boy (Johnny Sheffield) as Tarzan works to solve the mystery of the unexplained leopard attacks. Tarzan's family and a quartet of school teachers are captured and prepared for sacrifice—but, fortunately, the Leopard Men overlooked the resourceful Cheeta, who's always ready to bolster a timely escape.

Tarzan and the Leopard Woman offered a gruesome slant in its antagonists, who were based on cannibalistic clans that flourished in Central Africa during the early 20th century. The film's pressbook cited six non-fiction books as references for the killer cult, which had previously been featured in Edgar Rice Burroughs' novel *Tarzan and the Leopard Men*.

The film was initially announced as *Tarzan and the Intruder*, to be written by Griffin Jay and Marjorie Pfaelser, but the concept was changed to *Tarzan and the Leopard Men*. This, too, changed, when a suitable female villainess was found in the person of Acquanetta, a former Universal contractee who launched the *Captive Wild Woman* horror franchise as an ape-woman. Juvenile actor Tommy Cook was cast as Leopard Queen Lea's little brother, Kimba, an adversary for Boy to overcome.

The leopard men included some of Johnny Weissmuller's athletic colleagues, several of whom enjoyed busy careers as stuntmen. Donning the spotted capes were Miola Kalili, a middle-distance swimming champion; Stubby Kruger, a former Olympic backstroker; Paul Stader, a paddleboard champion-turned-stuntman; and Pete Weissmuller, Johnny's brother, who came in second to Johnny in national championships (and occasionally worked as Johnny's stand-in). Diving title holder Bill Lewin and football players Charlie McBride (all-American halfback) and Don Malmberg (UCLA tackle on the 1945 team) were also leopard men, as was Johnny Roth, who had served as the "Ice Cream Cup Tarzan" in a 1930s promotional campaign.

Professional wrestler Abe "King Kong" Kashey appeared as Tarzan's opponent Tongolo the Terrible, while Doris Lloyd (Mrs. Cutten in MGM's *Ape Man*) returned to the series as the school superintendent. Anthony Caruso played Mongo, Lea's lieutenant, and revisited the franchise in *Tarzan and the Slave Girl* and, later, as a guest star in the NBC *Tarzan* television series. The Zambesi maidens were portrayed by starlets Helen Gerald; Kay Solinas; Lillian Molieri, Miss Central America 1945; and Iris Flores, the granddaughter of former Costa Rican President Rafael Yglesias Castro.

Director Kurt Neumann associate-produced the script by Carroll Young. It was shot at the Arboretum and RKO lot from late July through September, 1945 for a February 1946 release. Cinematography was provided by Oscar-winning lensman Karl Struss, ASC (*Sunrise: A Song of Two Humans*, 1929), who introduced the first soft-focus lens into the film industry in 1916 and was eventually nominated for four Academy Awards. Olga Celeste, a renowned cat trainer from L.A.'s Luna Park Zoo, handled the leopards, and choreographer Lester Horton taught the leopard men their tribal dance.

Los Angeles Times Hollywood columnist Edwin Schallert reported in his March 25, 1948 column that the film was banned in East Africa for fear that it would offend a native tribe known as the "leopard men".

"There isn't a dull moment in Tarzan and the Leopard Woman. This latest one of the hardy perennial series follows the regular plot and action formula frankly and expertly. Script is tightly plotted, tells the story convincingly and keeps the exploits of Tarzan and his pals vivid but plausible. Production values are tops." – Daily Variety, February 8, 1946

EDGAR RICE BURROUGHS'

TARZAN
and the Leopard Woman

Starring

JOHNNY WEISSMULLER

BRENDA JOYCE ★ **JOHNNY SHEFFIELD**

with **ACQUANETTA**

Produced by **SOL LESSER**   ASSOCIATE PRODUCER AND DIRECTOR **KURT NEUMANN**

R K O RADIO PICTURES

1A

ORIGINAL STORY AND SCREEN PLAY BY CARROLL YOUNG
BASED ON CHARACTERS CREATED BY EDGAR RICE BURROUGHS

"Introduction of a femme menace into the yarn in the person of Acquanetta as high priestess of Leopard Men cult is all to the good. She displays plenty of what it takes to stir male interest and handles her acting chores adequately." – Daily Variety, February 8, 1946

ACQUANETTA

Lea the Leopard Priestess is a familiar archetype for readers of the Tarzan novels and similar lost-race pulp fiction; characters like La of Opar, Nemone, the mad queen of Cathne, or H. Rider Haggard's Ayesha were a staple in such tales. Acquanetta, whose exotic background was shrouded in mystery, was ideal for such a role.

Acquanetta arrived in Hollywood as the "Venezuelan Volcano", so dubbed by Hollywood columnist Walter Winchell, who helped craft her unusual backstory. She claimed to have been born Burnu Acquanetta, which meant "Burning Fire, Deep Water", on July 17, 1921 in Cheyenne, Wyoming, to an Arapaho mother who sent her to live with her father in Pennsylvania. He, she announced, was an illegitimate son of the British royal family.

Acquanetta further claimed that she left home at 15 to begin her modelling career in New York, working for Harry Conover and John Robert Powers. She crafted a Latin identity while residing in Spanish Harlem, or during a modelling trip to Miami (her story varied), and headed for Hollywood.

Walter Wanger of Universal contracted her as a preemptive strike against MGM when she screen tested for both on the same day. She debuted as Ishya in *Arabian Nights* (1942); the publicity hype led to a photo shoot for *Life* magazine, but her pictorial was bumped from the proposed cover story. She next played Luani, a cannibal king's daughter in *Rhythm of the Islands* (1943), and the only female lead in a Universal horror franchise when she portrayed Paula Dupree, the gorilla woman in *Captive Wild Woman* (1943) and its sequel, *Jungle Woman* (1944). Her final Universal role was opposite horror veteran Lon Chaney, Jr. in *Dead Man's Eyes* (1944).

When her Universal contract ended, Kurt Neumann cast her in *Tarzan and the Leopard Woman*. She declined Johnny Weissmuller's later invitation to join him in his Jungle Jim pictures, and moved to Mexico, where she married Luciano Baschuck, and had a son, Sergio. The couple separated, and Sergio died of cancer in 1952, age five. During the high-profile 1950 divorce proceedings (when she was unable to prove they were ever married), the *Los Angeles Sentinel* revealed that she was the former Mildred Davenport of Norristown, Pennsylvania, an alumna of the West Virginia State College for Negroes, one of five children born to William and Julia Davenport.

Undeterred by revelations about her past, Acquanetta married painter Henry Clive, 68, and returned to the screen as a jungle woman in the prehistoric land of *Lost Continent* (1951). Divorcing Clive, she married auto dealer Jack Ross and the two moved to the Phoenix area, where his auto dealership prospered. Their union lasted 25 years and produced four sons. Acquanetta became a local celebrity appearing in elaborate ads for the dealership and hosting Friday night movies on television.

Acquanetta died of complications from Alzheimer's disease on August 15, 2004 in Ahwatukee, Phoenix. She was survived by her four sons; seven grandchildren; and a brother. She was remembered locally not just for her flashy turquoise jewelry and colorful personality, but for the many philanthropies she supported. She maintained her claim to a Native American origin throughout her life.

Left: High Priestess Lea (Acquanetta) and Dr. Lazar (Edgar Barrier) plot to stop civilization's progress in their corner of the jungle.

Opposite top left: Jane (Brenda Joyce) and Boy (Johnny Sheffield) foil Kimba's (Tommy Cook) plot to steal Jane's heart.

Opposite top right: Boy, trapped by leopard men.

Oppposite middle left: Tarzan and his family rescue the school teachers.

Opposite middle right: The leopard men bring Tarzan before Dr. Lazar and Lea.

Opposite bottom: Lea prepares to sacrifice Tarzan.

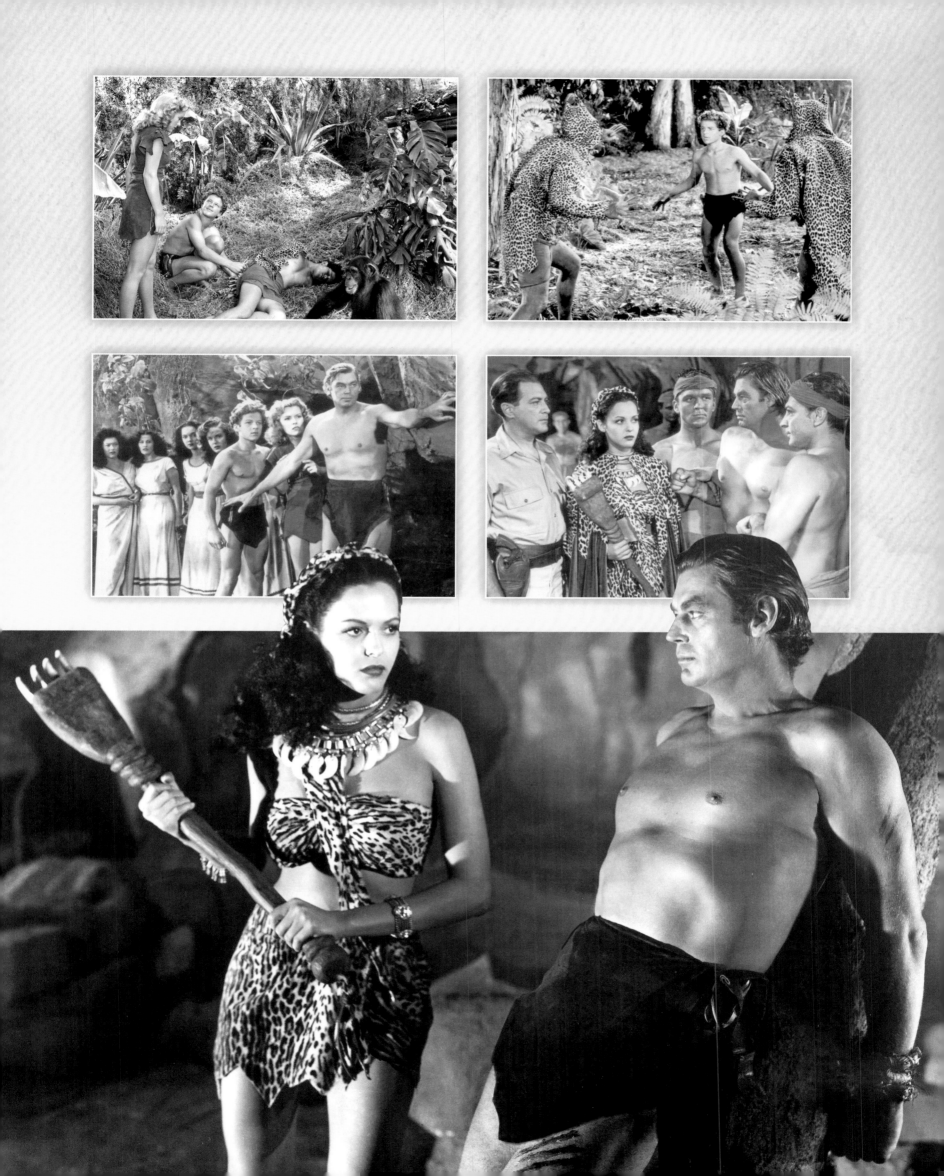

TARZAN AND THE HUNTRESS *1947*

Animal trainer Tanya Rawlins (Patricia Morison) and her crew arrive in Africa to trap wild beasts for zoos, which have become depleted during the war years. King Farrod (Charles Trowbridge) permits them to trap two of each species, but the greedy hunters cut a deal with his treacherous nephew, Prince Ozira (Ted Hecht) and ignore the quota—so Tarzan (Johnny Weissmuller) calls the animals to his side of the river, where hunting is forbidden. The trappers, ignoring Tarzan's warnings, move their operations into his jungle—with deadly consequences.

"Animal Hordes Scream Vengeance Against Invading Humans!"

After several fantastic outings with lost tribes and lands, Sol Lesser returned to a standard jungle formula for *Huntress*. His original concept was *Tarzan's Dangerous Game*, with Ewing Scott attached to direct but Scott departed the project, citing insufficient prep time. Associate producer Kurt Neumann stepped in to helm his third consecutive Tarzan film. Following *Leopard Woman*, Weissmuller was contracted for three more films, but bowed out after two.

Tarzan and the Huntress was the last appearance for the growing "Boy", Johnny Sheffield. Before departing, he shot a synchronized swimming sequence with Tarzan and Jane, and contributed his own heroics, joining Tarzan to sabotage the jungle invaders' scheme. In 1949, Sheffield debuted as Bomba, the jungle boy in a 12-film series based on the juvenile adventure stories of the Stratemeyer Syndicate under the pseudonym Roy Rockwood.

During *Huntress* pre-production, Lesser sent Kurt Neumann to New York to secure animals from Osa Johnson and Frank Buck for the picture, devoting plenty of screen time to the fauna, including elephants, lions, monkeys, and even South American kinkajous. Albert Antonucci, formerly head chimp trainer at Los Angeles Zoo, provided Cheeta. The little simian ate cold cream onscreen (actually strained peaches) and drank perfume (Coca-Cola), but balked at applying lipstick until mashed bananas were added to the "red goo".

B. Reeves "Breezy" Eason, director of the *Ben Hur* chariot sequence (1925) and the eponymous charge in *The Charge of the Light Brigade* (1936) directed the elephant stampede sequence, where it proved tough to get the pachyderms to break their non-destructive conditioning and stomp packing crates and uproot trees as needed.

Production designer Phil Paradise crafted a two-piece outfit for Joyce, a sarong and brassiere of African antelope skin that marked the first time since O'Sullivan's scandalous pre-Hays Code wardrobe that Jane's midriff was exposed. Leslie Charteris, creator of the hero Simon Templar, The Saint, contributed to the screenplay, credited to Jerry Gruskin and Rowland Leigh.

Barton MacLane (*Amazons*) was back for more Tarzan villainy, with Patricia Morison, a talented actress who found career-making success in the title role in *Kiss Me, Kate* on Broadway and in London; she later appeared on Broadway opposite Yul Brynner in *The King and I* and continued touring in musicals throughout her life.

The film shot at the Arboretum and RKO 40 Acres backlot sites from September to December 1946 and was released on April 5, 1947.

091

JOHNNY SHEFFIELD

Johnny Weissmuller personally selected Johnny Sheffield to play his onscreen son, from a cattle call of 300 aspirants. Sheffield's casting was confirmed when he joined Weissmuller at the Hollywood Athletic Club for lessons, and fearlessly dove into the deep water to begin his training. He eventually appeared in eight Tarzan films for MGM and RKO Studios.

He was a four-pound incubator baby, born John Matthew Sheffield Cassan in Pasadena, California, on April 11, 1931. His parents were British actor Matthew "Reginald Sheffield" Cassan, and his wife Louise Van Loon Cassan, a playwright and lecturer; he had an older sister and younger brother. Noteworthy ancestors included Benjamin Franklin and John Sheffield, the Duke of Buckingham.

Little Sheffield won his first professional role as Pud in the touring company of the Broadway play *On Borrowed Time*, and was called to New York in 1938 to replace the lead. The part was touted as having the most dialogue of any child's role ever written for the stage, but Sheffield, whose father also appeared on Broadway as a youth, was up to the task. Returning to Hollywood, his father answered a trade-paper ad asking "Do you have a Tarzan Jr. in your backyard?" and Sheffield's role in film history was sealed.

Weeks before filming began, he made daily visits to the MGM menagerie to befriend the chimps, elephants, and lions so that he could perform believably with them onscreen.

According to his father, he was so proud of his role that he wore his breech clout to bed. During production, Sheffield attended MGM's little red schoolhouse with other child actors for four hours daily, returning to public school between films. Following his Tarzan appearance, Sheffield won an RKO contract, appearing in *Little Orvie* and *Knute Rockne, All American*, among other films.

After outgrowing the Boy role, Sheffied played Bomba the jungle boy in a series of 12 films (1949–55), based on the popular juvenile books. Following his Bomba stint, he starred in a television pilot created by his father, *Bantu the Zebra Boy*, but it did not sell. Sheffield retired from acting, earning a BBA from UCLA and making lucrative real estate investments in Santa Monica, Malibu, and other coveted Southern California locales.

Sheffield farmed 3,000 acres in Yuma, Arizona, and it was there he met his wife Patricia Berg on a blind date, marrying in 1959. He later worked as a lobster importer before settling in Chula Vista, California, contracted to restore historic buildings in San Diego's Gaslamp Quarter. He continued to receive fan mail throughout his life, and responded to occasional interview requests.

Sheffield suffered a fatal heart attack at his Chula Vista home on October 15, 2010, survived by his wife, three children, and a grandson.

Opposite: *Huntress* was the final Tarzan film for Johnny Sheffield, who had outgrown the Boy role.

Top: Animal trainer Tanya Rawlings (Patricia Morison) and her crew—trail boss Paul Weir (Barton MacLane), Karl Marley (John Warburton) and Smitty (Wallace Scott)—decide that rules about taking sustainable quotas of animals don't apply to them.

Bottom: Rawlings and her gang don't realize their guns are no match for Tarzan!

TARZAN AND THE MERMAIDS *1948*

Tarzan (Johnny Weissmuller) catches a two-legged mermaid, Mara (Linda Christian), in his fishing net. She has fled a forced marriage to Balu, the god of her people, the Aquatanians, who live in idyllic seaside bliss (minus the tyrannical god part). When the Aquatanians capture her for return to Balu, Tarzan, Jane (Brenda Joyce), the commissioner (Edward Ashley) and Benji, the singing mailman (John Laurenz) follow. Tarzan's task is to expose the high priest and false god as a pair of pearl thieves (George Zucco and Fernando Wagner) so that Mara can marry her true love, Tiko (Gustavo Rojo).

Sol Lesser sought to bring A-list production values to *Tarzan and the Mermaids,* which boasted a $1 million budget. For his first location shoot, Lesser chose Acapulco, Mexico, the playground of the Hollywood elite. It was only the second film after *The New Adventures of Tarzan* to film outside the U.S.

Though he had two pictures left on his contract, this was Johnny Weissmuller's last Tarzan film. Johnny Sheffield had departed the series, with Boy's absence explained via the device of a letter from England, where he was in boarding school. Brenda Joyce was back as Jane, but Lesser had a new discovery, Linda Christian, as his focus.

Benji, the calypso-singing mailman, served as a comic foil, as did Cheeta, who had four understudies for the film, apes-in-training to become future stars. Edward Ashley, the commissioner, would later return to the series as a commissioner in *Tarzan's Peril* (1951). George Zucco, a staple villain of the Universal horror films of the 1940s, was well cast as the high priest Palanth, the mouthpiece of Balu. The troupe was complemented with local talent like Fernando Wagner, Gustavo Rojo, and Andrea Palma, dubbed "the Helen Hayes of Latin America", in her U.S. film debut as Christian's mother. The internationally famous water ballet of Club Deportivo at Chapultepec performed onscreen, with more than 60 female swimmers going through their paces.

Locations included La Quebrada Cliffs, famous for the cliff-diving locals, and Pie de Cuesta, a caverned lagoon five miles north of Acapulco. Teotihuacán ruins stood in for Balu's temple, with interiors shot at Churubusco Studios and exteriors in the nearby jungles.

The film was directed by Robert Florey from a story and screenplay by Carroll Young. Karl Struss returned as cinematographer. Lesser hired Dimitri Tiomkin (who won three Oscars in 17 nominations, along with six out of seven Golden Globe nominations) to compose and direct the music (John Laurenz wrote his own songs).

The developed infrastructure of the tourist locale notwithstanding, the crew experienced hardships that presaged the difficulties of future Tarzan location shoots. Exterior sets were destroyed by a hurricane, Sol Lesser suffered a heart attack and returned to the United States, and Florey lost 31 pounds from the stresses of filming. According to a July 31, 1947 *Hollywood Reporter* item, Weissmuller's stunt double Angel Garcia was killed in a high dive when the surf dashed him against the rocks.

Despite the adversity, Weissmuller became enamored of the location, and later purchased the Hotel Los Flamingos—which looked out over La Quebrada and its daredevil locals—with a consortium of his friends, the Hollywood Gang, which included John Wayne, Fred McMurray, and Red Skelton. Weissmuller spent his final months of life in Acapulco, and is buried there.

Tarzan unmasking a false god was common Burroughs trope, which was revisited in novels, comics, and various adaptations over the years. The octopus battle offered Weissmuller a novel underwater challenge in his final outing, after years of fighting the same crocodile.

Completed on September 15, 1947, the film was released the following spring. At 68 minutes, it is the shortest Weissmuller film, and marked the end of an era.

"The trouble is that a real jungle doesn't look like a Hollywood jungle. It's all matted growth and mud, with malaria, mosquitos, scorpions, crocodiles and little tigers that jump at you. When we'd get back from location every day, even a big guy like Johnny Weissmuller was buckling at the knees." – director Richard Florey

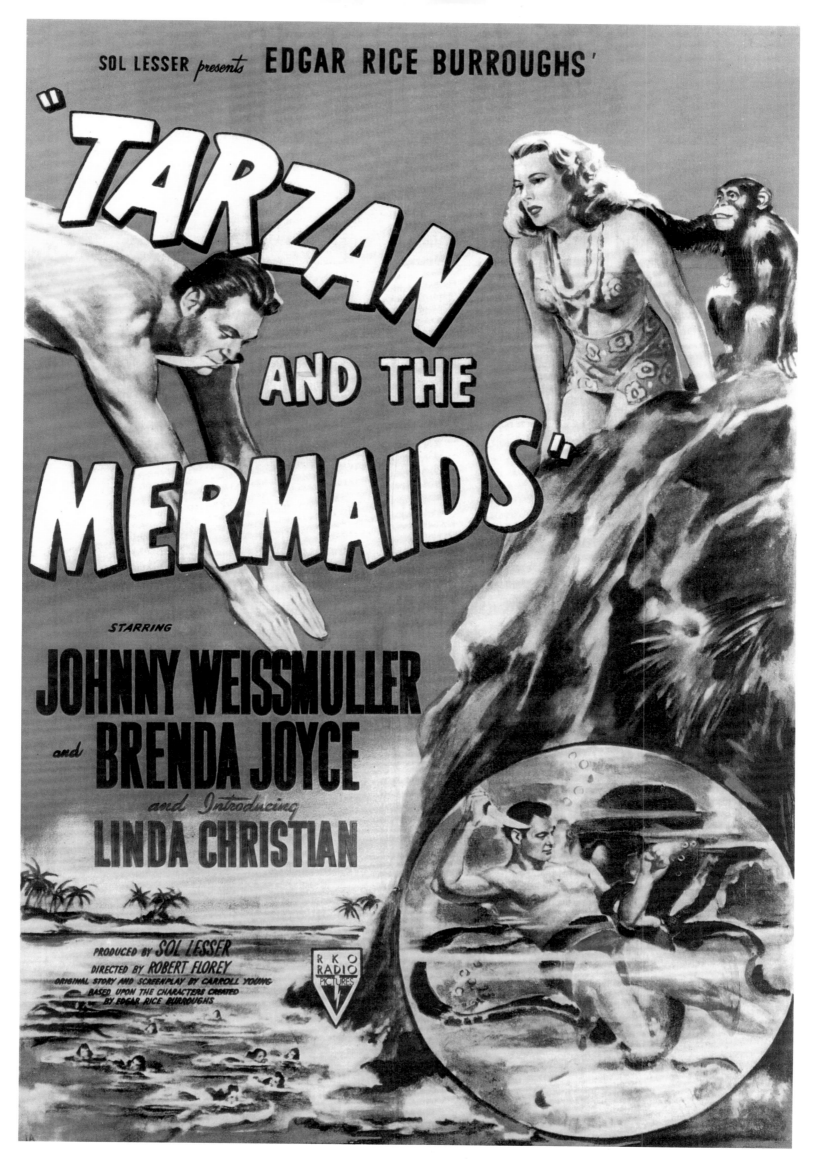

CHEETA

Cheeta the chimp (alternately spelled Cheetah, Cheta, and Chita) became a staple of the Tarzan films following the little ape's introduction in MGM's *Tarzan the Ape Man*. The primate's gender varied onscreen and in real life as a succession of simians portrayed the character over the decades.

The first apes cast in a Tarzan film were the chimpanzees Sally and Prince Charles, owned by the E & R Jungle Film Company, who cavorted with Gordon Griffith in 1918's *Tarzan of the Apes*. Joe Martin, the trained orangutan of the Universal menagerie, appeared in *Tarzan's Revenge* with Gene Pollar, and with Elmo Lincoln as Ara the Ape (doubled by a man in an ape suit) in *The Adventures of Tarzan*. Martin was captured as a baby in the wilds of Borneo in 1914 and named for one of the trappers, whom he resembled. As with Cheeta, there were several Joe Martins over the years, both orangutan and chimpanzee.

The first Cheeta was played by Emma, trained by Bud Barsky for *Ape Man*. Tony Gentry and his chimp Jiggs were employed for subsequent MGM films. Gentry started his career when he ran away from home to join the circus at age 16, and later worked for Frank "Bring 'Em Back Alive" Buck as a trainer before entering the film business.

Jiggs lived in a backyard bungalow, but dined at the table with Tony and wife Jackie, and brushed his teeth afterwards. He was taught trapeze tricks by Jackie's sister Rosalie, an aerialist. Jiggs enjoyed riding in the car, channel-surfing the radio, smoking cigars, and typing (he was forever intrigued by the fact that hitting the space bar produced no mark on the paper). Jiggs also had his own dog, Spanky, a border collie, but it was unclear (even to them) which was the master and which the pet, with Spanky herding Jiggs off the set at the end of the shooting day.

In addition to the MGM Tarzan films, Jiggs appeared in Our Gang comedies and Dorothy Lamour jungle pictures, earning (with the Gentrys) $2,000 per film. Jiggs also performed in the competing films of Buster Crabbe (*Tarzan the Fearless*) and Herman Brix (*The New Adventures of Tarzan*), renamed Nkima in the latter after Tarzan's monkey companion in the novels. Jiggs was fingerprinted and issued an ID card for international travel, and had his own stateroom on the cruise to Guatemala.

Jiggs died on February 28, 1938, after contracting pneumonia on the set of Paramount's *Her Jungle Love*. Jiggs II took over, later succeeded onscreen by Jiggs III and Jiggs IV. After Gentry joined the military for World War II, Jiggs II was donated to the Baltimore Zoo. Following the war, Gentry left Hollywood to train Ham, Enos and other chimps in NASA's space program.

When Sol Lesser assumed control of the Tarzan film series in 1943, he hired Albert Antonucci, formerly the head chimp trainer at the St. Louis Zoo, to wrangle the primates. During hiatus between films, Antonucci toured with circuses and appeared at zoos with the performing apes.

Other Cheetas and their Tarzans included Skippy (Weissmuller); Little Chim, Lucky, and Zippy from *The Howdy Doody Show* (Gordon Scott); Little Joe (Denny Miller); Dinky (Mike Henry); Vickie and Elmer (Ron Ely); Max (Joe Lara); and Archie (Wolf Larson).

Left: Tarzan finds a mermaid (Linda Christian) in his net.

Opposite top left: The Aquatanians live in fear of their god, Balu.

Opposite middle left: Tarzan always finds time to help distressed damsels.

Opposite bottom left: Tiko (Gustavo Rojo) threatens Tarzan at Balu's behest.

Opposite right: Weissmuller and Joyce posed for a series of publicity shots on the ruins of Teotihuacán.

TARZAN'S MAGIC FOUNTAIN *1949*

When Tarzan (Lex Barker) returns the diary of missing aviatrix Gloria James (Evelyn Ankers) to the authorities, he learns that her testimony can free Douglas Jessup (Alan Napier), imprisoned for life in England. Tarzan brings her out of the jungle, looking no older than when she disappeared 20 years prior. She soon returns to Africa from England, now married to Jessup, with hopes that Tarzan will guide them back to her home in the Blue Valley, with its fountain of youth. Tarzan refuses, having pledged to keep the Valley a secret for its residents, but Jane agrees to guide the couple there, accompanied by local traders Dodd (Charles Drake) and Trask (Albert Dekker). Tarzan follows to keep an eye on the party (and the misfortune that inevitably befalls them).

In April 1948, Sol Lesser, planning his next Johnny Weissmuller project, *Tarzan and the Fountain of Youth*, announced he would send a camera crew to East Africa in October to shoot location footage, negotiating with Clyde Beatty to head the expedition. When the aging athlete bowed out of the series, Lesser considered 1,000 applicants, including Sterling Hayden, Willard Parker, Johnny Sheffield, and Jock Mahoney.

Lesser eventually selected Lex Barker, insuring him for $100,000 against possible on-set injuries. The film's working title was changed to *Tarzan and the Arrow of Death*, and the plans for an African location shoot were scrapped. Lesser offered Elmo Lincoln a role in the film as an incentive to participate in a publicity stunt. When the expectant Lincoln arrived for work, Lesser asked him to don a loincloth for a photo session for *Life* magazine, touting Lex Barker alongside the oldest Tarzan. After the shoot, Lincoln was relegated to an inconsequential background role as a fisherman in a fight scene, earning one day's minimum pay for his free publicity. The film industry veteran was incensed by Lesser's gimmick.

The film's plot echoed that of the 1933 James Hilton novel *Lost Horizon*, which featured Shangri-la—a utopian civilization hidden from the outside world. The best-seller was adapted to a 1937 Columbia Pictures film directed by Frank Capra. *Magic Fountain* also capitalized on the mystery of flyer Amelia Earhart's 1937 disappearance. The fountain of youth trope appears in other Tarzan stories, such as the comic tales of Burne Hogarth and Joe Kubert.

In Burroughs' novels, Tarzan imbibed a youth elixir to avoid aging.

Brenda Joyce returned as the first of five Janes for Lex Barker, but retired from acting after the film to raise her family. Linda Christian, the ingénue from *Mermaids*, declined Lesser's offer to continue with the series. Popular horror-film heroine Gloria Ankers co-starred opposite Alan Napier, who reappeared as Commissioner Peters in *Tarzan's Peril* and is today remembered as Alfred, Bruce Wayne's butler, in the popular 1960s *Batman* television series. German-born Henry Brandon, who often played ethnic roles like the Indian chief Scar in John Ford's *The Searchers* (1956), played the Blue Valley guard Siko; he would revisit the franchise as M'Tara in *Tarzan and the She-Devil*.

The film was the directorial debut of Lee "Roll 'em" Sholem, nicknamed for his ruthless efficiency in remaining on schedule, and written by speculative-fiction novelist and horror-film scripter Curt Siodmak (*Donovan's Brain* and *The Wolf Man*) and Harry Chandlee. *Los Angeles Times* gossip columnist Hedda Hopper noted that author Burroughs earned $175,000 per picture without writing a word, simply leasing the rights to Lesser, who held them until 1965.

The production lensed in July and August 1948; Barker again donned his loincloth on October 14 for reshoots, because the "foliage of the trees did not match up properly" on the earlier filming. The movie opened in New York City on February 5, 1949. According to a February 12, 1949 article in *Cue* magazine, Tarzan pictures were being booked into 11,000 theaters per year.

"After all, it's a couple of chimpanzees, Cheta in particular, that bring delight and add a finishing touch to the entertainment. The creature's tricks are almost incredible. His chimp friend, too, is delightful, while elephants, tigers and snakes prowl around refreshingly." – David Bongard, *Los Angeles Daily News*, April 6, 1949

LEX BARKER

Lex Barker brought a dignified bearing to the Tarzan role, due to his society background and theatrical training. His five Tarzan films gave him his first breakout leading role; unable to capitalize on this domestically, he moved to Europe to become a star overseas.

Alexander Crichlow Barker, Jr. was born May 8, 1919, in Rye, New York, to Alexander C. Barker, a wealthy contractor and later stockbroker, and his wife Marion Thornton Beals Barker. Among his ancestors were Roger Williams, founder of Providence, Rhode Island, and Sir William Henry Crichlow, Governor-General of Barbados.

Barker enrolled briefly at Princeton, but dropped out to join a theater stock company. He appeared on Broadway in bit roles, and was cast in *The Five Kings* (1940) by Orson Welles. Unwilling to rely on family money, he did manual labor and worked in a steel mill to support himself.

Barker joined the army in February 1941 as a buck private serving as General Mark Clark's aide. He was wounded twice in North Africa, spent 19 months as a P.O.W., and was awarded several medals (including two Purple Hearts), mustering out as a major.

Upon return to civilian life, he signed a contract with 20th Century Fox and debuted in *Doll Face* (1945) as a Coast Guard captain, before bouncing to Warner Brothers and then RKO, where he remained on long-term contract. Writer Curt Siodmak (*Tarzan's Magic Fountain*) claimed he met Barker at the Polo Club, and introduced him to Lesser. Upon winning the role, the 6'4" Barker joined Terry Hunt's gym and lost 10 pounds, weighing in at 197.

Barker, who maintained his physique for his entire tenure as Tarzan, stayed active with swimming, golf, horseback riding, tennis, and squash. His more cerebral pursuits included art (charcoals and oil painting), backgammon, and gin rummy. His contract forbid him from drinking, nightclubbing, skiing, or riding on airplanes, all in an effort to protect Lesser's investment.

Offered a contract in 1953 for seven more Tarzan pictures, Barker asked to contract for one picture at a time. When Lesser refused, Barker signed with Universal-International and received the lead in Western *Yellow Mountain* (1954).

Hoping to play swashbuckling heroes, Barker dickered with Edgar Rice Burroughs for the rights to the medieval novel *The Outlaw of Torn*, but had to relocate to Europe to find such roles. In 1957, he became a Swiss citizen and founded Christopher Productions in Geneva. Fluent in French, Spanish, Italian, and German, he shot pictures in Brazil, Germany, Spain, Yugoslavia, Italy, Lebanon, and France. He maintained homes in Rome and Barcelona, and on Lake Geneva, where he enjoyed sailing his 50-foot yacht *Peter Pan*.

Barker credited Federico Fellini for resurrecting his film career when the director cast him in *La Dolce Vita* (1960) as Anita Ekberg's jealous boyfriend. Barker went on to become one of the highest paid stars and one of the biggest box office successes in Europe.

He was a German film hero due to his role as cowboy "Old Shatterhand" in film adaptations of German pulp novelist Karl May's Westerns. *Winnetou* (released domestically by Columbia as *Treasure of the Silver Lake* in 1965) was a surprise hit and the most profitable German film of 1963. Barker won the German Bambi Award for "Most Popular Foreign Actor".

Barker had five Janes, one for every jungle romp, and five wives: Constanze Rhodes Thurlow, actress Arlene Dahl, actress Lana Turner, Irene Labhardt, and Maria del Carmen Cervera, a former Miss Spain. He had two children with Thurlow, and a son with Labhardt.

Sadly, Barker's hopes for a Hollywood comeback never came to fruition—he was stricken with a fatal heart attack in New York City on May 11, 1973, on his way to a luncheon appointment.

Opposite: Newest ape man Lex Barker with Brenda Joyce and Cheeta.

Top left: Tarzan (Lex Barker) puts an end to Vredak's (Henry Kulky) bullying.

Top right: Siko (Henry Brandon) seeks to preserve the secret of the Blue Valley, but he's no match for Tarzan.

Second from top, right: Douglas and Gloria James Jessup (Alan Napier and Evelyn Ankers) find danger on the path to the Blue Valley with Tarzan.

Second from bottom: Those who enter the Blue Valley cannot leave.

Bottom: The secret of the Blue Valley—the Fountain of Youth.

TARZAN AND THE SLAVE GIRL *1950*

Women in Tarzan's jungle are being stolen by a mysterious tribe. Tarzan (Lex Barker) captures one of the men, whom Jane (Vanessa Brown) recognizes as suffering from the plague. Tarzan brings Dr. Campbell (Arthur Shields) from Randini, accompanied by his lusty nurse Lola (Denise Darcel) and her boyfriend, safari guide Neil (Robert Alda). The locals are inoculated, but Jane and Lola vanish. Tarzan, Dr. Campbell, Neil and Cheeta trail them to the lost city of Lionia, whose dying inhabitants seek to propagate their race with new brides. Dr. Campbell promises the tribal Prince (Hurd Hatfield) he can save his ailing young son and the populace—but the treacherous Sengo (Anthony Caruso) has other plans.

"Innocent Beauty Trapped for Pagan Pleasures—and Tarzan vows vengeance!"

As Lex Barker returned for reshoots on *Tarzan's Magic Fountain* in October 1948, Sol Lesser announced that the ape man would return to civilization in *Tarzan at the Olympics*, with star Barker demonstrating his athletic prowess onscreen. After commissioning an outline, Lesser abandoned the idea.

The following May, Lesser revealed that Brenda Joyce had departed the franchise, which would resume with *Tarzan and the Golden Lion*. He announced his search for a "panther woman" to play the role of "Jungle Lola". The finished script didn't feature Jad-bal-ja, Tarzan's lion companion, but did include a hidden civilization of lion-worshippers, the Lionians.

By July, Hollywood columnist Edwin Schallert wrote that Sally Forrest was rumored for Jane in the now-titled *Tarzan and the Slave Girl*, but wasn't confirmed; Lesser was also considering Peggy Knudsen, Lorraine Miller, Trudy Marshall, Lita Baron and Dona Drake, among others. Approximately 150 women attended the slave girl casting call in swimwear; those chosen for roles all wore more conservative one-piece suits, according to the pressbook. Young Freddie Ridgeway accompanied his sister Darla Lee to a screen test, and was cast as the sickly young prince. French import Denise Darcel was already cast as "Jungle Lola", and under consideration to "re-enact the role in other films".

Lee Sholem was hired for his second directorial effort, and interviewed 350 Jane contestants, selecting 10 finalists. He lobbied Lesser unsuccessfully to hire the unknown Marilyn Monroe to play Jane, bringing her in to read eight times, but Lesser decided to cast Vanessa Brown as Tarzan's newest lady.

Anthony Caruso, who played the head leopard man Mongo in *Leopard Woman*, returned to the series as the scheming Sengo. Robert Alda cancelled a local stage role to accept the part of Neil, Lola's overmatched boyfriend.

Russell Harlan photographed from a script by Hans Jacoby and Arnold Belgard. Harlan, who began his career on Hopalong Cassidy films, was eventually nominated for six Academy Awards, including twice in 1963 for *Hatari!* and *To Kill a Mockingbird*, respectively. The project filmed at the Arboretum, Iverson's Movie Ranch, and the RKO 40 Acres backlot from August 1 to September 3, 1949. Edgar Rice Burroughs toured the production with grandson Mike Pierce and Burroughs Bibliophiles founder Vernell Coriell; it was the author's last Tarzan set visit and his final public appearance. The film was released on March 18, 1950.

"There is no point in throwing any poisoned critical darts at Tarzan and the Slave Girl . . . the adventures of the jungle athlete have been going on for a long time now and probably will continue so long as little boys go to the movies." *– New York Times, June 24, 1950*

VANESSA BROWN

Producer Sol Lesser decided to cast against type, and chose UCLA student and intellectual Vanessa Brown to play opposite Lex Barker in his second Tarzan film. It was her only role in the series.

Brown was born Smylla Brind on March 24, 1928 in Vienna, Austria, the only child of historian and linguist Dr. Nahum "Nah" Brind, and Dr. Anna B. Brind, a clinical psychologist. Her father drilled her every morning over breakfast to increase her linguistic proficiency, and she was fluent in German, French, and Italian. Brown's first acting experience was dubbing a child's voice in German for the 1936 Fox film *Prisoner of Shark Island*.

The family fled Vienna when Hitler began his rise to power, emigrating to Paris and then New York City. There, Brown became Ann Blyth's understudy in Herman Shumlin's *Watch on the Rhine* for on Broadway, later touring with the company, credited as Tessa Brind. A child prodigy, she scored 165 on an I.Q. test at age 13, was placed in the Rapid Advance program (a school curriculum for gifted children), and began appearing on the radio show "Quiz Kids" while appearing onstage in Chicago.

Producer David O. Selznick saw her on Broadway in *Rhine* and signed her to a contract, debuting her in producer Val Lewton's *Youth Run Wild* (1944), on loan to RKO. Her family retained the fabled Paul Kohner as her agent; following her release from Selznick, Mervyn LeRoy signed her, and renamed her Vanessa Brown, inspired by the movie *Vanessa, Her Love Story* (1935).

Later contracted by 20th Century Fox, where studio head Darryl F. Zanuck promised her big things, Brown became a popular film ingénue in pictures like *Margie* (1946), *The Foxes of Harrow* (1947), *The Ghost and Mrs. Muir* (1947), *The Late George Apley* (1947), and *Mother Wore Tights* (1947).

Following her Hollywood High graduation, Brown enrolled in UCLA under her birth name, with most students unaware that a star was in their midst. Her friends on the *Daily Bruin* newspaper staff knew about her double life, teasing her about playing the ape man's mate. She enjoyed her part in the series—noting that Lesser paid well—but her contract wasn't renewed.

She married Hollywood plastic surgeon Dr. Robert Alan Franklyn and returned to Broadway in *The Seven Year Itch*, but grew tired of acting. Following her divorce from Franklyn, she wed director Mark Sandrich, Jr., with whom she had two children. She painted, worked as a journalist, and was politically active, but became disillusioned after the assassinations of John F. Kennedy and Martin Luther King, Jr. In her later years, Brown focused on her family, appearing sporadically in film and television.

Brown beat cancer three times before it claimed her life on May 21, 1999, at the Motion Picture Home in Woodland Hills.

Opposite: Jane (Vanessa Brown) has competition in the shapely form of Nurse Lola (Denise Darcel).

Top: Lex Barker's Tarzan demonstrates his archery skills.

Middle: Tarzan seeks to reclaim Jane, Lola, and their fellow captives from the Lionians.

Bottom left: Sengo (Tony Caruso) battles Tarzan over the lion pit.

Bottom right: Tarzan rescues the beautiful ensemble.

"Tarzan has gotten himself a new Jane in the form of Vanessa Brown, who rubs noses with him and shares his adventures quite as attractively as prior Tarzan mates. Vanessa has a tradition to uphold, and appears to relish the job." – *Motion Picture Herald*, March 18, 1950

TARZAN'S PERIL *1951*

Radijeck (George Macready), the agent for a hostile foreign power, escapes jail with the help of Trask (Douglas Fowley) and Andrews (Glenn Anders), intent on selling guns to the warlike Yorango tribe, led by King Bulam (Frederick O'Neal). Bulam attacks the peaceful Ashuba tribe, ruled by Queen Melmendi (Dorothy Dandridge), who has rebuffed his marriage proposal. It's up to Tarzan (Lex Barker) to save the day, with a little backup from Jane (Virginia Huston) and Cheeta.

Tarzan's Peril was the first film of the series to actually shoot location footage in Africa, rather than relying on stock location footage such as that taken from *Trader Horn*. Lex Barker travelled 25,000 miles round trip by air and safari, swimming in African rivers and swinging through African jungles, dressed as the ape man.

During a layover on his journey, the British press asked Barker to strip to the waist, but he modestly declined. As a consolation, they suggested that he tear a thick London telephone book in half. Slipping into the hotel kitchen, he borrowed a cleaver, hacked the insides of the book apart, and emerged to easily rip the book asunder for the delighted reporters.

African location filming began in July 1950 in British East Africa (Kenya), Uganda and Tanganyika (Tanzania). The six-week safari included Barker, 25 crew members, 12 native drivers, and 41 African porters, helmed by Phil and Cliff Brandon. Though the footage was shot in color, problems with development necessitated the final film's release in black and white.

The crew shot at Thika Falls, the Meru Jungle, the Great Rift Valley, Lake Naivasha, Fourteen Falls, the desert wastes of Isiolo, and the plains of Embu. It was the rainy season. Water was plentiful and the crew had a hard time obtaining animal footage (since the beasts weren't concentrated around water holes). Jungle scenes were photographed at 6,500 feet above sea level, in cloudy, wet weather; the natives, wrapped in lionskins, chuckled at Barker, shivering, near naked, standing next to a bonfire to stay warm between takes, his Southern California tan fading.

The safari ate kongoni, gerenuk, and Thompson's gazelle; the natives killed and ate a 14-foot crocodile during the Murchison Falls shooting, but Barker and the Americans declined to partake. A total of 250 natives were hired, including 53 Wakamba dancers, 120 Tharaka dancers, and Masai warriors acting in the jungle warfare segments—the latter paid in cattle. The dancers wore *kikois* (skirts similar to sarongs), and baboon-skin headdresses. African stilt dancers from Dar-es-Salaam also performed on camera.

Two villages were built to accommodate the Wakamba and Tharaka tribesmen, who travelled several hundred miles to participate. Animals photographed on location included lions, giraffe, zebra, Thompson's gazelle, wildebeest, warthogs, hippopotami, rhinoceri, and elephants. Peter Colmore served

as the on-set translator, and Buster Cooke as the white hunter.

Barker easily bested the local Wakamba tribesmen in spear-throwing and archery contests (their strategy was to get as close as possible to their prey to spear it, so their accuracy for distance shots was lacking, and their diet of *posho*—corn porridge—left them too undernourished to bend Lex's bow). He fared less well against the martial Masai, who bested the actor in tossing the caber, a sport introduced by the local district commissioner, a Scottish Highlander. The Masai gifted him with a shield and javelin out of respect for his prowess.

U.S. sequences were shot in October, on an eight-week schedule, from a script by Samuel Newman and Francis Swann, and directed by Byron Haskins, a special-effects expert known for his later sci-fi films like *War of the Worlds* (1953). Haskins claimed that it was the best pay he ever received on a picture, earning $50-$60,000, including a $10,000 bonus. Karl Struss returned as cinematographer for the remaining Barker films.

Co-stars who didn't make the traveling team included George Macready, who portrayed the gun-runner Radijeck, abetted by cronies played by Douglas Fowley and Glenn Anders. Alan Napier and Edward Ashley appeared as the ill-fated District Commissioners. Frederick O'Neal, (Chief Bulam), was a respected thespian, who had emerged from small town Brooksville, Mississippi, to co-found Harlem's prestigious American Negro Theater (ANT), which launched the careers of Sydney Poitier, Harry Belafonte, and other prominent actors.

Dorothy Dandridge gave a luminous performance as Queen Melmendi, her return to film after seven years of touring as a nightclub chanteuse; three years later, she received an Academy Award nomination for Best Actress for her lead in *Carmen*. David Kashner, a whip expert, wielded the nine-foot whip in the flogging scene. The industry's resident expert, Douglas Fairbanks, Sr., Errol Flynn, Bob Hope, Bing Crosby, Gregory Peck, and Ray Milland all felt his lash. Virginia Huston played Tarzan's mate Jane, whose role wasn't prominent this time, due to the tribal storyline and location footage.

The film's working title was *Tarzan's Mate in Peril*. California locations included the Arboretum, Iverson's Movie Ranch and RKO 40 Acres. Released March 10, 1951, it has been screened overseas under the titles *Tarzan and the Jungle Queen* and *Tarzan and the Jungle Goddess*.

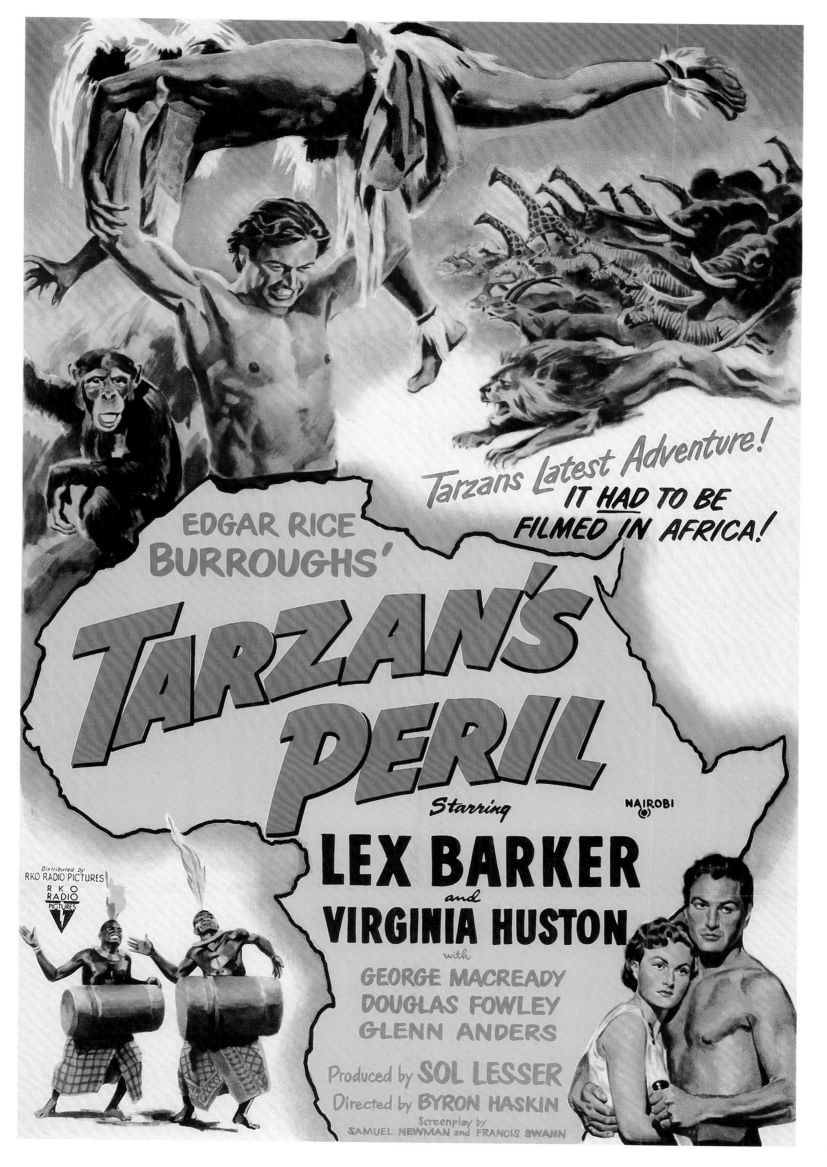

Tarzans Latest Adventure! IT **HAD** TO BE FILMED IN AFRICA!

EDGAR RICE BURROUGHS'

Tarzan's Peril

Starring

NAIROBI

LEX BARKER
and
VIRGINIA HUSTON

with

GEORGE MACREADY
DOUGLAS FOWLEY
GLENN ANDERS

Distributed by
RKO RADIO PICTURES

Produced by **SOL LESSER**
Directed by **BYRON HASKIN**
Screenplay by
SAMUEL NEWMAN and FRANCIS SWANN

VIRGINIA HUSTON

The role of Jane offered Virginia Huston a return to the silver screen after a year in convalescence, the result of a near-fatal car crash. The accident left her with a broken back, but she recuperated with an arduous regimen of physical therapy, and was able to swing from vines and swim as befitted Tarzan's mate.

Huston was the first child born to Marcus M. Huston, an American Airlines executive, and wife Mary Agnes in Wisner, Nebraska, on April 24, 1925, with two younger brothers. She launched her dramatic career at age 12, making her professional debut on the radio show *Calling All Cars*, soon followed by other roles. She attended the Duchesne Academy of the Sacred Heart in Omaha from kindergarten through high school, studying music and drama. She was a member of the tennis team and won several swimming competitions.

She began her stage career at the Omaha Community Theater, the training ground for Dorothy McGuire and Henry Fonda, and landed the title role in *Janie* at age 18. She also appeared in *Wuthering Heights*, *Judgement Day*, *Hay Fever*, and *The Philadelphia Story* there. In 1945, her family moved to Hollywood, where, according to her studio biography, she was discovered by an RKO Radio talent scout while dining at the trendy restaurant Romanoff's with her parents.

The studio kept her under wraps in its drama school until it found a suitably conspicuous role to launch her. She debuted in *Nocturne* (1946) as the second female lead opposite George Raft as a police detective trying to solve a murder. Huston played a nightclub singer, though her songs were dubbed. *Variety* magazine dubbed her performance "outstanding".

Next up was a role as Robert Mitchum's girlfriend in *Out of the Past* (1947), but after only two films in three years, she left RKO to freelance, landing a role in Warner Brothers' *Flamingo Road* (1949) as Zachary Scott's society wife (the television remake inspired a short-lived series in 1981–82). After appearing opposite Randolph Scott in *The Doolins of Oklahoma*, she received top billing in her fifth film, *Women from Headquarters* (1950), a fact-based tale of a female cop's crusade to clean up the Los Angeles streets.

Sol Lesser requested the blue-eyed blonde cut her locks for *Tarzan*, which was followed with roles in RKO's *Flight to Mars* (1951) and *The Highwayman* (1951). After a few more small roles, she married Manus Paul Clinton II, a Malibu real estate broker, and retired from film. She died of cancer on February 28, 1981 in Santa Monica, California, survived by her husband.

Left: Lex Barker and his third Jane, Virginia Huston.

Opposite left: Dorothy Dandridge reigns as Queen Melmendi of the Ashuba.

Opposite top right: Melmendi spurns the marriage offer of King Bulam's emissaries.

Opposite middle right: Radijeck (George Macready) and King Bulam (Frederick O'Neal) plot.

Opposite bottom right: Cheeta and Barker.

TARZAN'S SAVAGE FURY *1952*

Foreign spies Rokov (Charles Korvin) and Edwards (Patric Knowles) arrive in the jungle, with the latter impersonating Tarzan's cousin Oliver Greystoke, hoping to trick the ape man into leading them to diamonds held by the remote Wazuri tribe. Believing they are aiding England's Cold War efforts, Tarzan (Lex Barker), Jane (Dorothy Hart) and their young ward Joey (Tommy Carlton) guide the scoundrels across mountains and desert to the Wazuri—which sentences Jane to death when the men escape with the jewels, with Tarzan in hot pursuit.

Lex Barker's Tarzan experienced the joy of (adoptive) fatherhood, as Sol Lesser revisited the familiar scenario of Tarzan's nuclear family in *Tarzan's Savage Fury*. Chicago lad Tommy Carlton was chosen from a headshot submitted by his parents to portray the new Boy, Joseph "Joey" Martin, the orphaned son of missionaries. Joining them in the treehouse was Barker's fourth Jane, Dorothy Hart, who provided a performance that was both warm and feisty.

Scripted by Cyril Hume, the story evoked touches of Tarzan's literary roots, with an origin story that most previous sound films ignored. Tarzan's father, the ninth Earl of Greystoke, was a "scientist and explorer, with perhaps a touch of the missionary", who had previously befriended the Wazuri tribe; when Tarzan was orphaned, the apes carried him away to be reared in the jungle. Barker posed for the still photo of Tarzan's father, in safari togs, a beard and mustache. Though the actual location of Tarzan's domain remained vague, the coordinates given by Rokov in the film placed the Wazuri territory on the eastern shore of Lake Turkana in northern Kenya.

The film used the familiar rear-projection technique to show Tarzan and Joey squaring off against rhinos and lions, as the ape man taught his young charge the secret to mastering the animals: face the beast down, stare it in the eye, and shout "Umgawa!" to frighten it into scurrying for safety.

Charles Korvin launched his career as the French jewel thief in *Enter Arsène Lupin* (1944); his lust for baubles continued in *Savage Fury* as a villain who addressed his partner as "Comrade"—perhaps a takeoff on the literary Tarzan's nemesis, Nicholas Rokoff. British actor Patric Knowles essayed Rokov's ambivalent accomplice, whose impersonation of the murdered Lord Greystoke was troubled by conscience.

Cyril Endfield directed; a fan of prestidigitation, he included some sleight of hand in the plot. Endfield would later write and direct the excellent African historical film, *Zulu* (1964), about the battle at Rorke's Drift, and wrote the prequel *Zulu Dawn* (1969). Hume, who had done exceptional work on MGM's *Ape Man* and *Son!*, was aided on the script by Hans Jacoby and Shirley White. Karl Struss photographed the action.

Lesser noted that of female visitors to the set, only 43 asked to meet Barker, while nearly 150 asked to meet Cheeta. The little ape's antics were good for a "Award of Excellence" from the American Humane Association's Performing Animal Top Star of the Year (PATSY) award in the event's second year.

At the film's end, perhaps as an apology for the commuted death sentence, Hart's Jane wore a large diamond, which was actually the 67.89-carat Victoria-Transvaal diamond, provided by Circle of Light Diamonds. The gem now resides in the Smithsonian National Museum of Natural History, the gift of Leonard and Victoria Wilkinson.

The production shot at the Arboretum and RKO 40 Acres backlot, going afield to shoot the mountain and desert sequences in the Alabama Hills and Olancha Dunes near Lone Pine, California, and building the Wazuri village on Iverson's Movie Ranch, near the Garden of the Gods location (the former village site is now covered in condominiums). While shooting location footage in Kenya in 1950, the Tarzan film crew observed the natives killing and eating a large crocodile, which may have inspired the reptile-fishing sequence in the film (hopefully, using little boys for bait is a cinematic convention!).

Released in April 1952, the film played on a double-bill in some locations with the documentary *Under the Red Sea*. The Tarzan films continued to be a financial juggernaut, with exhibition in 14,000 U.S. theaters during their run. Sixty percent of the audience were adults. The films were dubbed in 15 languages, with an estimated gross of more than $2.5 million apiece.

"Just a trifle weary. Silly old legs. Fairly sticky trip, you know— absconding bearers, fever, impolite natives—awful bore."
– Lord Oliver Greystoke (Edwards)

Left: The latest incarnation of the jungle nuclear family: Joey (Tommy Carlton), Tarzan (Lex Barker), and Jane (Dorothy Hart).

Opposite top left: Sol Lesser commissioned a series of studio shots of the principals, including Barker and Carlton.

Opposite top right: Barker rides an elephant at Iverson Ranch.

Opposite middle right: Rokov (Charles Korvin) and Edwards (Patric Knowles) run afoul of Tarzan (Lex Barker).

Opposite bottom: Jane (Hart) gives Cheeta a reading lesson.

DOROTHY HART

Dorothy Hart brought warmth, charm, and strength to her role as Jane in *Tarzan's Savage Fury*, but she was unhappy with her career in Hollywood. Following her final film, *Loan Shark* (1952), she relocated to New York City, where she guest-starred on television programs and game shows before finding her calling as an observer and speaker for the United Nations.

Hart was born April 3, 1922 to Mr. and Mrs. Walter C. Hart of Shaker Heights, Ohio, attending elementary and high school locally. She graduated from Case Western Reserve University in Cleveland, where she studied English and drama and was Homecoming Queen and Fiftieth Anniversary Queen; her beauty also garnered the "Queen of the Air" title for the 1941 National Air Races. The aspiring actress burnished her resume by studying at the Cleveland Play House and appearing on local radio shows.

Sponsored by a reporter friend at the *Cleveland Press*, Hart beat 22,000 contestants for the title National Cinderella Cover Girl in a contest launched in conjunction with Columbia Pictures' 1944 film, *Cover Girl*. She declined the resulting contract offer, convinced she wasn't yet ready for Hollywood, and moved to New York City. There, Hart continued her drama studies, appeared on radio shows, and became a top cover model of the 1940s. Represented by the famed Harry Conover

Agency, the green-eyed, auburn-haired Hart's work included appearances on the covers of *Cosmopolitan*, *McCall's*, and *Esquire*, among other magazines.

In 1946, she accepted a second offer from Columbia, and was cast opposite Randolph Scott in *The Gunfighters*. Dissatisfied, she moved to Universal, where roles included Howard Duff's girlfriend in *The Naked City* (1948) and the female lead in *Undertow* (1949), and then Warner Brothers, where she essayed a Spanish accent for the Western *Raton Pass* (1951).

Photoplay magazine named her one of Hollywood's 10 Most Promising Actresses and awarded her their 1952 "Gold Key," but Hart had tired of Tinseltown. She relocated to New York City that year and later married Fred Pittera, an industrial research consultant, with whom she had a son. Hart experienced an epiphany and realized she wanted to contribute to her dream of world peace, so she became a U.N. observer and was named to the organization's speaker's bureau by Eleanor Roosevelt.

In 1966, Hart retired from acting for good and moved to Asheville, North Carolina. She died on Sunday, July 11, 2004 in Arden, North Carolina, of complications from Alzheimer's disease, survived by her son and sister.

TARZAN AND THE SHE-DEVIL *1953*

Ivory hunters Vargo (Raymond Burr) and Fidel (Tom Conway) have a problem: Tarzan (Lex Barker). Their boss-lady Lyra (Monique Van Vooren) has a solution: Jane (Joyce MacKenzie). It should be a simple matter to take Jane hostage, coercing Tarzan into participating in the elephant roundup, alongside the enslaved Lycopo tribe, but things are never that easy for criminals who invade Tarzan's jungle.

The final Tarzan film starring Lex Barker featured the fifth actress to play Jane in as many films, Joyce MacKenzie. She provided a lively performance as a woman who fights to survive when left injured and alone in the bush.

As Edgar Rice Burroughs' children assumed control of their late father's empire, they gave Lesser a vote of confidence by extending his contract for 20 years in return for 10 percent of the box office; this tripled Lesser's royalty payment, and he was happy to continue the profitable series with a new film: *Tarzan Meets the Vampire*, later changed to *Tarzan and the Ivory Thieves* and, finally, *Tarzan and the She-Devil*.

Always on the lookout for new talent, Lesser spied actress Monique Van Vooren, dubbed the "Belgian Bombshell", on *The Abbott and Costello Show*, and later flew her to Los Angeles from Paris to play the villainess Lyra, in her American film debut. Lesser hired costumer Jay Morley, Jr. to design six outfits to highlight the 5'7" starlet's 38-23-34 figure, with three new outfits for MacKenzie, too. Art director Carroll Clark, who accrued seven Academy Award nominations in his field, dressed Lyra's lair in $250,000-worth of African and Oriental art borrowed from museums and private collections—including ceremonial masks, wood sculpture, jade statuary, tapestries, furniture, and ornaments.

Raymond Burr (laboring in the cinematic trenches as a villain before gaining fame as lawyer Perry Mason and, later, as police detective Robert Ironside), supplied menace as the pitiless poacher Vargo. Tom Conway (*Tarzan's Secret Treasure*) returned to the series as Fidel, Lyra's sophisticated partner, who urges Lyra to retire, and is persuaded to join her for one more score. Actor Henry Brandon (*Tarzan's Magic Fountain*) allied with Tarzan for this appearance as M'Tara, leader of the besieged Lycopo tribe, whose beloved (played by Mara Corday) enlists Tarzan's aid.

Director Kurt Neumann, cinematographer Karl Struss, and writer Caroll Young all returned for their fifth and

final Tarzan film, with Karl Kamb sharing scripting credit. Neumann's career was cut short when he died in 1958 at age 50, before his best-remembered film, the horror classic *The Fly*, went into wide release.

The production filmed in the usual locations, the Arboretum and RKO 40 Acres backlot, in October–November 1952. Stock footage of the vine-swinging from *Tarzan the Fearless* was incorporated, as was the elephant stampede and leopard–python battle from the 1934 Frank Buck documentary *Wild Cargo*. Jane's feverish flashbacks included footage of the charmed cobra from *Leopard Woman*, Tarzan's battle with the octopus in *Mermaids*, and the giant spider from *Desert Mystery*. Clocking in at 76 minutes, *She-Devil* was released June 8, 1953.

"The screen thunders with a stampede of ACTION . . . when the Lord of the Jungle clashes with a killer . . . more devil than woman!"

JOYCE MACKENZIE

Joyce MacKenzie's Jane is no wilting African violet, but a strong, capable mate for the ape man, who outwits Lyra's thugs and escapes into the jungle, foiling their plot to hold her hostage. It was the athletic, blue-eyed, auburn-haired thespian's only appearance in the Tarzan series.

MacKenzie dreamed of acting from childhood, when she studied drama, dance, and music. She was born in Redwood City, California, to dentist Norman MacKenzie and wife Alice, with one brother, Gordon. She captained the tennis team at Sequoia Union High School, won top academic honors, and underwrote her acting ambitions with a variety of jobs including waitressing, modelling, and working as a retail clerk.

During World War II, she moved with her mother to San Francisco, where she served as a carpenter's assistant in the San Francisco shipyards, earning the nickname "Joycie the Joiner". She endured the usual hazing rituals, spending half a day looking for a "left-handed monkey wrench" at her co-workers' behest, since she was a lefty. She also worked as a salesgirl at The Emporium in San Francisco for $3.62 a day.

After the war, she moved south and enrolled at the Pasadena Community Playhouse to study acting, and was discovered by talent agent Ivan Kahn while she was serving a stint in the ticket booth to help pay her tuition. She made her film debut as Cherry Davis in *Tomorrow is Forever* (1946), followed by a small role as a Goldwyn Girl in *The Kid from Brooklyn* (1946).

Signing a contract with 20th Century Fox, she played a nurse opposite Gregory Peck in *Twelve O'Clock High* (1949),

and one of four dance-hall girls (along with Marilyn Monroe, Barbara Smith, and Marion Marshall) in *A Ticket to Tomahawk* (1949). She thought her role as one of the townsfolk in *Broken Arrow* (1949) would provide her big break; her onscreen footage, alas, was largely edited from the film, leaving her with one line. She won her first lead as Laura Mansfield in *Destination Murder* (1950) for RKO, and later departed Fox.

Following her turn as Jane, she appeared in RKO's 3D *The French Line* (1954), cast because her measurements matched Jane Russell's (the pair switch identities). The Western *Rails Into Laramie* (1954) was her final film, followed by several television appearances.

MacKenzie retired from film to focus on her family, which included two sons with then-husband Walter H. "Tim" Leimert, Jr., son of a prominent local family of Los Angeles real estate developers. Though her Tarzan scenes were filmed in Southern California, she later realized a life-long ambition when she traveled to South Africa and stood on the Cape of Good Hope.

In 1959, MacKenzie resurfaced as the producer and host of *Court of Small Claims*, a syndicated weekly series inspired by her own experience of suing a cleaner in Santa Monica Small Claims Court three years prior (she lost). She later moved to Laguna Niguel, where she taught at Niguel Hills Middle School and married for the third time, to fellow teacher Victor Benedict Hassing. MacKenzie remained an active athlete, taking daily swims, and cited losing the lead in the Lassie series to June Lockhart as her greatest acting career disappointment.

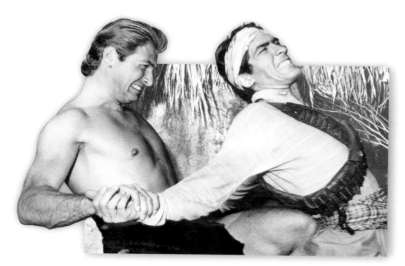

"The thing is that I adored what [Tarzan] stood for. Here was the manifestation of strength and courage. He represented the Spartan life combined with truth and honor. We need more figures like that today."
– Joyce MacKenzie, OC *Chronicle*, December 8, 1976

TARZAN'S HIDDEN JUNGLE *1955*

Game hunters Burger (Jack Elam) and DeGroot (Charles Fredericks) can't meet their quota for ivory, hides, and rendered fat unless they can slip into Sukulu country, which teems with animals revered by the local tribe. They trick Dr. Celliers (Peter Van Eyck) into allowing them to "film" his work among the suspicious tribe so they can scout game and drive it back toward their camp. Realizing the danger the hunters pose, Celliers' nurse Jill Hardy (Vera Miles) and Tarzan (Gordon Scott) race to stop the hunters before their planned slaughter destroys the goodwill Celliers seeks to cultivate with the reclusive tribe.

Gordon Scott's debut as Tarzan offered producer Sol Lesser a chance to spruce up the series with some modern conveniences like jeeps and a United Nations medical clinic in an attempt to bring progress to the jungle. It was the twelfth and final RKO Tarzan picture and the last of the Tarzan theatrical films shot in black and white.

Former beauty queen Vera Miles was cast as Jill Hardy, a capable woman who still needs a hand from Tarzan when she becomes lost in the jungle. Though there was no onscreen romance, Miles and Scott married the following year.

Popular screen heavy Jack Elam played the lead baddie, while Rex Ingram, who had battled Elmo Lincoln in 1918, returned to the series as the Sukulu chief, with Maidie Norman as Suma, his wife. Jester Hairston, a choral director later renowned for his preservation and presentation of gospel music, played the witch doctor after years of serving as an extra in the Tarzan films. His reaction to his only speaking role in the series? "Good gracious, I've been promoted!"

Ike Jones, a former UCLA football player and the first black graduate of the school's film program, played Malenki, Burger and DeGroot's headman. The enthusiastic Scott accidentally knocked Jones unconscious when he hurled him to the ground in a fight scene.

Zippy, a regular on the children's television show *Howdy Doody*, played Cheeta, with Lucky as his chimp companion. The little apes had never been caged, and had to be gradually taught to accept this element of the plotline. They had also never been naked, and their response to this newfound liberty was to caper about the set, climbing high into the trees.

Production began on August 13, 1954, at the World Jungle Compound in Thousand Oaks; shooting continued at the

RKO 40 Acres lot, the last Tarzan picture to film there. Harold Schuster directed from a script by William Lively, a co-creator of the East Side Kids films who also served as a writer on the *Jungle Girl* serial starring Frances Gifford.

The film was released on February 16, 1955. Though it continued the Tarzan series' profitable reign, Lesser realized it would take more than a couple of jeeps and some U.N. references to remain relevant in the marketplace, and began planning a franchise upgrade, starting with more authentic location footage shot in Africa.

"One noteworthy feature is the introduction of a new Tarzan in Gordon Scott, a good-looking lad with a husky physique that would make the ordinary male cut his own throat in pure frustration."
– Hollywood Reporter, February 11, 1955

GORDON SCOTT

Gordon Scott was working as a lifeguard at the Sahara Hotel and Casino in Las Vegas, when a pair of Hollywood agents discovered him and convinced him to audition for Tarzan producer Sol Lesser. Scott made his acting debut as the lead in *Tarzan's Hidden Jungle*, eventually shooting five Tarzan features and three pilot episodes released as a telefilm.

Scott was the youngest of nine children born to Stanley Griffith and Alice Irene Johnson Werschkul, entering the world on August 3, 1926 in Portland, Oregon, as Gordon Merrill Werschkul. He attended school in Portland, and enrolled in Oregon University upon graduation.

After one term studying physical education, Scott dropped out of Oregon to join the Infantry at Fort Lewis, Washington, during World War II. He earned his sergeant's stripes and became a drill instructor, specializing in close-order drill, the use of the rifle, bayonet and pistol, judo, and hand-to-hand combat. He also served as an MP, transporting dangerous prisoners. He was honorably discharged in 1947, and worked as a firefighter, and as a cowboy on his brother's ranch near Baker, Oregon, before his move to Las Vegas.

"During the six hours of the test, in addition to running, jumping, swimming and doing 120-foot leaps on swinging vines, I had to help test five girls trying out for the female lead," the newly christened Gordon Scott recalled of his Tarzan audition. Scott was conspicuously more muscular than his predecessors, with a 50-inch chest, 30-inch waist, and 19-inch biceps on a 6'3", 218-pound frame.

He found romance with his *Hidden Jungle* co-star, Vera Miles, and the two were married on April 15, 1956 in Yuma, Arizona; son Michael Griffith Scott was born in 1957. The couple divorced in 1959.

Following three pictures for Sol Lesser, and an unreleased television pilot, Scott severed relations when the new franchise owner, Sy Weintraub, refused to give him a non-exclusive contract. As a sign of his new independence, Scott cut his hair, grew a thick beard, and revealed to Hollywood columnist Bob Thomas that he was talking to producers about Western roles.

Weintraub announced a worldwide competition to find the new Tarzan in July 1958, but was dissatisfied with the applicants for the role. When he learned that MGM was remaking *Tarzan the Ape Man* with UCLA basketball player Denny Miller in the title role, Weintraub cancelled his star search and re-signed Scott to four pictures with a raise, with the agreement he could act in other roles, but not play villains. Together, Weintraub and Scott made what are deemed by fans to be among the best Tarzan pictures in the series, *Tarzan's Greatest Adventure* and *Tarzan the Magnificent*, before parting ways.

Scott moved to Italy, where he appeared as the lead in 42 films in 8 years, by his accounting. In addition to portraying strongmen like Samson, Hercules, and Goliath, he played Zorro, Buffalo Bill, and other roles in Westerns, spy pictures and historical adventures. Scott returned to the States in 1970, but declined further film offers. Later in life, he was a regular on the fan convention circuit, selling signed stills, Tarzan documentaries, and special-edition Tarzan knives.

Scott died April 30, 2007, age 80, at Johns Hopkins Hospital in Baltimore, Maryland, of complications following heart surgery. He is buried in Kensico Cemetery in Valhalla, New York.

Opposite: *Tarzan's Hidden Jungle* was Gordon Scott's film debut.

Top left: Shooting an elephant in Tarzan's jungle is never a good idea.

Right: Scott's brawn and fight training were used to good effect in the series' action sequences.

Second from top, left: Gordon Scott and leading lady Vera Miles married after falling in love on set.

Second from bottom, left: Mr. Johnson (Don Beddoe) warns Burger (Jack Elam) that he'd better make his quota of fat, skins, and ivory, while DeGroot (Charles Fredericks) observes.

Bottom: Thirty-seven years after his film debut, battling Elmo Lincoln in *Tarzan of the Apes*, Rex Ingram returned to the series as the Sukulu chief.

TARZAN AND THE LOST SAFARI *1957*

A plane carrying bickering socialites Gamage Dean (Yolande Donlan), Carl Kraski (George Coulouris), the married couple Diana and Dick Penrod (Betta St. John and Peter Arne) and gossip columnist "Doodles" Fletcher (Wilfrid Hyde-White) crashes in Tarzan's jungle. It's up to the ape man (Gordon Scott) to lead them to safety, but he's hindered by meddling ivory hunter "Tusker" Hawkins (Robert Beatty), who wants to seduce Diana and deliver the others as human sacrifices to the hostile tribe of Opar, in return for a bounty in ivory.

With RKO Pictures' fortunes declining, Sol Lesser struck a distribution deal with MGM, a first for them since the six Weissmuller films, providing a needed infusion of cash to the series. The studio released two films as part of the deal: *Tarzan and the Lost Safari* and *Tarzan's Fight for Life* (1958), the first color films in the series.

On the upgraded budget, Lesser was able to commission location footage, announcing that big game hunter and author Alexander Lake and his colleague Harry Selby would serve as consultants. Documentarian Miki Carter and his wife Peg made six trips to Africa to shoot wildlife, tribal rituals, and scenic vistas. On their first foray, they roamed Africa for six months in a specially designed jeep, including areas never before filmed, in British East Africa, Portuguese East Africa, French Equatorial Africa, North and South Rhodesia, and parts of the Sudan, capturing the Zambesi waterfall, the Murchison Falls above the Nile, and Mount Kilimanjaro. Gordon Scott accompanied them, playing with a rhino and baby elephant and riding a giraffe for their cameras. Two months into the shoot, Scott broke his foot while filming at Thompson Falls in British East Africa.

Carter's camera assistant was a Wakamba youth named David, who began working with Carter at age 16, spoke nine languages, and harbored no desire to return to tribal life. Filming techniques included being lowered inside a cage into a pack of hyenas to film them at short range, and digging a pit and enticing a lion to leap over the camera to feed. Aerial footage of stampeding hoof stock and veldt fires was also shot, as well as scenes of local tribal life.

The Carters' location footage was also featured in the documentary series *Bold Journey*, hosted by Jack Stevenson, titled "Cartoon King in Africa". Animal species subsequently appearing in Tarzan films included lions, leopards, cheetahs, hyenas, wildebeest, topi, jackals, elephants, rhinos, hippos, gazelle, antelope, duiker, dik-dik, waterbuck, and reedbuck. Birds included ostriches, pelicans, buzzards, vultures, hornbills and secretary birds.

While doing publicity with the film at a Nairobi press conference, Scott posed with his co-star Bobby, a mature 500-pound lion who had previously appeared in *Mogambo*. A reporter's flashbulb startled the feline, and it swatted Scott, who quickly leapt a table to get out of its range, not realizing the cat's claws were extended. The trainer hustled the lion out of the room, and Scott hustled to the hospital for 32 stitches in his calf and a cycle of antibiotics.

Scott returned to England, where the film was shot entirely on the soundstages (other than the location footage) of Associated British Pictures Corp. Studios, Elstree, in Borehamwood, England, with locally hired British and American expatriate actors. Victor Stoloff was announced to direct, but was replaced by Bruce "Lucky" Humberstone, who also helmed the following Lesser Tarzan film. Scripted by Montgomery Pittman and Lillie Hayward, the film offered no romance for Tarzan, other than a bit of one-sided flirtation from the females.

The film includes a brief discussion of the ape man's origin, which was usually overlooked in Lesser's films, when Tarzan tells the safari party of his upbringing by the female ape "Kerchak" who found him orphaned, and says he learned English from hunters and missionaries. Although the tribe of hostile natives in the film are referred to as the Men of Opar, they bear no relation to the Oparians in Burroughs' Tarzan novels. The native dances and village sequences were shot on the soundstages of London, arranged by Harold Holness.

"Did you see the way he caught that fish?" – Diana
"Yeah—I'll bet he does everything well!" – Gamage

ALL NEW!
GREATEST OF ALL!
FIRST TIME IN COLOR!

M·G·M presents

TARZAN and the LOST SAFARI

Starring GORDON SCOTT AS THE NEW "TARZAN"

Co-starring
ROBERT BEATTY · YOLANDE DONLAN · BETTA ST. JOHN · WILFRID HYDE WHITE

Screen Play by
MONTGOMERY PITTMAN and LILLIE HAYWARD

TECHNICOLOR® Based on the characters created by EDGAR RICE BURROUGHS Directed by BRUCE HUMBERSTONE Produced by JOHN CROYDON A Sol Lesser Production An M·G·M Release

BETTA ST. JOHN

Though she never played Jane, Betta St. John won principal roles in the Tarzan series from two producers, Sol Lesser and Sy Weintraub. Both of her characters were women in troubled marriages; one enjoyed a happy outcome, the other fell prey to her own baser instincts.

St. John was born Betty Jean Strigler in Hawthorne, on the outskirts of Los Angeles, on November 26, 1929, to George and May Strigler. Her parents enrolled her in a Saturday drama school to help her overcome shyness and improve her posture and diction. She appeared in several small, uncredited roles at this time, most notably as the girl singing "Little Joe" in the wagon at the end of *Destry Rides Again* (1939).

At 15, she won a role in the chorus of Rodgers and Hammerstein's *Carousel* on Broadway, which led to a bigger role as the native girl Liat in *South Pacific*. Richard Rodgers gave her the stage name Betta St. John.

The show moved to London, where she fell in love with the only Englishman in the cast, Peter Grant, who played Lieutenant Joseph Cable, her onstage romantic interest. They married in 1952 and were together for 40 years until his 1992 death.

Having spent five years onstage in two productions, St. John won an MGM contract at age 21, and began screen testing in London for Hollywood parts. She was now typecast in exotic roles, due to her stage success, and her adult debut

came as Princess Tarji of mythical Bukistan in *Dream Wife* (1953) opposite Cary Grant.

She played a Polynesian girl in *All the Brothers Were Valiant* (1953), Miriam in *The Robe* (1953), and the lead in *High Tide at Noon* (1957) about a Nova Scotia fishing community.

After a few years in California, she and Grant sold their Los Angeles home and returned to London so he could resume stage work. St. John signed a contract with the Rank Organization, and won the role of unhappy wife Diana Penrod in *Lost Safari*. She returned to the Tarzan series to play another dissatisfied spouse stranded in Africa with Gordon Scott's ape man in *Magnificent*.

After a few more television appearances, St. John retired from acting in the early 1960s to focus on her family, which included three children.

"When mate call, you go, quick!"
– Tarzan

"Quick? Not where I come from."
– Diana

"Way of jungle better."
– Tarzan

TARZAN'S FIGHT FOR LIFE *1958*

The jealous witch doctor Futa (James Edwards), aided by his strongman Ramo (Woody Strode), opposes the work of Drs. Sturdy and Warwick (Carl Benton Reid and Harry Lauter), who, aided by Jill Sturdy (Jil Jarmyn), seek to bring medical advances to the jungle. With Jane (Eve Brent) hospitalized by appendicitis, Tarzan (Gordon Scott) must expose Futa's plot so a vaccine can be administered to the Nagasu chief's dying son.

"The Tarzan films are, perhaps, the film industry's greatest tradition."
– Lowell E. Redelings, *Hollywood Citizen-News*, June 10, 1958

The ape man returned to a California soundstage for Sol Lesser's last Tarzan feature. Gordon Scott finally settled down in a nuclear family, with Eve Brent as his Jane and Rickie Sorensen playing Tartu, a Boy role, in a standard jungle adventure offering an evil witch doctor as Tarzan's opponent.

The film lensed in Metrocolor on Stage 12 at Desilu-Culver Studios, formerly RKO-Pathé, with a simulated jungle, treehouse, and 75-foot water tank for a jungle waterhole. The picture re-used African location footage shot by Miki Carter, including Tarzan's meeting with pygmies, riding a giraffe, and eventual capture by natives and transport by canoe.

James Edwards gave a convincing performance as Futa, a witch doctor driven mad by the prospect of losing his status to the civilized interlopers. Woody Strode, a physically imposing former athlete and professional wrestler bowed in his first Tarzan appearance as Futa's muscle; he would make several more memorable contributions to the franchise, and provided a powerful, credible adversary for the ape man.

Lucky Humberstone returned to the megaphone, directing from a script by Thomas Hal Phillips. The film rolled in February and March 1958, for a July debut. Upon its wrap, Lesser shot three television pilot episodes immediately, using the same cast of Scott, Brent and Sorensen; these episodes were later combined to create the telefilm *Tarzan and the Trappers*.

The press campaign noted that *Fight for Life*'s release marked the 40th anniversary for the Tarzan film franchise. According to a July 8, 1958, *Daily Variety* brief, an "elaborately planned and projected promotion campaign for personal appearances by Gordon Scott" was scrapped due to the demise of further contract negotiations between Scott and Sol Lesser Productions, and Scott was "proceeding with other plans".

Despite the film's familiar setting, Lesser stressed to *Los Angeles Examiner* columnist Neil Rau that Tarzan remained fresh. He recognized that World War II had changed his audience. Men were returning from war with experience in international travel and jungle warfare. If they were going to enjoy Tarzan with their children, they would need additional enticements—better choreographed stunts and fights, more sophisticated scripts, less Cheeta humor, and color film. It would remain for Sy Weintraub to deliver on this promise of an updated Tarzan.

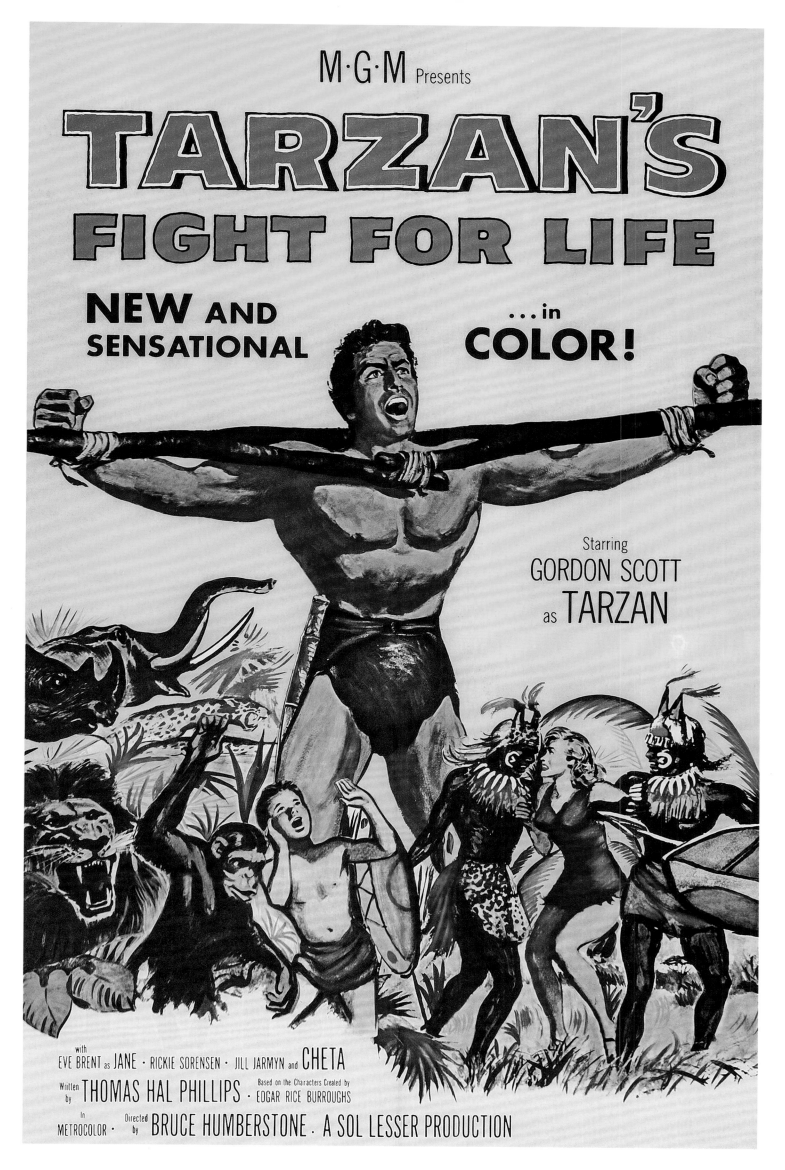

> *"Down at the bottom of my acting resume, I have a little star and it says, 'Eve played Jane in two Tarzan movies', and I'm telling you, that gets me work! People just love that!"* – Eve Brent, December 11, 1997

EVE BRENT

Blue-eyed blonde Eve Brent played Jane twice opposite Gordon Scott in *Tarzan's Fight for Life* (1958) and *Tarzan and the Trappers* (1958).

Born Jean Ann Ewers in Houston, Texas, on September 11, 1929, Brent grew up in Fort Worth. The daughter of a printing shop owner and a legal secretary, she had one brother and a sister. As a child, she decided to be an actress, and listened to the radio to cultivate her voice and eliminate her Texas drawl. She began dramatizing fairy tales on the air during her teens.

After a year at Texas Wesleyan College, she dropped out to marry Jack Lewis, a young Air Force captain, and the two began traveling, appearing in small theater. Their son James Marshall Lewis was born on November 12, 1951, in Texas.

The couple moved to Los Angeles, where the marriage ended. Brent won small television roles under her married name, Jean Ann Lewis, and began training at the renowned Pasadena Playhouse. Survival jobs for the young single mother included selling classified ads in the newspaper and working as a nightclub photographer.

Her big break came when director Samuel Fuller cast her as the ingénue lead, gunsmith Louvenia Spangler, in *Forty Guns*, renaming her Eve Brent after silent film actress Evelyn Brent. When the opportunity arose to play the ape man's mate, she was uncertain about interviewing until her son talked her into it. Only six of the women auditioning were screen tested, and Brent won the role. She got along well with Scott: "We hit it off right away, and worked well together"—and her co-star Cheeta, though she carried a scar on her wrist thereafter, from being bitten when she knocked the amorous ape off her leg, where he clung tightly.

Following the film and her typecasting, she felt the need to re-establish herself, and began touring in stage productions, and working as a casting director, while booking commercials and small film and television roles. She married actor Michael Ashe in 1978 and turned to Buddhism for help through the lean times.

Brent won a Saturn Award for Best Supporting Actress from the Academy of Science Fiction, Fantasy, and Horror Films for her role as Aunt Stella, the overbearing guardian of a troubled young man who finally avenges himself on his tormentors in *Fade to Black* (1981). Leading actor Dennis Christopher and the film also won Golden Scrolls. In 1988, Brent returned to the Pasadena Playhouse stage for their 71st-season opener in the West Coast premiere of *Steel Magnolias*, playing the role of Claree.

In 1999, she appeared in *The Green Mile* as Elaine Connelly, opposite Dabbs Greer as the elderly version of protagonist Paul Edgecomb (Tom Hanks). One of her final roles was in *The Curious Case of Benjamin Button* (2008). Brent died of natural causes on August 27, 2011 at Pacifica Hospital of the Valley in Sun Valley, two weeks shy of her 82nd birthday.

Left: Gordon Scott finally gets a Jane in Eve Brent.

Opposite top left: Futa the witch dotor (James Edwards) recruits Molo (Nick Stewart) to kill Jane, as Ramo (Woody Strode) watches.

Opposite top right: Lesser insisted that Woody Strode cut his hair into a Mohawk; after filming, Strode shaved his head so the hair could grow back evenly, but elected to retain the bald head for future film roles.

Opposite middle left: Gordon Scott was nearly strangled while wrestling an 18-foot python.

Opposite, bottom: The film's elaborate production design and sets took full advantage of the Metrocolor film stock.

TARZAN AND THE TRAPPERS *1958*

Trappers Shroeder (Lesley Bradley) and René (Maurice Masac) arrive in Tarzan's jungle, accidentally kill a local tribesman, shoot a mother elephant to capture her baby, then cage Cheeta and kidnap Boy (Rickie Sorensen). Tarzan (Gordon Scott) pursues them on giraffe-back, calling the elephants to the rescue, freeing the animals and leaving the titular trappers unconscious for the Randini authorities. Shroeder's brother Sykes (Saul Gorse), angered at his sibling's seven-year prison sentence, comes to hunt Tarzan, teaming up with Lapin the trader (William Keene) to take Tarzan's ally Tyana (Sherman Crothers) hostage and loot the lost city of Zarbo. Tarzan must stalk them into the city's catacombs to stop them. Meanwhile, back at the treehouse, Jane (Eve Brent) whips up a mean curlew egg omelet.

In 1956, Sol Lesser partnered with Jack Denove to develop a Tarzan television show for NBC. Walter White, Jr. and his Commodore Productions, producer of the 1951–53 Tarzan radio show, claimed that his contract included first refusal rights to television programming, and threatened to sue Lesser to halt production. Lesser offered a deal to White: finance a series of 39 episodes, paying Scott $1,500 per episode and Lesser $500,000 and 20 percent of the profits. White could not afford this, so he and Lesser worked out a more equitable agreement.

With the rights now cleared, Lesser shot the film immediately after *Fight for Life*, using the same cast (Scott, Brent, Sorensen) and sets. Stock footage from Africa, including Scott riding a giraffe, was recycled, and the snake puppet from *Peril* graced the opening credits. The episodes were directed by Charles F. Haas and Sandy Howard, and written by Frederick Schlick and Robert Leach.

The episodes racked up a record cost of $249,000, and no sponsor could be found to shoulder the expense. When Lesser, Denove, and NBC couldn't sell the pilot, it was shelved. It was included in the Tarzan film library purchased by Sy Weintraub, a former television syndication executive, who sold it as part of a package of 24 films to air as a television movie in 1966.

"Africa is the Dark Continent, where the struggle for survival is a never-ending drama. A savage land, where instant death or narrow escape is a part of everyday life ... At the sound of [Tarzan's] mighty yell, the antelope knows he is safe; the lion knows he must beware; the crocodile seeks the safety of the water and the great elephant answers the call of his friend Tarzan. The mighty ape man befriends the weak, helps the distressed, and enforces the jungle's primitive code of justice in this vast land where there is no other law."

– narrator's introductory voiceover

Opposite: Gordon Scott befriends a co-star on set.

Top left: Eve Brent returned as Jane for the television pilot.

Bottom left: Rickie Sorensen and Cheeta also remained for the television episodes, which were shot immediately following *Fight for Life*.

Right: When the pilot didn't sell, Scott asked to be released from his contract if Lesser insisted on an exclusivity clause.

TARZAN'S GREATEST ADVENTURE *1959*

Renegades Slade (Anthony Quayle), O'Bannion (Sean Connery), Dino (Al Mulock), and Kruger (Niall MacGinnis) rob the Mantu outpost, killing some of the residents. They travel upriver to excavate a diamond mine with their stolen supplies, pursued by Tarzan (Gordon Scott), who has a prior history with the malevolent Slade. The ape man's quest is complicated when he rescues Angie (Sara Shane), a downed bush pilot, while he stalks the wily criminals.

On April 2, 1958, producer Seymour "Sy" Weintraub, 34, purchased the rights to the remaining years on the 20-year Tarzan contract from Sol Lesser for $3 million. This included Lesser's library of 14 ape man pictures and television rights. Lesser estimated two billion people worldwide had seen a Tarzan film, with a cumulative gross of a half-billion dollars worldwide. The Tarzan comic strip ran in 315 domestic newspapers, and Tarzan comic books sold 13 million copies per year. Weintraub, a former television syndication executive and radio station owner, noted that no Tarzan film had ever lost money.

Weintraub announced that the next film would be *Tarzan's World Adventure*, with the biggest budget in franchise history, shot on locations worldwide, including Johannesburg, Tokyo, London, Munich, Rome, Paris and the African interior. By October, the film was re-titled *Tarzan's Greatest Adventure*, to be directed by Theodore B. Sills, who was later replaced by John Guillerman.

Gordon Scott walked over a contract dispute, but was rehired in late November, incentivized by a raise and a non-exclusive pact, and departed for East Africa in January. The picture, patterned after the popular Western films of the day, was lauded by critics as the first "adult" Tarzan film, certainly the first since the early MGM films to place the character in such a mature, life-or-death scenario, as the crooks are eliminated by the ape man and their own greed. The climactic battle between Quayle and Scott was shot without stuntmen, with both men secured atop the cliff with safety wires.

"I'm giving them a Tarzan they can believe in," Weintraub told Associated Press writer Norman J. Badderly on location. "Kids of today are a lot brighter than they used to be. They want action and adventure, so I'm emphasizing the action of the story rather than the simple story line. Tarzan the Ape Man who used to grunt and groan is now articulate and a lot more exciting." His was the first educated Tarzan since Herman Brix in *Tarzan and the Green Goddess*.

Weintraub's vision of a modern Tarzan didn't include Jane and Boy: "Previously he was going to work in the jungle and coming home again just like a suburban city worker. A bachelor figure is a lot more exciting than a man who comes swinging home through the jungle every night to tell his little woman what's been happening during the day." A baby chimp was retained to play Cheeta, imported 340 miles to set, garbed in a mini-loincloth, but was too scared to perform in the wild, so the little ape was written out early in the storyline.

The political upheaval in Africa was a concern. "While we never encountered an actual skirmish we did see the Mau Mau practicing rites in the valley below us," recalled Weintraub. "The impending danger added extra excitement." Three hundred Kenyan extras went on strike, demanding shorter hours, higher wages and free *posho* (porridge), along with liberation from British colonialism. Weintraub was unable to grant the fourth request.

The location work was concluded at Shepperton Studios in London. Due to work restrictions, only Scott and Guillerman travelled from the U.S.; American Sara Shane was already in England, where the other actors and crew were hired.

Trailers for the film included a kiss between Scott and tough-talking Angie, who was *not* Jane, but the ardor was trimmed from the film. The cast was complemented by the presence of an ensemble of talented thespians in the antagonist roles. It was the American film debut of Scilla Gabel, Sophia Loren's former stand-in, who played Quayle's girlfriend Toni.

The film was directed by John Guillerman, who co-wrote the screenplay with Berne Giler, from a story by Les Crutchfield, a prolific Western scripter who contributed heavily to the *Gunsmoke* radio and television shows. Guillerman returned to the series in 1962 for *Tarzan Goes to India*; subsequent notable credits include *The Blue Max* (1966), *The Towering Inferno* (1974), *King Kong* (1976), and *Sheena* (1984), the latter also shot in Kenya. Cinematographer Ted Scaife shot *Greatest Adventure* in Eastman Color, and returned to the series to direct photography on *Tarzan the Magnificent* and *Tarzan's Three Challenges*.

"Tarzan's Greatest Adventure is Tarzan with a vengeance."
– Philip K. Scheuer, *Los Angeles Times*, July 19, 1959

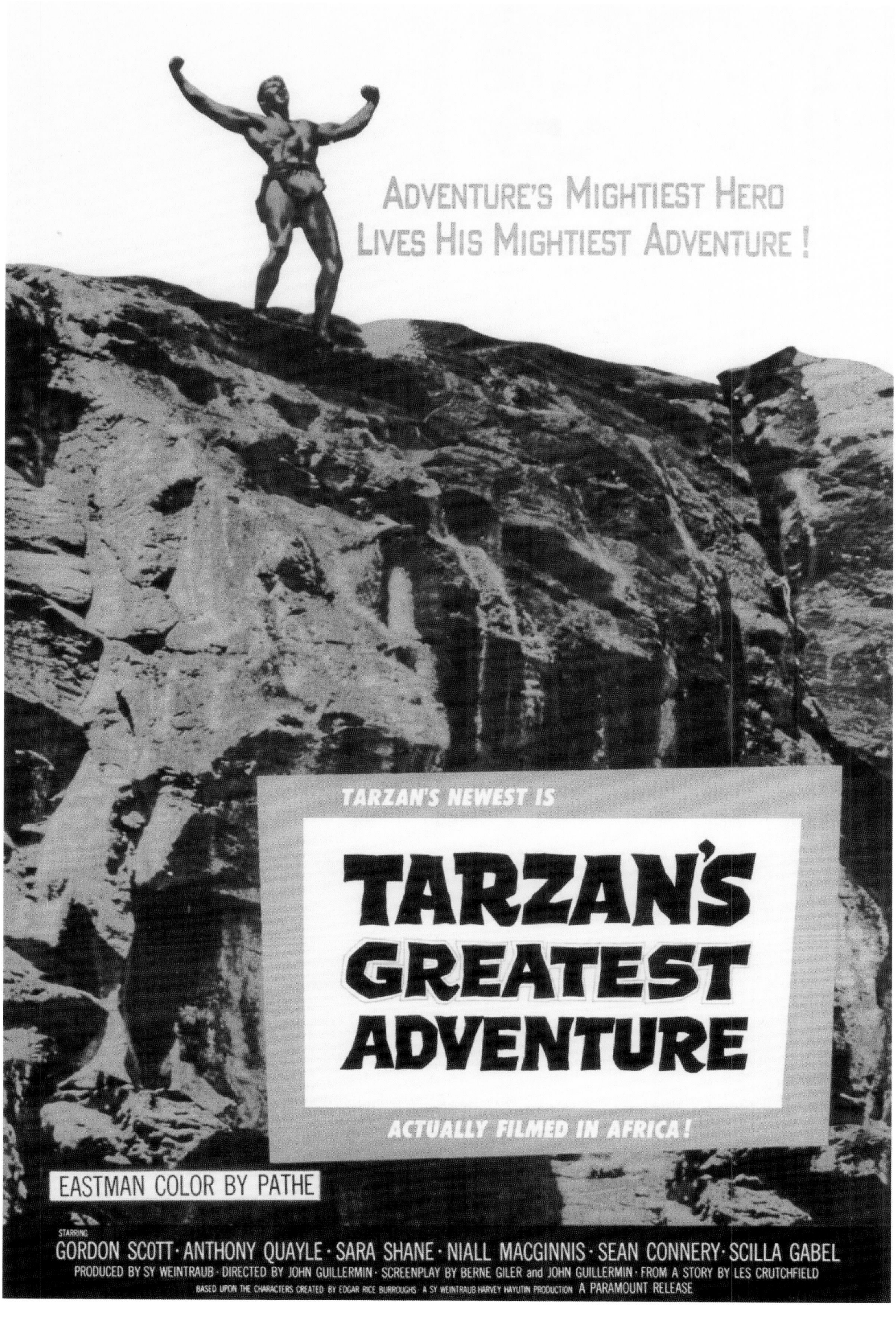

ADVENTURE'S MIGHTIEST HERO
LIVES HIS MIGHTIEST ADVENTURE!

TARZAN'S NEWEST IS

TARZAN'S GREATEST ADVENTURE

ACTUALLY FILMED IN AFRICA!

EASTMAN COLOR BY PATHE

STARRING
GORDON SCOTT · ANTHONY QUAYLE · SARA SHANE · NIALL MACGINNIS · SEAN CONNERY · SCILLA GABEL
PRODUCED BY SY WEINTRAUB · DIRECTED BY JOHN GUILLERMIN · SCREENPLAY BY BERNE GILER and JOHN GUILLERMIN · FROM A STORY BY LES CRUTCHFIELD
BASED UPON THE CHARACTERS CREATED BY EDGAR RICE BURROUGHS · A SY WEINTRAUB-HARVEY HAYUTIN PRODUCTION · A PARAMOUNT RELEASE

133

SARA SHANE

Sara Shane's turn as Angie the bush pilot in *Tarzan's Greatest Adventures* is one of fans' favorite "non-Jane" roles in the film series. Her character is brave, resourceful, and a fit partner for Gordon Scott's ape man as he tracks a band of killers through the bush.

The only child of Alden Sterling and his wife, residents of the St. Louis suburb Kirkwood, she was born Elaine Sterling on May 18, 1928. From early childhood, she wanted to be in the movies; shortly after graduating from high school, she began modelling for John Robert Powers in New York City, and moved to Hollywood with a girlfriend a few months later.

She signed a contract with MGM and had small roles in *Easter Parade* (1948) and *Neptune's Daughter* (1949) before marring wealthy realtor William I. Hollingsworth and leaving the profession. A son, Jamie, was born in 1951.

Tiring of her socialite lifestyle, she returned to acting in 1953 at the urging of her friend Hedy Lamarr. Public relations man Russell Birdwell renamed her Sara Shane (after the Western film) and ran a sexy full-length photo of her, split in half, in two Hollywood trade papers to garner attention. It generated a contract with Universal International and roles in *Magnificent Obsession* (1954) and *Sign of the Pagan* (1954).

Her roles got bigger, as she earned a starring part opposite Clark Gable in *The King and Four Queens* (1956) and played leads in *Three Bad Sisters* (1956) and *Affair in Havana* (1957), the latter opposite Raymond Burr.

In 1958 Shane divorced Hollingsworth and moved to London, to pursue stage work in the West End, when she attended a casting call and won the role of Angie. It was her final feature film role, though she continued to appear on television through 1964. She fell in love with Africa while filming, and vacationed there several times in the succeeding years.

Shane became enamored of the Caribbean while shooting *Affair in Havana* in Cuba. She moved to Haiti, where she and her friend, actress Yvette Mimeux, founded Partners in Paradise, selling textiles crocheted and embroidered by Haitian women. While there, she caught dengue fever, which damaged her liver; she attributed her recovery to a better diet, which stimulated her interest in alternative medicine.

After returning to Los Angeles, she bought and remodeled houses, selling them for profit. Shane tired of the smog, congestion and crime and moved to Australia, where, today, she works as director of the Hippocrates Health Centre in Queensland and has authored several books.

> *"... the most fun I had [acting] was the Tarzan picture, because of going to Africa and running around in the jungle and working with all of those fantastic guys. I just had a wonderful time."*
>
> – Sara Shane, *Classic Images*, August 25, 2006

Opposite: Sara Shane's rescue from her plane crash was shot on a soundstage in London.

Top left: Scott and Shane proved a memorable pairing.

Top right: Angie's desperate bid to steal medicine for the wounded Tarzan results in her capture by Slade (Quayle), Kruger (Niall MacGinnis) and Toni (Scilla Gabel).

Middle: Before he was James Bond, Sean Connery stalked Tarzan in the jungle with Anthony Quayle.

Bottom: Scott and Quayle wore safety wires for their climactic cliff-top battle.

TARZAN, THE APE MAN *1959*

Jane Parker (Joanna Barnes) *returns to Africa to join her father* (Robert Douglas) *and his partner Harry Holt* (Cesare Danova), *just as local tribesmen, angry over Holt's rescue of a rival Watusi, destroy the partners' trading post. Seeking the riches of the fabled African graveyard, the trio set off, guided by the Watusi* (Leon Anderson). *Tarzan* (Denny Miller) *observes, saving them from a stalking leopard and romancing Jane after rescuing her from a charging elephant. Reclaiming her, Parker and Holt are suspicious, until Tarzan saves them again. Captured at a lost city, the trio are marked for sacrifice, but Tarzan arrives to foil the plan.*

As Sy Weintraub made news with his acquisition of Sol Lesser Productions, MGM assigned producer Al Zimbalist to remake *Tarzan the Ape Man*, for which the studio held full rights. The plan was to save costs by filming entirely on MGM's Culver City lot, reusing Academy Award-winning color footage from *King Solomon's Mines*, which shot on location in Africa. As with *Trader Horn* in the 1930s, the *Mines* location footage appeared in numerous films thereafter, including the film's sequel, *Watusi* (1959), also produced by Zimbalist and shot in California.

MGM contractee and UCLA basketball player Denny Miller was signed as Tarzan, with starlet Joanna Barnes as Jane and Robert Douglas and Cesare Danova as Colonel Parker and Harry Holt, all contracted for a planned film trilogy. Italian import Danova brought his wife, British actress Patricia Matthews, to help him master the dialogue. The film was directed by Joseph Newman from a script by Robert Hill. Shorty Rogers provided the jazz score.

The principals were dressed in wardrobe to match that of the *Mines* cast so that long-shots of the trek to King Solomon's treasure source could double for the *Ape Man* journey to the elephants' graveyard. A tribal attack and animal stampede were among the *Mines* scenes used, as Tarzan calls the zebras (rather than elephants) to the rescue. *Mines* producers spooked 6,000 hoofstock in Africa, including zebras, impala, gazelle and wildebeest. When the wily animals refused to follow direction, and veered off course, the studio re-shot close-ups of the *Mines* principals hiding behind the rock barrier at the studio, with goats and donkeys painted to resemble zebras.

To film the native charge, *Mines* producers hired 400 Wakamba tribesmen, but the crowd swelled to 1,500, and they became so excited by their pre-fight ritual that they actually hurled their spears at the camera crew. Fortunately, no one was injured.

Ape Man also recycled the only matte-painting scene in *Mines*, an establishing shot in the desert with the snow-capped "White Twins" in the distance. This sequence was actually photographed in the Mojave Desert, since the proper landscape wasn't available on location. *Mines* filmed the climb through the mountains at 15,800 feet of elevation on Mount Kenya, but producers decided to restage the scene, since the blizzard that arose in Africa seemed too unrealistic to use.

Ape Man director Newman staged a battle between Miller and the mechanical crocodile from *Tarzan and His Mate*, but when Miller tackled the aging relic, it sank like a submarine, ruining the shot. Archival footage of Johnny Weissmuller's battle with the giant reptile was tinted and incorporated instead, along with prior sequences of aerial work by Alfredo Codona and the elephant stampede through the pygmy village.

A scene of Miller and Barnes swimming underwater was superimposed over stock footage of hippos. The water in the pool was so cold that Barnes' teeth began chattering uncontrollably, so the crew gave her brandy to warm her up—with the result that non-drinker Barnes began slurring her words.

In the climactic sacrificial-pit sequence, the actors crawl around an 11-foot-tall, 3,000-pound fiberglass idol of Baal that previously appeared in the Lana Turner film *The Prodigal* (1955) and later resurfaced in George Pal's *Atlantis, the Lost Continent* (1961). The idol was later displayed in front of a travel agency in Smyrna, Delaware, and now resides in Philadelphia, Pennsylvania.

Ape Man's studio photography was completed in eight weeks. Jordan's King Hussein, in town for a state visit, insisted on a tour of the Tarzan set, signing autographs for the cast and crew and posing for photos while chatting with them.

The film was released on October 23, 1959, in New York. It was reissued theatrically in 1972.

> **"'Tarzan the Ape Man'** *might best be described as an African* **'Hellzapoppin.'** *Almost everything that's happened to Tarzan since his creation happens all over again . . ."* – Hollywood Reporter, October 16, 1959

DENNY MILLER

Denny Miller planned to earn a physical education degree and coach basketball when he was plucked from the UCLA basketball court, given an MGM contract, and cast as Tarzan.

Physical fitness was a way of life for the Miller clan. Denny's father, Ben W. Miller, headed the P.E. department at UCLA. After earning All-City honors as a guard at University High, Denny accepted a basketball scholarship to UCLA.

His love of basketball was a birthright; he entered the world on April 25, 1934 in Bloomington, Indiana. Both parents, Miller's grandfather, and his great-grandfather were all Indiana University alumni, and his younger brother Kent was even bigger and more athletic than the 6'4", 212-pound Denny.

The family moved to Los Angeles in Miller's senior year when his father accepted the job at UCLA. Miller declined a scholarship from Indiana University, preferring to play for UCLA's Coach John Wooden. College was interrupted for army service. Miller was stationed in Germany during the Korean War, after which he returned to UCLA to rejoin the team alongside Kent and decathlon standout Rafer Johnson.

Miller was discovered by a talent agent while earning extra money moving office furniture on Sunset Boulevard. He signed with MGM after a screen test by George Cukor. His greatest regret was resigning from Coach Wooden's team at the studio's behest.

For his Tarzan screen test, Miller emerged from a pool and recited the 23rd Psalm to Joanna Barnes (Jane). "That was more than I said in the entire film," he later recalled. He recommended his friend and workout buddy Bill Smith for the role, but MGM wanted Miller.

He modeled several loincloths for producers, including a beaded version, vetoed because it rattled when he walked. He was fitted with rubber soles to protect his feet, but discarded them after he bounced out of them upon his first vine-landing.

Miller only worked 8 weeks of the 20 months he was on contract with MGM, earning $175 per week, and became a bit self-conscious about drawing a paycheck for doing nothing. He stayed in shape during filming by working out three nights a week and swimming almost daily.

He was introduced to the animal menagerie to build a rapport with them, but still asked for a stuntman on the day he was to wrestle a live cheetah. The cat, a house pet of a private collector, spooked when the stuntman started batting at its face, and slashed out with its claws. The stuntman was hospitalized, and Miller was given a rubber knife and stuffed cat to wrestle. Miller earned his stripes in the actual manner shortly after when a young lion slashed his back during their wrestling scene.

His next major break came when he was cast as scout Duke Shannon on *Wagon Train* (1961–64), though producers insisted he change his name to Scott Miller. Miller went on to become a prolific character actor and television guest star in the 1960s to 80s, with hundreds of roles on shows including *Gilligan's Island*, *Gunsmoke*, *Battlestar Galactica*, *Charlie's Angels*, *The Incredible Hulk*, *Magnum P.I.*, and *Lonesome Dove*. Due to his imposing size, he was frequently cast as a heavy.

He was also a popular commercial pitchman in myriad campaigns, serving as Big Wally, the Brawny paper towels giant, and the Gorton's fisherman. He continued to work with senior citizens as a personal trainer throughout his life.

Miller was married twice, first to Kit Smythe (the original Ginger on *Gilligan's Island*, and a busy commercial actress), with whom he had two children, and then to Nancy Gordiner. In 2004, Miller published his autobiography, *Didn't You Used to Be What's His Name?*

Miller died at home in Las Vegas on September 9, 2014, age 80, of ALS, survived by wife Nancy. He is remembered as a fan-favorite Tarzan for the friendships he cultivated at industry convention appearances throughout his life.

Left: Denny Miller, with Cheeta, won his first major film role in *Tarzan the Ape Man.*

Opposite top left: The film's publicity touted Joanna Barnes' academic credentials and society background (color tinting by Danny Proctor).

Opposite top right: Jane (Joanna Barnes), her father Colonel James Parker (Robert Douglas), and Harry Holt (Cesare Danova) recruit the Watusi (Leon Anderson) to guide them to the elephants' graveyard.

Opposite middle: The party struggles through the desert on their trek.

Opposite bottom: Journey's end for Tarzan, Cheeta, Jane, and Holt.

> *"I remember it as just being great, huge fun, a grand adventure. How often in your life do you get to ride on an elephant's back?"*
> – Joanna Barnes, December, 1997

JOANNA BARNES

Joanna Barnes, who made a career playing socialites and ice queens, was a rising starlet when she was cast in *Tarzan the Ape Man*. Like Denny Miller, she went on to a long and varied screen career.

The daughter of John Pindar Barnes, the treasurer of New England Mutual Life Insurance Company, and Alice Weston Mutch Barnes, she was born November 15, 1934 in Boston, Massachusetts, and had two younger sisters. Barnes attended Milton Academy Girls School, and was launched at the Boston Cotillion in the 1952–53 debut. She graduated Phi Beta Kappa from Smith College where she studied literature and edited the *Smith Review*, following classmate Sylvia Plath's stint on the latter.

She spurned employment offers from Time, Inc. and *Life* magazine and moved to California after graduation to research the film industry for a magazine article. Relying on an old family friend (former silent actress Carmel Myers) as a reference, she received contract offers from Warner Brothers, Paramount, and Columbia, and signed with the latter, despite her lack of acting experience. Columbia immediately began casting her in television roles, but she soon moved to Warner Brothers.

Barnes made her breakthrough as the young socialite Gloria Upson in *Auntie Mame* (1958). She was soon typecast as sophisticated society types, which reflected her real-life background. She reported to the set of *Ape Man* on a Monday morning after wrapping *Spartacus* the previous Friday night, her blonde hair darkened on that set to distinguish her from co-star Nina Foch.

In 1961, she played Brian Keith's gold-digging fiancée in *The Parent Trap* (1961), and was invited back to play the character's mother in the 1998 remake. She continued her prolific television appearances, including her favorite part, as Peter Falk's ex-wife in *The Trials of O'Brien* (1965–66). She also hosted the daily ABC talk show *Dateline Hollywood* (1967) and wrote a newspaper column on home decorating.

She married three times, to Richard Edward Herndon, actor and director Lawrence Dobkin (who had provided voices for the 1950 Tarzan radio show, and later directed NBC *Tarzan* television episodes), and architect Jack Warner.

Barnes also wrote novels, including *The Deceivers* (1970), *Who is Carla Hart?* (1973), *Pastora* (1980), and *Silverwood* (1985). She was the last actress to play Jane on the big screen until Bo Derek essayed the role in 1981.

TARZAN THE MAGNIFICENT *1960*

Tarzan (Gordon Scott) captures murderer Coy Banton (Jock Mahoney), to deliver him to Kairobi, the nearest police outpost. The pair are trailed by Banton's father Abel (John Carradine) and brothers, who destroy a riverboat to impede Tarzan. The ape man sets out overland, but is now accompanied by a disparate group of stranded travelers, including the blustering coward Ames (Lionel Jeffries) and his unhappy wife Fay (Betta St. John), Conway (Charles Tingwell), a former doctor, and his girlfriend Laurie (Alexandra Stewart), and Tate (Earl Cameron), the only capable one of the five. The Bantons pursue the party, determined to free Coy and kill Tarzan.

For *Tarzan the Magnificent*, Sy Weintraub returned to the formula that had proved so successful for *Tarzan's Greatest Adventure*, a Western-style face-off against an ensemble of hardened criminals, set in the wilds of Africa. The Mantu settlement was again the setting, with the local settlers' unwillingness to help Tarzan bring an outlaw to justice recalling the plotline of *High Noon* (1952).

Writer Bern Giler was re-hired to script, with Robert Day stepping in to direct after Weintraub saw his film *First Man into Space* (1959) in Picadilly and offered him the job. It was a providential choice, as Day would go on to direct three more Tarzans in three films (*Three Challenges*, *Valley of Gold*, and *Great River*) and the NBC *Tarzan* television episode "A Life for a Life". Principal photography began in Kenya on January 25, 1960, and ran through late March, finishing at Shepperton Studios in London. As with its predecessor, the picture was shot in Eastman Color by cinematographer Ted Scaife. It was released by Paramount in July 1960.

Weintraub extended invitations to the quartet of actors who played Tarzan's adversaries in the prior picture, but only Al Mulock returned, as brother Martin Banton. With Anthony Quayle shooting *Lawrence of Arabia*, John Carradine was hired as the patriarch of the Banton clan, a felonious family molded in the image of the Clantons of O.K. Corral shootout fame. Gary Cockrell, who played Johnny Banton, made his film debut; a former gymnast, he earned his acting break as a dancer in *West Side Story* (1957) on Broadway.

As with *Lost Safari*, Tarzan must lead a disparate group of travelers to safety in the bush. In lieu of romance the film offered an ensemble supporting cast with individual character arcs. Australian Charles "Bud" Tingwell, who portrayed Conway, had previously played Tarzan on the radio in his homeland, following in the footsteps of Rod Taylor in the role and in his subsequent onscreen career. Betta St. John (*Lost Safari*) returned as one of Tarzan's charges, the target of Coy Banton's (Jock Mahoney) amorous intent. St. John was doubled by Joy Adamson and Elsa the lioness of *Born Free* fame in the lion attack scene.

Weintraub claimed that the Swahili spoken between Tarzan and the native tribesmen was a first for a Tarzan picture; although MGM and Sol Lesser sprinkled the African language throughout their films, this ape man actually conversed in a native tongue. The film used stock shots of the native dance from *Lost Safari* (shot on a London soundstage) over opening credits and later when the tribe celebrates a child's birth.

The film culminated in a battle royale between Scott and Mahoney, who did their own stunts in a display of athleticism that garnered critical praise. One lighter note of their rivalry was relayed by Mahoney to AP Hollywood columnist Bob Thomas. "We were doing a fight during the London interiors, Gordon Scott and I," he recalled. "I had him in a tight grip and he suddenly let out a yell. I was afraid I might be breaking his arm, and I released him immediately." Mahoney noticed Scott's loincloth on the floor, and "there was Gordon, naked and running for cover!"

Mahoney's work ethic and physical skill were enough to earn him an offer to play lead in the succeeding Tarzan film. He packed nylon briefs in his travel bag as a safeguard against future loincloth malfunctions.

"In the current Tarzanian thriller, athletic Gordon Scott hunts down bank bandits in Kenya, in bravest High Noon fashion, and shows killers Jock Mahoney and John Carradine that nobody, but nobody can tangle with the trapeze-swinging tree-boy and win the decision." – Cue, July 23, 1960

TARZAN GOES TO INDIA *1962*

The Maharajah (Murad) and his beautiful daughter, Princess Kamara (Simi), ask Tarzan (Jock Mahoney) to help relocate a herd of 300 elephants that will otherwise drown when a new dam inundates their forest home. The task is thorny: the elephants are led by a killer rogue, and the project's engineers O'Hara (Mark Dana) and Bryce (Leo Gordon) won't brook interference from a jungle man.

A seasoned world traveler, producer Sy Weintraub decided it was time to cement Tarzan's international appeal (and capitalize on cheap overseas labor) by reinventing Tarzan as a globe-trotting troubleshooter. He bought out his silent partner Harvey Hayutin and formed Banner Productions, then inked a deal with MGM to distribute two Tarzan pictures, starting with *Tarzan Goes to India*. Weintraub departed for Madras in December 1961 to arrange filming for January to March 1962, before the monsoon season began.

John Guillerman (*Greatest Adventure*) returned to the director's chair. Screenwriter, novelist, and former *Chicago Daily News* writer Robert Hardy Andrews scripted; it was his final feature film screenplay. Cinematographer Paul Beeson shot the $1.1 million film in Metrocolor on Cinemascope.

Jock Mahoney was cast as Tarzan; at 42, he was the oldest actor to accept the role. "Sy was grateful for the help I gave him during the shooting of that film (*Magnificent*) in Africa," commented Mahoney. "He says I saved him thousands of dollars doing my own stunts and he told me he'd always find a place for me in his next Tarzan pictures. But I never expected to wind up with a vine of my own!"

The movie filmed entirely on location in India with the cooperation of the forestry departments of Mysore and Madras. Local hires included the elephant boy, Jai, 10, and leading lady Simi Garewal in her film debut. Feroz Khan, who later became famed as the "Indian Clint Eastwood" for his filmmaking style and industry stature, played a young engineer, with Murad, a Bollywood veteran, cast as the Maharajah. Music by Ravi Shankar and Panchal Jaikishan added a touch of authenticity to the production, which featured 5,000 Indian laborers hauling rocks in the dam-building scene, filmed at an actual construction site.

Gajendra, the giant lead elephant, was portrayed by the 67-year-old, 11-foot-tall mount of the Maharajah of Mysore, with his successor, Rajendra, serving as his stand-in. The elephant stampede was filmed last, after the rest of the film was in the can, so that if Mahoney was hurt, it wouldn't postpone production. It was a complicated scene: when Mahoney, astride the elephant, shot his arrow in a high arc during the 35-mile-per-hour charge, the pachyderms overran it; the quick-thinking actor snatched the descending arrow out of the air, and let it fly again, but this snafu was edited from the film. After charging the elephants through the bamboo barricade, it took two or three miles to stop them. Mahoney received 127 cuts and scratches when his out-of-control mount ran through some underbrush, and later compared the experience to "riding a skateboard on a Los Angeles freeway on a wet Saturday night."

The original script had both Bryce (Leo Gordon) and O'Hara (Mark Dana) dying in the final elephant charge, but was re-written to kill Bryce earlier and allow O'Hara to survive and atone for his callousness. Gordon, a popular film and television heavy who was killed hundreds of times onscreen (he noted this was his first death by elephant), returned to bedevil Ron Ely in the *Tarzan* television series.

A veteran stuntman, Mahoney did most of his stunts; though the Indian government forbade his dive from the airplane into a lake, he later told friends he did a jump anyway, in a long-distance shot. Mahoney wisely declined to wrestle a tiger whose mouth had been sewn shut; when Guillerman produced a leopard the next day, he again refused. Stuntman Gerry Crampton, a British bodybuilder who later earned the sobriquet "Mr. Mayhem" stepped in, and was mauled by the cat, carrying the scars to his grave.

Mahoney went on a press tour to support the film, visiting 51 cities in 60 days in July–September. Released on a double bill with *The Tartars*, it was the highest-earning Tarzan picture in history, a "phenomenal success" according to *Los Angeles Times* film columnist Philip K. Scheuer, and the biggest hit for MGM in two years.

Air India International noticed a conspicuous uptick in tourist travel to India after the feature was released, and attributed it to the Tarzan film, which extended thanks to the airline in the picture's credits. Following the film's success, Weintraub announced that Mahoney would resume the role in the next movie, perhaps set in Japan or the Philippines.

"A Tarzan picture is always playing somewhere. The sun never sets on him." – Sy Weintraub

JOCK MAHONEY

At 42, Jock Mahoney was the oldest actor to accept the Tarzan role. After two films, he became the oldest actor to retire from the role at age 44; Johnny Weissmuller bowed out at age 43.

Jacques Joseph O'Mahoney was born on February 7, 1919 in Chicago, Illinois, to Charles James and Ruth Eugenia Miller O'Mahoney. The family usually went by the name Mahoney, with young Jacques earning the nickname "Jocko" during school.

In 1920, the family moved to Davenport, Iowa, where Charles worked as a railroad switchman and a manager at Rock Island Arsenal. Mahoney attended public school in Davenport; he was a football, basketball, gymnastics and swimming star.

Mahoney won a swimming and diving scholarship to the University of Iowa, where he also played football and basketball while working odd jobs like busboy and delivery boy and studying pre-med. He dropped out after two years and moved to California, working as a swim instructor, and doing occasional film extra work.

He married USC co-ed Lorraine O'Donnell, and had two children. In 1943, he joined the Marine Corps, serving as a pilot scouting for enemy submarines in the Atlantic Ocean. After the war, he worked as a horse trainer and stuntman, doubling for Charles Starrett in the Durango Kid series. He later doubled leads like Jon Hall, Errol Flynn, Gregory Peck, and Randolph Scott, and became a top earner, renowned for his fearlessness and athletic ability.

When the marriage failed, Mahoney dated a series of starlets, including Shelley Winters, Yvonne De Carlo, and Irish McCalla.

In 1952, he married actress Margaret Field, mother of two small children, including future Academy Award-winning actress Sally.

He had speaking roles in Westerns and Three Stooges shorts, and won the lead in the cowboy series *The Range Rider* (1951–53). Mahoney received a contract with Universal Studios and appeared in feature films for three years before launching *Yancy Derringer* (1958–59), which lasted one season on television.

Mahoney auditioned to replace Johnny Weissmuller as Tarzan, but lost out to Lex Barker. Though he was touted as Barker's replacement five years later, he declined to audition. His first contribution to the franchise came as the villainous Coy Banton opposite Gordon Scott in *Tarzan the Magnificent* (1960). Mahoney's athleticism and work ethic won an offer from producer Sy Weintraub to play Tarzan when Scott left the role.

Mahoney added 20 pounds of muscle to his 6'4" frame, expanding his chest to 50 inches atop a 31-inch waist, while maintaining his lean, corded appearance at 215 pounds. When Mahoney's health was ravaged by disease on the set of *Tarzan's Three Challenges*, he and Weintraub agreed that rest and recuperation were vital, and terminated their agreement.

It took nearly two years for Mahoney to regain his health, whereupon he was offered three roles in the NBC *Tarzan* television series. Mahoney later assisted friend John Derek in auditioning and casting Miles O'Keeffe in *Tarzan the Ape Man* (1981) and served briefly as a stunt coordinator on location in Sri Lanka.

Returning to Hollywood, Mahoney made numerous television guest appearances and did stunt work on popular shows like *BJ and the Bear* and *The Fall Guy*, before retiring to Poulsbo, Washington, with his third wife, actress Autumn Russell.

On December 12, 1989, Mahoney, 70, had a stroke while driving, and after a serious car accident was hospitalized in Bremerton, Washington. He died on December 14, his wife Autumn and daughter Princess by his side. His was cremated and his ashes were scattered over the Pacific Ocean. The senior-most jungle lord is remembered by friends as an outgoing, garrulous, good-natured, fun-loving practical joker.

Left: Tarzan (Jock Mahoney) is recruited to rescue a herd of elephants endangered by an Indian hydroelectric project.

Opposite top: Lead engineer O'Hara (Mark Dana) has a deadline to meet and ignores the request of Princess Kamara (Simi Garewal) and Tarzan (Mahoney) to allow them to save the elephants, though local engineer Raju Kumar (Feroz Khan) is sympathetic to their cause.

Opposite, second from top: Tarzan and Simi take cover when the elephants, led by a rogue named Bala bent on destruction, storm through their refugee caravan.

Opposite, second from bottom: Tarzan finds an ally in the small elephant boy Jai and his huge mount, Gajendra.

Bottom left: Gajendra and Bala battle.

Bottom right: Tarzan leads the elephant charge!

"Tarzan is the original superman, fighting for the rights of the underdog. He's a terror to all villains, be they human or beast. He never enters into politics and rules his jungle domain with a minimum of spoken words and a few well-pitched yells, hence he's understood by all. He represents pure escapist entertainment."
– Jock Mahoney

TARZAN'S THREE CHALLENGES *1963*

Tarzan (Jock Mahoney) is recruited to escort a small boy, Kashi, the Chosen One (Ricky Der) and his governess Cho San (Tsu Kobayashi) to his ordination ceremony as the new Tarim, spiritual leader of his people. The party is pursued by the boy's bitter uncle, Khan (Woody Strode), who wants to install his own son as ruler. At the event, Khan challenges Tarzan to the Test of Might—a grueling athletic competition to the death—to determine the boy's fitness to rule.

Sy Weintraub was always ready to capitalize on a trend: after the success of *Tarzan Goes to India*, he set another Asian picture in Thailand, again starring Jock Mahoney. His plan to accurately portray Thai culture won the cooperation of the prime minister, who granted unprecedented entrée to formerly inaccessible locales. Budgeted at $1.2 million, *Three Challenges* was the first major foreign film since Merian Cooper's *Chang* (1927) to film entirely in-country.

Robert Day (*Magnificent*) returned to the helm, re-writing a script by Berne Giler (making his third contribution to the franchise). Lead cameraman Ted Scaife also returned for his third Tarzan picture. Filming ran from February 10 to April 10, 1963; as per Weintraub's practice, dialogue and sound effects were dubbed during London post-production to avoid complications from outside noise on set and speed location production. British actor George Pastell's regal tone replaced Woody Strode's voice, which was considered unsuitable for the character.

Strode (*Fight for Life*) returned to the Tarzan series in dual roles as the evil Khan and his benevolent brother, Tarim. Weintraub continued to omit romantic adventure for the ape man; platonic female support was provided by American actress Tsu Kobayashi as the young Kashi's guardian, Cho San. Ricky Der made his film debut in the role of the diminutive Chosen One. With Cheeta remaining in Africa, Hungry the baby elephant elevated the cuteness factor.

The production shot in several unique locations, including Wat Phra Phutthabat, the Temple of Buddha's Footprint, which allowed cameras for the first time; the Buddha-filled caves of Phetchaburi; and the Buddhist temple at Wat Suan Doc in Chiang Mai, complete with 40-foot high, 500-year-old gold Buddha.

When the temple's monks decided at the last minute that it would be improper to appear in the film, director Day hired local townspeople, placing bowls on their heads to give them the proper haircuts. More than 1,000 Thai girls staged a native dance; they were trucked to the Chiang Mai temple from nearby villages. The crew also filmed in remote, never-before-filmed jungles within 11 miles of the Chinese border, at risk from communist infiltrators and sympathizers, and members of the Karim hill tribe, who raided the locals for livestock and brides.

Color was also provided by sixty native archers, who fired primitive teak bows with bone triggers (similar to a crossbow) at Mahoney and Strode, in a scene written on location to capitalize on their proficiency with their weapons. Mahoney and Strode shot the beginning of their bungee-jump sequence (jumping 30 feet from the bridge into a net), which relied on dummies—which were torn apart by the force of the fall—for the distance shot. Production was hampered following the sequence with water buffalo challenging Mahoney in a test of strength; afterward, his arms were so sore that he couldn't lift them for days, and had to be spoon-fed. Mahoney took his own camera equipment to Thailand, hoping to film a documentary on the people and their royal family, but such aspirations were forgotten when he began a struggle for his life.

Problems arose when Mahoney filmed a scene swimming in the Klong River, which was polluted with human waste and garbage. Ingesting the water led to a series of near-fatal illnesses, including dysentery, dengue fever, and pneumonia; Mahoney's weight plunged as he lost 40 pounds, down to 175, finishing the film in gaunt, haggard condition. Scenes were filmed largely in order, and Mahoney's decline throughout the film is apparent.

Following the final sequence, the delirious Mahoney, who was fainting several times a day, was rushed back to the hotel, where Strode put him in an ice bath and fed him antibiotics like candy. "Anybody else would have died but Jock Mahoney," recalled Strode, in his 1990 autobiography, *Goal Dust*. "He believed he was Tarzan. That's what made him great."

Upon his return to the States, Mahoney and Weintraub agreed that rest was in order, and they dissolved his contract. Weintraub renewed his contract with Edgar Rice Burroughs, Inc. through 1972, and the search was on for a new leading ape man.

"On meeting an enemy, after a thousand-mile journey, of what would you make sure?"

TARZAN AND THE VALLEY OF GOLD *1966*

When a small boy, Ramel (Manuel Padilla, Jr.), emerges from the wilderness, criminal mastermind Augustus Vinero (David Opatoshu) kidnaps the child, planning to loot his homeland, the hidden city of Tucumai. Accompanied by his moll Sophia Renault (Nancy Kovack) and Mr. Train (Don Megowan), his massive enforcer, Vinero gathers a small army, equipped with sophisticated modern weapons. It's up to Tarzan (Mike Henry) and his animal friends to stop Vinero, and save the lost valley's pacifistic inhabitants.

After his success in re-imagining Tarzan as an African Western starring Gordon Scott, and later a global problem-solver in the person of Jock Mahoney, Weintraub decided to follow the hit *James Bond* series and give Tarzan an air of international mystery.

The one-time ape man was now a society sophisticate who helicoptered into danger, attaché case in hand, to face a diabolical supervillain and his hulking Man Friday, and rescue an imperiled damsel, all while making the world a safer place. Titled *Tarzan '65*, the film updated the notion of a lost Utopian civilization like *Lost Horizon*'s Shangri-la, with this city's treasure hoard coveted by ruthless criminals armed with modern weaponry.

Filming on *Tarzan '65* began on January 25, 1965. Starlet Sharon Tate was announced for the lead, but her manager Marty Ransohoff cancelled the agreement, believing she was destined for greater things. Nancy Kovack replaced her. David Opatoshu, who got his start in Yiddish theater, brought acting chops to the role of the evil genius Vinero, and Don Megowan, a 6'6" 230-pound USC football alumnus, provided a credible threat to Mike Henry's ape man. Manuel Padilla, Jr. played the small boy Ramel, providing a performance that earned an invitation to return for the following film and the NBC *Tarzan* television series. Tarzan was joined in the film by Blanco the leopard, Major the lion, and Dinky the chimpanzee.

The film was directed by Robert Day from a script by Clair Huffaker, a prolific Western novelist who adapted his own novels into films, as well as scripting original features and television episodes. His *Tarzan* script was novelized by Hugo Award-winning speculative-fiction author Fritz Leiber. The book's first chapter, which features Tarzan facing a *toro* in the ring, wasn't based on the movie, but written by Leiber as an audition for the assignment.

The production filmed entirely in Mexico, using locations around Acapulco and Mexico City. Tarzan sentences a thug to death-by-giant-Coke-bottle in the famed Plaza de Toros. Chapultepec Castle served as Vinero's lair; the Cacahuamilpa Cave served as the passage to the lost city, which was portrayed by the Teotihuacán ruins. Sound dubbing and interiors were recorded at Estudios Churubusco. The picture was shot by Irving "Lippy" Lippman, whose 60-year career began on Roscoe "Fatty" Arbuckle comedies in 1922 and ended with an episode of *The Love Boat* in 1982; he died at age 100 in 2006.

According to a *Los Angeles Times* profile, Phill Norman won several design awards for the opening titles. He was later nominated for 10 Emmy Awards for his title designs, winning four of them; he created openings for shows like *Charlie's Angels*, *The Love Boat*, and *Dynasty*, and films like *Out of Africa* and *On Golden Pond*. He also contributed to the two subsequent Henry films and the NBC TV series, credited with Cinefx.

Weintraub held permits from the National Institute of Anthropology and History, a subsidiary of the Mexican Department of Education, to shoot for five days at the pyramids, paying 5,000 pesos (US $400) daily, plus $40 for an Institute official to oversee filming. He also posted a $40,000 bond against any damages, and hired the Teotihuacán villages for $2,400 a day to participate.

On March 11, Mexican playwright and poet Salvador Novo wrote in *El Universal* that the film was "degrading to a national monument". Though the Mexican film trade unions disagreed, noting that domestic productions shot there, filming permission was withdrawn with a demand that the film be submitted for censorship or face confiscation.

Weintraub had plans to shoot his next Tarzan film and a television series in the area, but he quickly reversed course, smuggled the film out of the country, and decamped to Brazil to produce his next two films. When the re-titled *Tarzan and the Valley of Gold* was released on September 14, 1966, it was a hit for American International Pictures, their only Tarzan film release.

> ## "You can take Tarzan out of Africa, but you can't take Africa out of Tarzan."
> – Vincent Canby, *New York Times*, March 30, 1967

MIKE HENRY

Shooting three Tarzan films in just over a year took a toll on Henry, who was no stranger to physical hardship—he had broken his nose four times on the gridiron. Following a severe chimp bite, dysentery, food poisoning, and various infections, he declined the lead in the Tarzan television series and sued Banner Productions for $800,000 for "maltreatment, abuse, and working conditions detrimental to my health and welfare", and $75,000 for a chimp bite that "resulted from human error". He eventually settled out of court for an undisclosed amount.

Henry was born August 15, 1936, in Boyle Heights, Los Angeles, to a family of film editors. He attended Bell High School and was an All-City tackle his senior year. He received a football scholarship to the University of Southern California, earning co-captain and Outstanding Lineman honors in 1956 and '57.

He was drafted by the Pittsburgh Steelers, but began moonlighting as an extra in Hollywood. As his football prowess and playing time increased, he caught the attention of William T. Orr, head of Warner Brothers television, who offered him a standard seven-year contract. He appeared in several television shows, including *77 Sunset Strip*, *Hawaiian Eye*, and *Surfside Six*, and the movie *Spencer's Mountain*, but Steelers coach Buddy Parker wasn't happy with a bi-coastal player, and traded him to the Los Angeles Rams.

Henry played for the Rams from 1962–64. When his Warner Brothers contract was cancelled, he produced the football documentary *Men from the Boys* for network television.

Meanwhile, Sy Weintraub, seeking a young Burt Lancaster-type for the Tarzan role, was dissatisfied with his 400 applicants, which included former New York Giants halfback Frank Gifford. A Rams fan, Weintraub saw Henry's documentary and called him for an interview. The football star was "honored" to accept the role; less happy was his Rams traveling roommate Cliff Livingston, whom the rest of the squad immediately nicknamed "Jane". Weintraub asked the 6'3" Henry to shed 20 pounds from his playing weight of 228, and he complied; during his stint as Tarzan, the muscular Henry retired from football and relied on calisthenics, rather than weightlifting, to maintain his physique.

After quitting *Tarzan*, he was cast in a Screen Gems pilot *Tay-Gar, King of the Jungle*, which lampooned the jungle genre, but was shelved after a lawsuit by Banner Productions and Edgar Rice Burroughs, Inc., alleging trademark infringement.

Henry worked as a commercial producer and resumed acting, appearing with John Wayne in *Green Berets* (1968) and *Rio Lobo* (1970), and alongside Charlton Heston in *Number One* (1969), *Skyjacked* (1972), and *Soylent Green* (1973). He returned to the football field as a malicious prison guard in *The Longest Yard* (1974), and guest-starred on numerous television series of the era.

Henry, who married wife Cheryl in 1984, has a daughter from a previous relationship, and avoids the limelight in his retirement.

Right: Nancy Kovack and Major the Lion starred with Mike Henry in his debut as Tarzan.

Opposite top left: Crime boss Augustus Vinero (David Opatoshu) plots to stop Tarzan, with his bodyguard Mr. Train (Don Megowan) and paramour Sophia Renault (Nancy Kovack).

Opposite, second from top, left: Tarzan and Major escort the young boy Ramel (Manuel Padilla, Jr.) home to the lost city of Tucumai.

Opposite, second from bottom, left: Vinero employs helicopters, tanks, sharpshooters, and machine guns to stop Tarzan.

Opposite, bottom left: Tucumai's ruler, Manco Capak (Francisco Riquerio), is willing to surrender the city's treasure to preserve its inhabitants' lives, but Tarzan knows one cannot barter with a terrorist.

Opposite right: When Vinero tires of Sophia, he gifts her with an explosive necklace and leaves her in the jungle to die.

NANCY KOVACK

The only child of Michael A. and Bertha Kovach, Nancy Diane Kovach was born March 11, 1935 in Flint, Michigan. She graduated from high school early, thanks to an IQ of 158, and enrolled at the University of Michigan at Ann Arbor on scholarship at age 15. She worked as a television newscaster and hosted her own radio show, graduating in 1955 with a BA in Speech. She also won numerous beauty pageant titles during her college years.

After moving to New York, Kovack became one of Jackie Gleason's Glea Girls, then served as a presenter on *Beat the Clock* (1950), as an anchorwoman on *Today* (1952) and for *The Dave Garroway Show* (1953), while modelling and doing commercials.

A small Broadway role in *The Disenchanted* won her a Columbia contract and film debut in *Strangers When We Meet* (1960). Later film roles included Medea in *Jason and the Argonauts* (1963) and Nellie Bly opposite Elvis in *Frankie and Johnny* (1966).

The natural brunette bleached her hair to play Annie Oakley in *The Outlaws Is Coming* (1965) and chose to stay blonde. In 1969, she was nominated for an Emmy for Best Supporting Actress in a Regular Dramatic Series for her role on crime drama *Mannix*.

That year she married Zubin Mehta, then conductor of the Los Angeles Philharmonic Orchestra. After a few more television appearances in the 1970s, she retired from acting.

TARZAN AND THE GREAT RIVER *1967*

Barcuna (Rafer Johnson) has revived the ancient jaguar killer cult, burning villages and killing or enslaving the survivors. Tarzan (Mike Henry) is recruited to stop him, traveling upriver with crusty riverboat captain Sam Bishop (Jan Murray) and his little first mate, the orphan Pepe (Manuel Padilla, Jr.), who are ferrying medical supplies to Dr. Ann Phillips (Diana Millay). Assisted by Tarzan's animal allies, they join forces to stop Barcuna and free the villagers.

After cancelling plans to continue filming in Mexico, Sy Weintraub announced the next Tarzan picture would be *Tarzan, Spain*, and then *Tarzan, Brazil*. Basing the production in Rio de Janeiro, he finally arrived on the working title *Tarzan and the Big River*.

The project and its leading man suffered a setback during the second week of filming when Mike Henry was bitten viciously on the chin by Dinky the chimp, an injury that sidelined him for three weeks with monkey fever and 18 stitches in his face. Filming continued around his scenes as he recuperated. Henry finished the film, and the subsequent one, but later sued the production, asserting that he had warned the crew that the chimp was noticeably agitated before filming the scene.

Rafer Johnson, the 1960 Olympic decathlon champion volunteered to step in as Tarzan, but remained in his role as the evil Barcuna, the leader of a jaguar cult. Woody Strode had originally been offered the Barcuna part, but was unavailable, committed to a film shooting in Europe.

Comedian Jan Murray played crusty riverboat Captain Sam Bishop, a throwback to Humphrey Bogart's *African Queen* role. Murray enjoyed his time in Rio, but crashed the boat into the pier on his first day, and nearly strangled the chimp, Vicky, who became entangled as Murray frantically tied up to the dock. Manuel Padilla (*Valley of Gold*) returned as Pepe, Murray's sidekick, and Diana Millay appeared as Dr. Ann Phillips. Once again, Weintraub's Tarzan was denied a romantic storyline, as the protagonists resolved the plot without a dalliance.

Though the film was set in South America, stock footage of hippos and battling lions was inexplicably intercut into the action. Major the lion (once again playing Tarzan's ally, this time named Baron), escaped the production while filming in a park and had to be chased down by Henry. In another scene, he took his method acting too far, biting an onscreen adversary on the foot.

The film was director Robert Day's fourth and final Tarzan picture, with cinematographer Irving Lippman returning from *Valley of Gold*. It was scripted by Bob Barbash, from a story collaboration with Lewis Reed (Barbash later served as a story editor and producer on the NBC *Tarzan* series with Ron Ely). Finally titled *Tarzan and the Great River*, the feature was released by Paramount in September, 1967.

"You know the penalty for escaping—take him to the pit!"

TARZAN SWINGS INTO THE MOST DANGEROUS JUNGLE ADVENTURES OF ALL TIME!

TARZAN... kills the ferocious jaguar barehanded!

TARZAN... trapped by the erupting volcano!

TARZAN... plunges into the raging rapids from which no man ever returned!

PARAMOUNT PICTURES PRESENTS

TARZAN AND THE GREAT RIVER

Starring

MIKE HENRY · JAN MURRAY · MANUEL PADILLA, JR. · RAFER JOHNSON · DIANA MILLAY

Produced by SY WEINTRAUB · Directed by ROBERT DAY · Screenplay by BOB BARBASH · From a Story by BOB BARBASH and LEWIS REED
Based upon the Characters Created by Edgar Rice Burroughs · IN PANAVISION® AND COLOR

A PARAMOUNT PICTURE

DIANA MILLAY

Diana Millay's most memorable big screen role was Dr. Ann Phillips, a physician whose quest to stop an epidemic is targeted by the jungle terrorist Barcuna in *Tarzan and the Great River*. She went on to star in the ABC television gothic soap opera *Dark Shadows* as Mrs. Laura Collins, wife of Roger Collins (Louis Edmonds). Her character was revealed to be an immortal phoenix when the show took a turn towards the supernatural. She reprised the role in the second feature film based on the soap, *Night of Dark Shadows* (1971).

The only child of a Rye, New York, insurance executive, her interest in entertainment began when she received a standing ovation for tap dancing in her second grade play. Millay became a popular Conover child model and appeared in local summer stock productions during high school.

She made her film debut as a juvenile delinquent in *Street of Sinners* (1957), followed by her Broadway debut that year as Janet in *Fair Game*; this was followed with the role of Sandy Wendell in *Drink to Me Only* (1958). She also toured for a year onstage opposite Eddie Bracken in *The Seven Year Itch*.

Millay became a popular guest-star on television programs of the 1950s and '60s. Working bi-coastally, she earned $50,000 from acting in 1960, when the average annual salary of a Screen Actors Guild performer was $1,000. She filmed more than 30 television shows that season, shooting a different show almost every week, flying back and forth from New York to Los Angeles.

She married Broadway producer Geoffrey Jones in 1966, and had a son the following year (the marriage ended in 1968). Millay retired from acting to raise her son, and published a cookbook titled *I'd Rather Eat Than Act*, which was re-released in 2004. She continues to appear at *Dark Shadows* conventions and events.

Opposite top: Dr. Ann Phillips (Diana Millay) delivers health care to the people of Coliba.

Opposite bottom: Barcuna (Rafer Johnson) doesn't brook outsiders' interference with his megalomaniacal plans.

Top left: Riverboat Captain Sam Bishop (Jan Murray) becomes Tarzan's reluctant ally.

Top right: Baron the lion accompanies Tarzan (Mike Henry) on this adventure.

Middle: Barcuna fights to eliminate Tarzan's threat to his plans.

Bottom: Johnson and the elaborate bamboo set would return for the next film, *Tarzan and the Jungle Boy*.

TARZAN AND THE JUNGLE BOY *1968*

Photojournalists Myrna Claudel (Alizia Gur) and Ken Matson (Ronald Gans) parachute into the jungle, seeking the whereabouts of Erik Brunik (Steve Bond), a boy who disappeared years before and has been recently sighted in the area. They enlist Tarzan's (Mike Henry) help, but outsiders are not permitted in the uncharted Zugunda country, where two brothers—Nagambi (Rafer Johnson) and Buhara (Edward Johnson)—battle for the fate of their tribe.

Mike Henry hoped to take a break after shooting two Tarzan films back-to-back, but it was not to be. Planning to take advantage of favorable weather, Sy Weintraub began production on the tentatively titled *Tarzan No. 22* immediately upon wrapping *Tarzan and the Great River*.

Following a brief trip home, Henry returned to Brazil in December 1965, but the seasonal torrential rains had arrived, overwhelming the Rio de Janeiro sewer system and causing a typhoid outbreak during catastrophic flooding. Henry, still suffering the after-effects of the chimp bite, contracted dysentery and food poisoning (as did many in the cast and crew), followed by an ear infection and viral liver infection. Despite these trials, Henry later cited the now-titled *Tarzan and the Jungle Boy* as the favorite of his three films.

This time, the story was set in Africa, but re-used Brazilian sets like the bamboo scaffolding from *Great River*. The storyline offered Rafer Johnson a chance to resume his onscreen villainy in the person of Nagambi, the cruel son of a chieftain willing to kill anyone, even his brother, in his quest for power. Johnson's younger brother Edward played his screen sibling Buhara; their decathlon-style competition is a highlight of the story.

Robert Gordon helmed from a script by Steven Lord; former director Robert Day returned to the franchise as a producer, while Turkish cinematographer Özen Sermet committed the beautiful scenery to film.

Weintraub's practice of casting beautiful women in non-romantic roles continued with the hiring of Alizia Gur as a determined photojournalist. The film also featured Ronald Gans, whose distinctive bass voice yielded a prolific voiceover career.

Steve Bond played Erik Brunik, dubbed Junkara, or "Boy of the Trees" by the natives. It was the film debut for the former Shlomo Goldberg from Haifa, Israel, who had emigrated to New York two years prior with his mother, and begun learning English. Bond went on to a successful career in television and film, best remembered as leading man Jimmy Lee Holt on the popular soap opera *General Hospital*.

All three of Mike Henry's films, shot in barely more than a year, wrapped before the first one, *Valley of Gold*, screened in May, 1966. *Tarzan and the Jungle Boy*, released two years later, heralded the 50th anniversary of the popular series, which had boasted 32 sound films in 36 years, but also presaged a 16-year drought of new Tarzan features.

ALIZIA GUR

Alizia (Aliza) Gur's career was launched when she was crowned Miss Israel 1960, and became a Top 15 semi-finalist at the Miss Universe contest in Miami (Miss USA Linda Bement won the crown). Relocating to Hollywood, Gur portrayed exotic and mysterious characters in films that included *Night Train to Paris* (1964) and *Beast of Morocco* (1968) and on popular television programs such as *Get Smart* and *The Wild Wild West*.

She joined the James Bond franchise as the battling gypsy girl Vida in the second Sean Connery 007 film, *From Russia With Love* (1964). Two years later, she was in Brazil working in what was then the most profitable film franchise in history (until Bond overtook it in the 1970s), as Myrna Claudel, the headstrong photographer bent on completing her assignment opposite Mike Henry in *Tarzan and the Jungle Boy* (1968).

She was a native of Ramat Gan, born to parents who had fled Nazi Germany for the British Mandate of Palestine. She and her brother were raised in Haifa; in the 1970s, her parents followed her to America, living the rest of their lives in Cleveland, Ohio.

Gur was married to Seymour "Sy" Schulman, director of Hollywood's Cedars of Lebanon Hospital, and later to Sheldon Shrager, a production manager at Columbia Pictures. Following her appearance in the 1973 telefilm *Portrait: A Man Whose Name Was John*, she retired from acting and became active in social and philanthropic efforts in Beverly Hills, California.

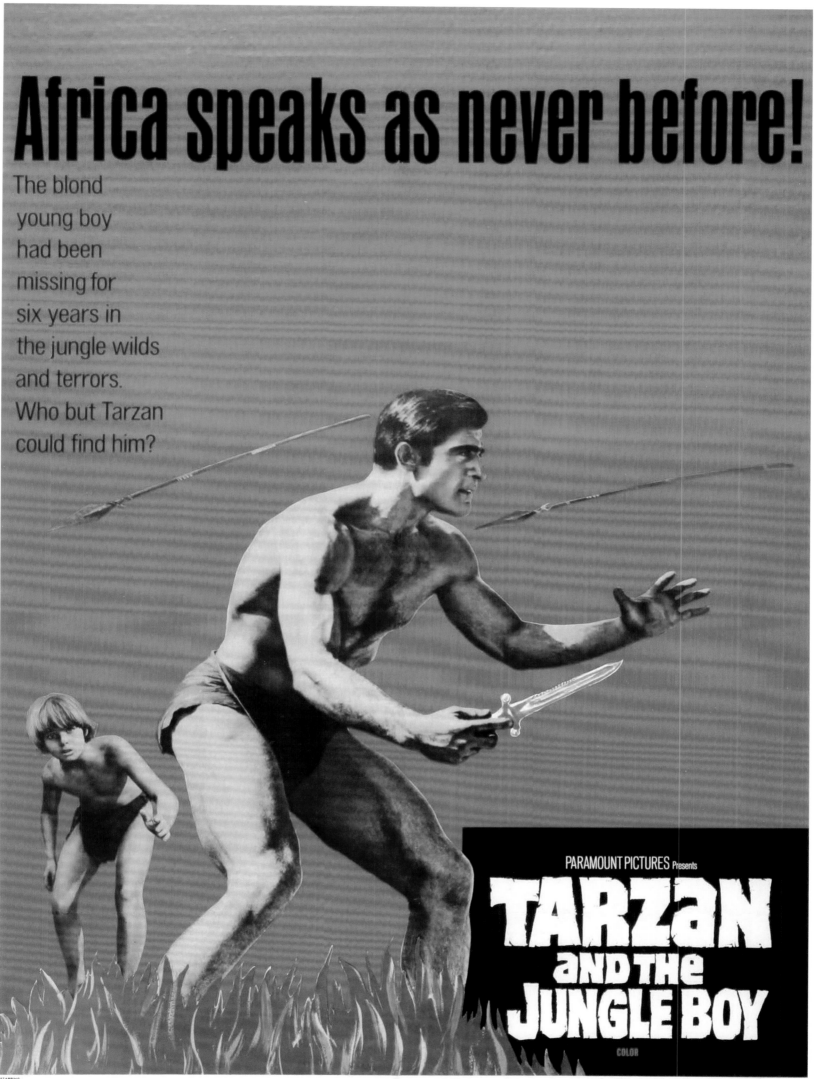

Africa speaks as never before!

The blond young boy had been missing for six years in the jungle wilds and terrors. Who but Tarzan could find him?

PARAMOUNT PICTURES Presents

TARZAN AND THE JUNGLE BOY

COLOR

STARRING MIKE HENRY · CO-STARRING RAFER JOHNSON · ALIZIA GUR · STEVE BOND · AND WITH ED JOHNSON · RONALD GANS · EXECUTIVE PRODUCER SY WEINTRAUB · PRODUCED BY ROBERT DAY · DIRECTED BY ROBERT GORDON · SCREENPLAY BY STEPHEN LORD · BASED UPON THE CHARACTERS CREATED BY EDGAR RICE BURROUGHS · PANAVISION® · A PARAMOUNT PICTURE

TARZAN *1966-68*

Sy Weintraub purchased Sol Lesser Productions with the intention of producing a Tarzan television series, but became side-tracked shooting profitable feature films. When he finally launched the series, it boasted A-list production values, but was beset by hardship on location, including inclement weather, uncooperative animals, and a star whose insistence on authenticity in the action sequences led to a series of injuries, all pushing the budget beyond sustainability.

On January 15, 1966 a *Los Angeles Times* news brief noted that Mike Henry would star in a proposed Tarzan series: seven episodes to be filmed on location in Brazil, returning to Hollywood to complete the 26-episode order. He was also scheduled for a fourth feature film, beginning in March or April.

On January 20, Weintraub flew to Los Angeles to find a replacement for the upcoming series; injuries and fatigue had taken a toll on Henry, who bowed out of the series after three feature films. Within 48 hours, Ron Ely was on a plane to Brazil, and he was announced as Tarzan number 15.

The show, simply titled *Tarzan*, offered an educated, articulate ape man in a contemporary setting. Manuel Padilla, Jr. played Tarzan's sidekick, the jungle boy Jai, with a series of attractive female co-stars vying for Tarzan's attention in lieu of a Jane character.

Production difficulties quickly arose. Driving rains destroyed the sets, leaving behind knee-deep mud, clouds of mosquitoes and dysentery. Sets were rebuilt, but six weeks later, more rains and flooding swept them downriver where they destroyed private property, generating a hefty lawsuit. The production was now $450,000 over budget.

Filming the first episode took more than a month, an impossibly slow pace for a weekly series. After five months, with only six episodes completed, the company moved to Mexico, where veteran production personnel could help speed up the pace of shooting. Before departing Brazil, the $110,000 village set was burned to be captured for B-roll footage, and Ely was filmed running through the destruction. A local entrepreneur, who planned to refurbish the village as a tourist attraction, threatened to sue.

Weintraub rented 25 acres of jungle outside Mexico City from Churubusco Studios, and spent nearly $200,000 building new sets to resemble the Brazilian locations. Co-stars Alan Caillou and Rockne Tarkington were released, though the latter returned in occasional guest-star roles.

Unwilling to coast on high production values, breathtaking scenery, and adventure, Weintraub sought to beef up Tarzan's critical appeal with a weekly parade of respected thespians. The incentive of a working vacation in Mexico attracted big-name guest stars like Ethel Merman, Helen Hayes, Julie Harris, and Diana Ross and the Supremes, as well as former Tarzan film veterans like Jock Mahoney and Woody Strode. The series offered a showcase for rising black actors like Robert DoQui, Lloyd Haynes, Geoffrey Holder, Yaphet Kotto, James Earl Jones, William Marshall, and Nichelle Nichols.

The show's opening credits took full advantage of the Brazilian location, with a shot of Ely at Iguaza Falls. Episodes opened with a theme song, *Tarzan's March* by Sydney Lee, with music composed and conducted by Walter Greene, and orchestration by Emil Cadkin.

To promote the show, a Tarzan reunion was staged at Churubusco Studios, with Johnny Weissmuller, Mahoney (sporting a bruised forehead from his guest-starring appearance), and Jim Pierce joining Ely for publicity photos.

Tarzan debuted one week early on Thursday, September 8, 1966 airing opposite *Batman* and rating 51st out of 100 new shows that week. Though feature film director Robert Day shot the pilot episode "A Life for a Life", the series opened with "Eyes of the Lion". NBC paid the highest price ever for a show in that timeslot; the show was the second most expensive show—in cost-per-1,000-viewers—on the air.

The program moved to its regular slot on Friday nights, competing against *The Wild, Wild West* on CBS and *The Green Hornet* on ABC. The second week, it gained a point (from 17.3 to 18.3) and rose to 38th place. By the end of the first season, the family series found an unexpected audience; it was the second most popular show on television with women aged 18-34, a coveted demographic for advertisers.

For the second season debut, "Tiger, Tiger", Ely wrestled a 350-pound tiger and later directed the episode "Hotel Hurricane", based on *Key Largo*. Injuries began to mount for the star, who suffered numerous cuts, falls, sprains, strains, broken bones, and animal bites. His role was often reduced in episodes to allow him to recuperate from his wounds.

On August 11, 1967, Weintraub sold Banner Productions and all affiliated companies, including 28 Tarzan films in the library, to National General Corporation. The series, which had climbed to 28th place, was not renewed for a third season.

"[Ron Ely] won't use a double. In a scene the other day he jumped off a cliff on to his lion's back ... I believe that Ron really thinks he can take this lion in a no-holds-barred battle."

– Sy Weintraub, *Lawrence Daily Journal-World*, December 22, 1967

RON ELY

Ron Ely holds two distinctions in his role as Tarzan: most screen time (2,964 minutes of programming in 57 episodes) and most injuries (more than two dozen). He was initially invited to audition for the Tarzan role when Gordon Scott vacated it but declined. After Jock Mahoney left the role Ely auditioned for Weintraub, who awarded him the television series lead when Mike Henry resigned.

Ronald Pierce Ely was born in Hereford, Texas, on June 2, 1938, to Vernon H. and Sybil Stephen Ely. His father died when he was a toddler, and he and his sister moved with his mother to Amarillo.

While at Amarillo High School, Ron played sports and won the Texas State Poetry Reading Contest in 1956, reciting Kipling in a Cockney accent; this victory gave him an indomitable feeling of confidence in future endeavors. He worked summers as an oilfield roughneck, before enrolling in Texas University in Austin.

Eager for a film career, Ely dropped out of school and moved to Hollywood with a friend, where he signed up for drama lessons with Estelle Harmon. While visiting the 20th Century Fox lot to interview for the New Talent program, he secured a small role on *South Pacific* (1958) and, later, a contract with the studio.

More film and television roles followed, including a regular part in *The Aquanauts*, later re-titled *Malibu Run* (1960–61). Upon accepting the Tarzan role, the 6'4" Ely was fitted with a $30 bespoke African antelope hide loincloth and started walking barefoot to toughen up his soles; he was eventually able to painlessly stub out cigarettes with his thickly calloused feet.

Determined to provide a convincing portrayal of the ape man, Ely did his own stunts; he felt that the element of realism would be compromised if other performers, whose physique didn't match his in a loincloth, were intercut into action sequences. He suffered numerous injuries on set, including a 25-foot fall from a vine that separated his shoulder, requiring surgery (he finished the story in a sling after producers filmed the episode's villain shooting him off the vine). A second vine fall broke the other shoulder. His first day on set, a lion's fangs punctured his skull during a wrestling sequence, and he was dragged by the head 100 yards through the brush by the spooked cat before he could battle free. Fortunately Weintraub had paid $65,000 for an insurance policy on Ely with Lloyds of London, worth $3 million.

Following the cancellation of *Tarzan*, Ely worked in European films and was a popular guest star on U.S. television series like *The Love Boat* and *Fantasy Island*. He also worked as an emcee, on the game show *Face the Music* (1979) and the Miss America Pageant (1980–81).

Ely portrayed another iconic pulp hero in the feature *Doc Savage: The Man of Bronze* (1975) and guest-starred on the 1990s *Tarzan* series as big-game bow-hunter Gordon Shaw, who stalks Wolf Larson's Tarzan. He also battled former Tarzan Denny Miller on the pilot *The Seal* (1981), which wasn't picked up for a series.

In 1981, while in Florida for a celebrity tennis tournament (which he won), he met future wife Valerie Lundeen, 1981's Miss Florida USA and a Miss World finalist. They married on March 10, 1984, and have two daughters and a son. Ely retired from acting to spend time with his family in their Santa Barbara home, and penned two Jake Sands mystery novels: *Night Shadows* (1994) and *East Beach* (1995). With his children grown, he recently returned to the screen in the film *Expecting Amish* (2014).

"Ever read the original Tarzan stories? They're beautiful. About an educated man who returns to the environment he knows best, the jungle. There he seeks truth, honor, and man's lost humanity to man. This Tarzan is the part I've been waiting for all my life." – Ron Ely

Opposite: Davis Roberts as Kanzuma in "Pride of the Lioness", with Ron Ely as Tarzan.

Top left: Ron Ely broke both shoulders in high falls during vine-swinging sequences.

Right: The series omitted Jane, but provided plenty of feminine sex appeal in the guest stars.

Bottom left: Child star Victoria Meyerink appeared in the episode "Jungle Dragnet".

TARZAN'S DEADLY SILENCE *1970*

The Colonel (Jock Mahoney), a crazed warhawk, plans to establish an empire in the jungle—'the last great battlefield'—where he can wage war without rules. Aided by Sergeant Marshak (Woody Strode) and Chico (Gregorio Acosta), an army of locals, and his razor-sharp whip, he is opposed by Tarzan (Ron Ely). The Colonel and his men attempt to leverage Jai's (Manuel Padilla, Jr.) safety to obtain their ends, but even deafened and injured by grenade blasts, Tarzan is more than a match for them.

"I know a thousand ways to kill. Killing is a science."
– The Colonel

Having battled Gordon Scott's Tarzan in *Tarzan the Magnificent*, and then donned the loincloth himself for two movies, Jock Mahoney returned to action in Banner Productions' *Tarzan* television series. He played injured game warden Hoby Wallington in the second episode, "The Ultimate Weapon", before an upgrade to a scenery-chewing villain in the two-parter, "The Deadly Silence". Also along for the ride as his right-hand man was Tarzan movie veteran Woody Strode, who appeared in a total of six NBC *Tarzan* episodes. Bob (Robert) DoQui, as good-guy tribesman Metusa, and Nichelle Nichols—who had just been cast as Lieutenant Uhuru on *Star Trek*—as his wife Ruana filled out the cast.

The episodes, which aired October 28 and November 4, 1966, were popular enough to merit release by National General Pictures as a feature film on the children's Saturday matinee circuit. Prolific director and actor Lawrence Dobkin (who was, at the time, married to former "Jane" Joanna Barnes) helmed one episode, Robert L. Friend the other; both shot three episodes for the series. Scripting duties were shared by Lee Erwin, Jack H. Robinson, and writer-actor brothers John and Tim Considine.

Top: Tarzan (Ron Ely) gives the Colonel (Jock Mahoney) a first-class ticket to a lion pit. Fortunately for the Colonel, it's a round-trip.

Middle: Tarzan (Ron Ely) holds Sergeant Marshak (Woody Strode), responsible for Jai's (Manuel Padilla, Jr.) injury.

Bottom: The Colonel (Jock Mahoney), Sergeant Marshak (Woody Strode) and Chico (Gregorio Acosta) plot Tarzan's demise.

Guns, grenades and an army of men roar through the jungle to destroy the most dangerous animal alive... TARZAN!

NATIONAL GENERAL PICTURES
presents

TARZAN'S DEADLY SILENCE

STARRING
RON ELY AS **TARZAN** WITH **JOCK MAHONEY** • **WOODY STRODE** AND **MANUEL PADILLA, JR.** AS JAI
PRODUCED BY LEON BENSON • WRITTEN BY LEE ERWIN • JACK A. ROBINSON • JOHN CONSIDINE • TIM CONSIDINE
DIRECTED BY ROBERT L. FRIEND AND LAWRENCE DOBKIN • EXECUTIVE PRODUCER SY WEINTRAUB • IN COLOR
Based on the "TARZAN" TV Series

G
ALL AGES ADMITTED
General Audiences

TARZAN'S JUNGLE REBELLION *1970*

Aspiring despot Colonel Tatakombi (William Marshall) dupes archaeologist Dr. Henry Singleton (Sam Jaffe) and his daughter Mary (Ulla Strömstedt) into fronting the excavation of the lost city Kulu and its "Blue Stone of Heaven", so Tatakombi can fulfill an ancient prophecy and his megalomaniacal dreams. When local tribal leader Matto (Lloyd Haynes) falls under the Colonel's thrall, it's up to Tarzan (Ron Ely) to discredit Tatakombi and avert a jungle rebellion.

Top left: Tarzan (Ron Ely) is held for a climactic human sacrifice by Colonel Tatakombi's men.

Top right: Jai (Manuel Padilla, Jr.), Mary (Ulla Strömstedt), Matto (Lloyd Haynes) and Cheeta plot Tarzan's rescue.

Bottom: Adventure's end for Tarzan and Mary Singleton.

The success of *Tarzan's Deadly Silence* on the matinee circuit inspired National General to release a second Tarzan feature edited from a two-part television episode. "The Blue Stone of Heaven" originally aired in *Tarzan*'s second season on October 6 and 13, 1967, and was re-titled *Tarzan's Jungle Rebellion* for theatrical exhibition.

William Marshall, at 6'5" and 250 pounds, with a resonant voice and commanding presence, made a fitting villain, while green-eyed, blonde Swede Ulla Strömstedt fit the bill as leading lady. They were supported by Sam Jaffe as the well-meaning scientist, Jason Evers as his more pragmatic assistant, and Harry Lauter as Tatakombi's toady whose greed runs afoul of his boss's designs. Jai (Manuel Padilla, Jr.) and Cheeta provided assistance as needed.

The episodes were part of six directed by William Witney, who, with former partner John English, directed many of the great serials of the sound era, including *Jungle Girl* (1941), inspired by Edgar Rice Burroughs' story. Jackson Gillis scripted the two episodes, from his total of eight *Tarzan* scripts. The episodes were filmed at the Mayan ruins of Zaculeu in Guatemala.

"He who stands to the right of the Blue Stone of Heaven shall rule the world!" – Colonel Tatakombi

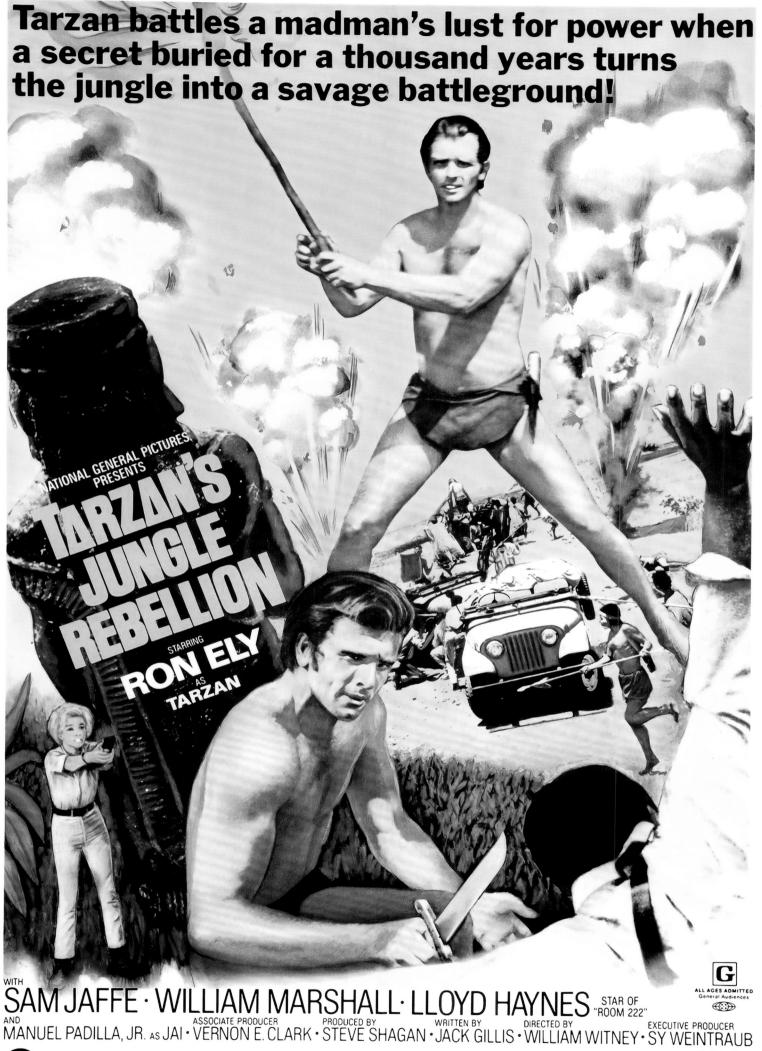

Tarzan battles a madman's lust for power when a secret buried for a thousand years turns the jungle into a savage battleground!

NATIONAL GENERAL PICTURES PRESENTS

TARZAN'S JUNGLE REBELLION

STARRING

RON ELY AS **TARZAN**

WITH **SAM JAFFE · WILLIAM MARSHALL · LLOYD HAYNES** STAR OF "ROOM 222"

AND **MANUEL PADILLA, JR.** AS JAI · ASSOCIATE PRODUCER **VERNON E. CLARK** · PRODUCED BY **STEVE SHAGAN** · WRITTEN BY **JACK GILLIS** · DIRECTED BY **WILLIAM WITNEY** · EXECUTIVE PRODUCER **SY WEINTRAUB**

G ALL AGES ADMITTED General Audiences

Based on the "TARZAN" TV Series IN **COLOR**

TARZAN, LORD OF THE JUNGLE *1976-84*

"The jungle: here I was born, and here my parents died when I was but an infant. I would have soon perished, too, had I not been found by a kindly she-ape named Kala, who adopted me as her own, and taught me the ways of the wild. I learned quickly, and grew stronger each day. And now I share the friendship and trust of all jungle animals. The jungle is filled with beauty and danger, and lost cities filled with good and evil. This is my domain, and I protect those who come here for I am Tarzan, Lord of the Jungle."
– from the show's weekly introduction

Lou Scheimer, president and co-founder of Filmation Studios, lived on a hilltop in Tarzana, California, where he would occasionally hear the Tarzan cry ring across the hillsides. Deciding that the ape man was an ideal property for a Saturday morning children's show, he descended into the San Fernando Valley to visit the Edgar Rice Burroughs, Inc. offices and broker a deal. There he met the source of that Tarzan cry, the author's grandson, Danton.

A deal was struck, and *Tarzan, Lord of the Jungle* debuted on CBS on Saturday, September 11, 1976, with 16 episodes in the first season. Six more episodes were filmed for the next year's *The Batman/Tarzan Adventure Hour*. The following season, *Tarzan and the Super 7* included six new *Tarzan* episodes, but the programs were shortened to 11 and 17 minutes to fit an abbreviated anthology format. Eight more full-length episodes were filmed for the following season, for

a total of 36. *Tarzan* continued to air reruns, later paired with *Lone Ranger* and *Zorro* episodes, until 1984.

The storylines followed a basic formula as Tarzan solved his fellow jungle inhabitants' problems with his physical might and righteous jungle morality, aided by his sidekick, the tiny monkey Nkima. Tarzan was patterned after Burroughs' original creation, intelligent, articulate, and innately noble.

The jungle setting was deliberately timeless, with occasional science-fiction elements added to lend a modern atmosphere. Lost cities, a staple of Burroughs' novels, were a common plot element. An added bonus was the use of Burroughs' ape language, including compound words like "Tand unk!" (don't go) and "Unk nala!" (climb).

"We wanted this to have a lush, illustrative feel to the art and animation, like the work of famed Tarzan comic strip artist Burne Hogarth," noted Scheimer. Filmation's aesthetic was also heavily influenced by the formative creative influences of Scheimer's childhood: Alex Raymond's *Flash Gordon* and Hal Foster's *Prince Valiant* newspaper comic strips.

Tarzan's origin was told in the opening montage, storyboarded and laid out by Bob Kline. Len Janson and Chuck Menville scripted the pilot episode, "Tarzan and the City of Gold", adapted from Burroughs' original novel. Other novels were also mined for content, including *Tarzan and the Golden Lion, Tarzan and the Forbidden City*, and *Tarzan, Lord of the Jungle*.

Robert Ridgely recorded Tarzan's dialogue, while Scheimer voiced Nkima the monkey's shrieks. Danton Burroughs' Tarzan cry was used, recorded in a variety of emotions, like angry, defiant, and triumphant. Veteran voiceover performers, including Linda Gary, Joan Gerber, Jane Webb, Barry Gordon, Alan Oppenheimer, and Ted Cassidy, portrayed the supporting characters.

A bartender from the nearby watering hole The Dug-Out, an animator hang-out, was hired and filmed walking, running, jumping, diving, and swinging for the realistic rotoscoped animation sequences. Aerialist Alfredo Codona's footage from early Tarzan pictures was also incorporated.

The Burroughs estate requested an episode with Jane, and Filmation complied; she had not been featured onscreen since 1959, and the corporation wanted to re-assert its rights to the character. The episode followed the usual formula, with no hint of romance, as Tarzan rescued Jane and her befuddled father from a series of perils, including the bullying ape Terkoz.

Eventually, Filmation was bought by L'Oreal and disbanded. Scheimer founded Lou Scheimer Productions in Woodland Hills, California, in 1989, and re-purchased the Tarzan animation rights. He was, however, unable to secure the John Carter of Mars rights he initially sought, which were under option by Walt Disney Studios, then in their first phase of preparing a feature film.

A new series, *The Fantastic World of Tarzan*, was conceived to use elements from the novels, like Jane, now a photojournalist, and animal characters Tantor, Nkima, and Jad-bal-Ja the Golden Lion. Environmental, science-fiction, and prehistoric elements were added to the mix, as Tarzan battled the mad scientist Dr. Mu-Tant; La, the alien Queen of Xenopia, stranded in her spaceship *The Opar*; the cutthroat Achmet Zek; and pirate Nicholas Rokoff. Scheimer was convinced he had a "terrific concept", but was unable to persuade the networks to buy the series.

In his autobiography *Creating the Filmation Generation* (2015), Scheimer remembered *Tarzan, Lord of the Jungle* as "one of our most beloved shows," which generated the most requests for DVD release. "I mean, it eventually sold like hotcakes all over the world. It was very, very successful," recalled Scheimer.

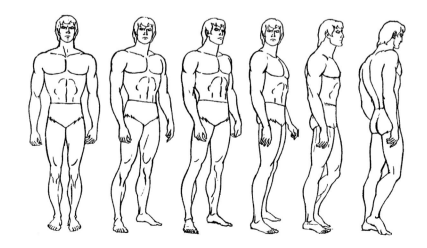

ROBERT RIDGELY

Actor Robert Ridgely's richly modulated voice was ideal for heroic roles on animated programs like *Tarzan, Flash Gordon, Thundarr the Barbarian* and more. He was also in demand as a commercial actor, both on-camera and as an announcer, and made occasional stage appearances.

Ridgely, born December 24, 1931, in Teaneck, New Jersey, began his career as a cabaret entertainer, honing his engaging comedic delivery in live appearances. In the 1960s, no doubt unaware he would one day play Tarzan, he released the novelty song "She Was a Mau-Mau", singing about Tanganyika Tillie. He also began guest-starring on popular television shows of the era, such as *Surfside 6, Maverick,* and *Sea Hunt.*

A member of Mel Brooks' ensemble, he appeared in several Brooks films, including a comic turn as Boris the Hangman in *Blazing Saddles* (1974), *High Anxiety* (1977), *History of the World Part I* (1981), *Space Balls* (1987), *Life Stinks* (1991), and *Robin Hood: Men in Tights* (1993), returning to a hangman role for his final Brooks film.

Ridgely appeared in six Jonathan Demme films, beginning their collaboration by playing game show host Wally "Mr. Love" Williams in *Melvin and Howard* (1980). He co-starred with Christopher Walken and Susan Sarandon in the 1982 PBS *American Playhouse* production of "Who Am I This Time?" from the Kurt Vonnegut story. Additional

collaborations were *Something Wild* (1986), *That Thing You Do!* (1996), and the PBS anthology series *Trying Times* pilot episode "A Family Tree" in 1987. His final role for Demme was portraying Walter Kenton, a senior partner who turns on the ailing Andy (Tom Hanks) in *Philadelphia* (1993).

Other memorable roles include that of Beverly Hills Mayor Ted Egan in *Beverly Hills Cop II* (1987); Craig Davis, the manager of Club Horizon in *The Wild Life* (1984); and Carter Brooks, a recurrent character on the sitcom *Coach.*

A resident of Toluca Lake, California, Ridgely died of cancer on February 8, 1997, at age 65. He was survived by his wife Patricia and a brother. His final role was The Colonel James in the posthumously released *Boogie Nights* (1997), a part that was written especially for him by director Paul Thomas Anderson; the film was dedicated to him and Anderson's father. Filmation founder and president Lou Scheimer remembered Ridgely as "one of the funniest men I ever met."

Above: Tarzan concept art.

Opposite: Storyboards by Bob Kline for the opening title sequence.

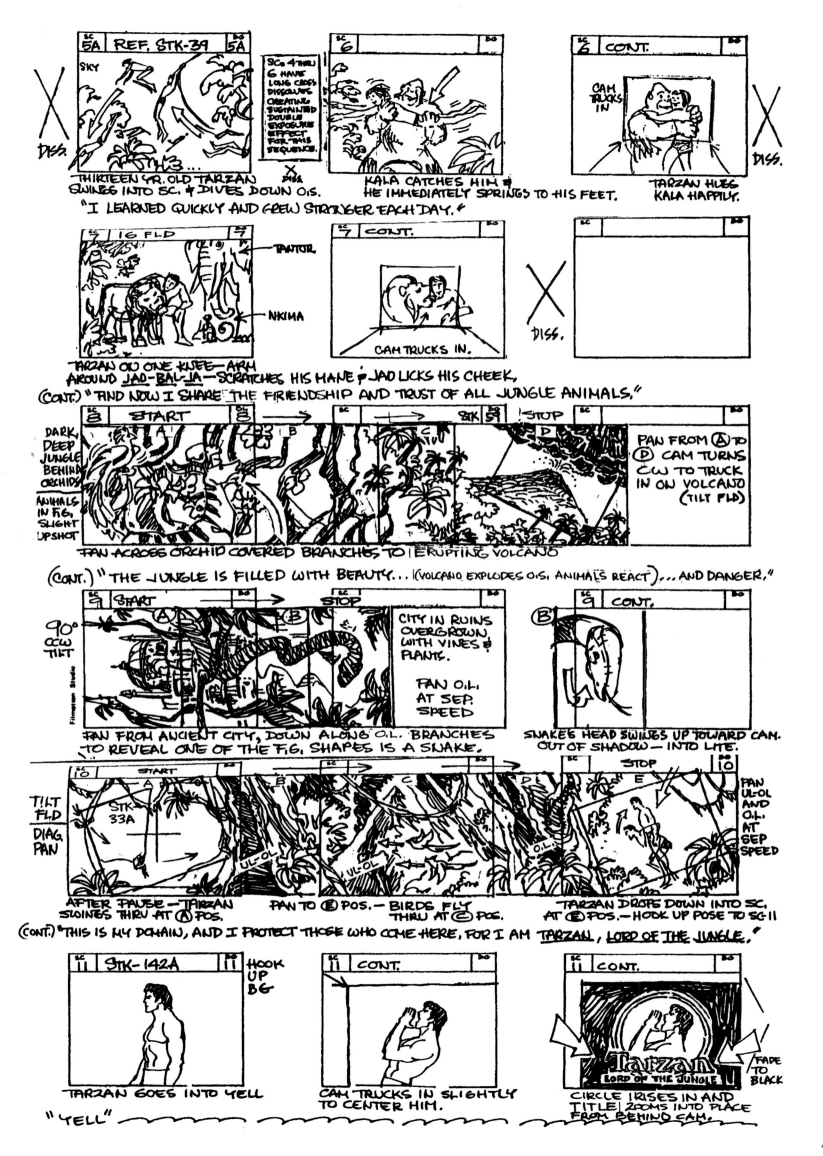

REF. STK-39

SKY

DISS.

SCs 4 THRU 6 HAVE LONG CROSS DISSOLVES CREATING SUSTAINED DOUBLE EXPOSURE EFFECT FOR THIS SEQUENCE.

DISS.

CAM TRUCKS IN

DISS.

THIRTEEN YR. OLD TARZAN SWINGS INTO SC. & DIVES DOWN O.S.

KALA CATCHES HIM & HE IMMEDIATELY SPRINGS TO HIS FEET.

TARZAN HUGS KALA HAPPILY.

"I LEARNED QUICKLY AND GREW STRONGER EACH DAY. ♦"

16 FLD

TANTOR

NKIMA

CAM TRUCKS IN.

DISS.

TARZAN ON ONE KNEE — ARM AROUND JAD-BAL-JA — SCRATCHES HIS MANE & JAD LICKS HIS CHEEK.

(CONT.) "AND NOW I SHARE THE FRIENDSHIP AND TRUST OF ALL JUNGLE ANIMALS,"

START

STK 59 STOP

DARK, DEEP JUNGLE BEHIND ORCHIDS

ANIMALS IN FG. SLIGHT UPSHOT

PAN FROM Ⓐ TO Ⓓ CAM TURNS CW TO TRUCK IN ON VOLCANO (TILT FLD)

PAN ACROSS ORCHID COVERED BRANCHES TO ERUPTING VOLCANO

(CONT.) "THE JUNGLE IS FILLED WITH BEAUTY... (VOLCANO EXPLODES O.S. ANIMALS REACT)... AND DANGER,"

START STOP

90° CCW TILT

CITY IN RUINS OVERGROWN WITH VINES & PLANTS.

PAN O.L. AT SEP. SPEED

Ⓑ CONT.

PAN FROM ANCIENT CITY, DOWN ALONG O.L. BRANCHES TO REVEAL ONE OF THE FG. SHAPES IS A SNAKE.

SNAKE'S HEAD SWINGS UP TOWARD CAM. OUT OF SHADOW — INTO LITE.

START STOP

TILT FLD DIAG PAN

STK 33A

UL-OL

UL-OL

O.L.

PAN UL-OL AND O.L. AT SEP SPEED

AFTER PAUSE — TARZAN SWINGS THRU AT Ⓐ POS.

PAN TO Ⓔ POS. — BIRDS FLY THRU AT Ⓒ POS.

TARZAN DROPS DOWN INTO SC. AT Ⓔ POS. — HOOK UP POSE TO SC 11

(CONT.) "THIS IS MY DOMAIN, AND I PROTECT THOSE WHO COME HERE, FOR I AM TARZAN, LORD OF THE JUNGLE,"

STK-142A

HOOK UP BG

CONT.

CONT.

FADE TO BLACK

TARZAN GOES INTO YELL

CAM TRUCKS IN SLIGHTLY TO CENTER HIM.

CIRCLE IRISES IN AND TITLE ZOOMS INTO PLACE FROM BEHIND CAM.

"YELL"

TARZAN, THE APE MAN *1981*

Jane Parker (Bo Derek) arrives in the jungle seeking her father, the wandering adventurer James Parker (Richard Harris). She finds him and photographer Harry Holt (John Philip Law) preparing a safari to find the fabled elephants' graveyard. Jane accompanies them and is abducted by Tarzan (Miles O'Keeffe) for a jungle idyll. Jane returns to her party, whereupon they are taken captive by hostile natives. Only Tarzan can save them now.

Bo Derek became a cultural icon after her appearance in Blake Edwards' romantic comedy *10* (1980), and she and husband John Derek, who managed her career, were swamped with offers for their next film. The couple signed a three-picture deal with MGM, under which John would make his major studio directorial debut.

The pair mulled over making a Tarzan picture titled *Me Jane*, but Warner Brothers, prepping *Greystoke*, held the Tarzan option. MGM, however, held remake rights to their previous Tarzan films, and Bo Derek's next vehicle was confirmed—a remake of *Tarzan the Ape Man*.

The studio urged the couple to follow the previous script closely, and suggested they shoot it at the Los Angeles Arboretum. The pair scouted Brazil, visiting the Amazon jungle and Iguazu Falls, which had appeared in the opening credits of the NBC *Tarzan* television show.

Derek, who didn't want to pay for pachyderm shipping, decided that he needed a location with a natural elephant population. The pair considered Kenya, until the president announced that a native Kenyan would play Tarzan, or no deal would be made. The two decided to shoot in Sri Lanka and the Republic of Seychelles in the Indian Ocean.

The project, based in the tiny seaside village of Trincomalee, filmed from January 12 to March 9, 1981, finishing ahead of the scheduled March 20 end date, thanks to 15–18-hour workdays. MGM green-lit a $5.3 million budget; the final cost was reported in the trades as $3 million, with $1 million in advertising, a little more than double the expenditure for MGM's *Tarzan and His Mate*, nearly 50 years prior.

Lee Canalito, who portrayed Sylvester Stallone's brother in *Paradise Alley* (1978) was initially cast as Tarzan, but left the production for undisclosed reasons after four days and was replaced by Miles O'Keeffe, making his feature film debut. Former screen Tarzan Jock Mahoney served briefly as the film's stunt coordinator.

Bo wanted Oliver Reed to play her screen father, but family friend Richard Harris was eventually cast, with John Philip Law in the Harry Holt role. Wilfrid Hyde-White, who had portrayed Doodles Fletcher in *Lost Safari* (1957) returned to the series to perform voiceover work as a club member in the opening, along with Laurie Mains and Harold Ayer.

Derek, whose only previous directorial experience was small

independent productions featuring his wives, preferred to shoot with a long lens, believing it to be less intrusive to the actors. Tom Rowe and Gary Goddard scripted, with Perry Botkin scoring.

The 17-foot python that ambushed Derek's Jane was caught in Thailand, and had its mouth taped shut for safety purposes. Declining to wrestle the principals, it disappeared in the water, causing some nervous moments for the actors (a corral around the set prevented it from escaping). Rocky the Lion was originally cast and spent time getting accustomed with Bo, but was replaced by Dandy Lion, a young, inexperienced cat whose front paws were declawed, though he retained his teeth. During filming, Dandy's prey instincts were triggered and he nervously rushed the struggling, squealing Derek and mauled her, bruising her and biting her shoulder, but O'Keeffe heroically stepped in to ward him off.

Derek's Jane is the focus of the picture, with Tarzan essentially a silent cipher. Derek was dressed in Gibson girl fashions to be "picked off, piece by piece," as she told Army Archerd of *Variety*.

Burroughs' estate, concerned that the project would impact the one under development at Warner Brothers, sought an injunction to halt filming. As a compromise, four minutes of nudity was eventually cut to allay concerns that the picture would undermine the franchise's family-friendly image. It is the only R-rated Tarzan film.

In the wake of a 1980 strike by the Screen Actors Guild, Hollywood studios were suffering a shortage of product, so post-production was fast-tracked to get the film into theaters by July 24. C.J. the orangutan embarked on a national publicity tour with the Dereks, accompanied by trainers Paul Reynolds and Bill Gage of Gentle Jungle, while O'Keeffe stayed home, ostensibly to preserve the Tarzan mystique.

The picture opened at #1 against five new films, earning $6,700,809 over the weekend at 930 theaters for a $7,205 per theater average—the largest MGM opening ever. After one week, it set another record for MGM, earning $10.1 million—and it hadn't been released in 70 New York City-area theaters.

Ape Man earned $17 million after two weeks, setting another record for MGM. It also set a studio record for the biggest three-day opening in New York City and most profitable first three weeks. The final tally was more than $36 million, making the film a surprise commercial hit of 1981.

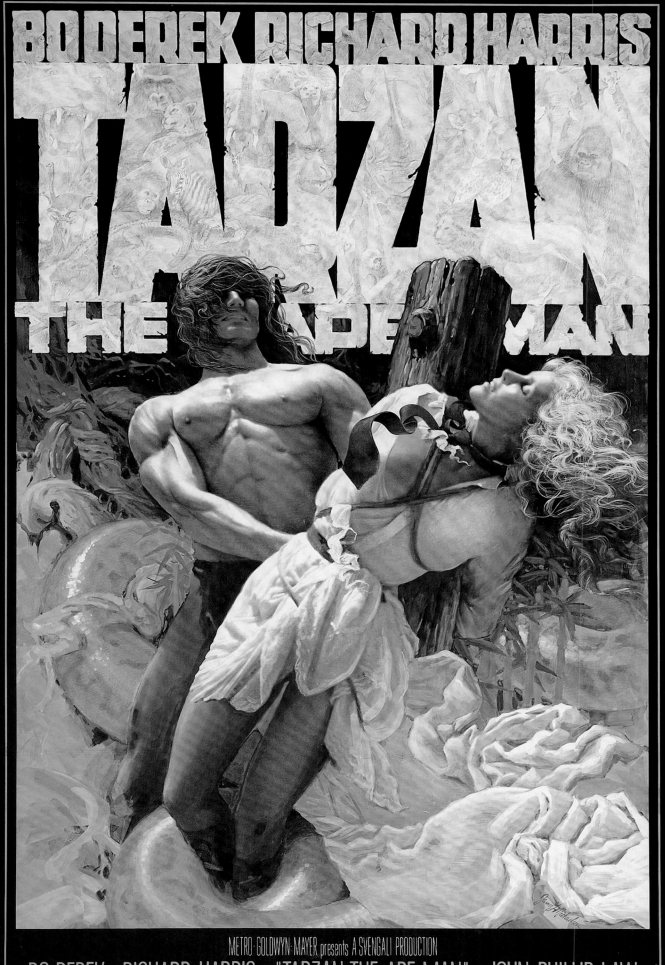

MILES O'KEEFFE

Miles O'Keeffe made his screen debut as Tarzan and won praise from fans for his chiseled physique, which evoked the idealized character conceived by Edgar Rice Burroughs. Unfortunately, his ape man never spoke a word and was offstage for much of the film.

Born June 20, 1954, O'Keeffe grew up on a farm in Ripley, Tennessee, where he attended high school. His father was an automobile dealer and prison counselor, his mother a school teacher.

O'Keeffe attended the U.S. Air Force Academy prep school, where he played halfback on the freshman football team. He won a scholarship to Mississippi State University and played on the offensive line before transferring to the University of the South in Sewanee, Tennessee, where he continued to excel on the gridiron.

"He was a heck of a football player," recalled his coach, Horace Moore. "I remember him breaking the game wide open at Millsaps. He caught a little dump pass, read the linebacker real well and went 80 yards for a touchdown. You didn't catch him when he got ahead."

O'Keeffe appeared onstage in theatrical productions, and studied political science and psychology. Upon graduation he worked as a prison counselor in Tennessee, before moving to Berkeley, California, where he played semi-professional rugby and worked in construction. In 1980, he moved to Los Angeles in search of dramatic work.

After submitting his photo to John Derek, he was called in to interview for Tarzan. He auditioned for stunt coordinator Jock Mahoney by doing flips and quarter turns on a trampoline and climbing ropes in a small circus outside Los Angeles, then posed for photos while wearing a wig and swinging from a tree in a local park. The studio put him under contract and told him to let his hair grow, but informed him that he was the backup, as a more experienced actor was preferred for the leading role.

Six months after his initial interview, in February 1981, O'Keeffe was quickly hired to replace Lee Canalito, and hopped a plane for Sri Lanka from Tennessee. Twenty-four hours later, he was 8,000 miles away, wearing a loincloth and doing his own stunts. Workplace hazards included mud, insects, leeches, lacerated feet, and recalcitrant lions and pythons.

Upon his return to the States, O'Keeffe was contractually forbidden from talking about the project (as was his predecessor, Canalito), and was left behind on the press junket. O'Keeffe did manage to capitalize on his image by playing the lead in three Italian sword-and-sorcery *Ator* films before moving on to portray a variety of roles onscreen.

"We all grew up watching Johnny Weissmuller on TV on Saturday afternoons. For most kids, I think it's the ultimate fantasy, to be this powerful man who's thrown into this untamed environment and learns to master the jungle and all its inhabitants. For a couple of weeks, I got to pretend just that."
– Miles O'Keeffe, *Starlog*, July 1990

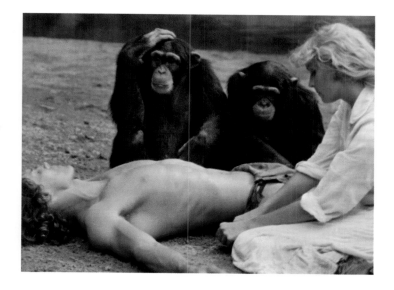

BO DEREK

Bo Derek became one of the 1980s' pre-eminent sex symbols as Dudley Moore's object of desire in *10*, portraying an idealized vision of beauty in cornrowed hair, running on the beach in a nude-tone bathing suit. Following the film, offers poured in, including the lead in *Sheena, Queen of the Jungle*.

Instead, Bo and husband John Derek chose Jane of the jungle, and announced that their newly formed Svengali Productions (an inside joke on critics' accusations that Derek was controlling his young wife) would film the MGM remake of *Tarzan the Ape Man*.

The pair met when actor-turned-filmmaker John cast 16-year-old Mary Cathleen Collins in *Once Upon a Time*, shot in Mykonos, nicknaming her Bo as their romance blossomed. They married on June 10, 1976. It was her first marriage and John's fourth, following unions to ballerina Patty Behrs, with whom he had two children, and actresses Ursula Andress and Linda Evans.

Bo, who briefly reigned as Miss Teen California, declined offers to star in *King Kong* and *Mandingo*, but accepted *Kong* producer Dino De Laurentiis' follow-up offer to appear in *Orca*

(1977), which didn't repeat the box office success of *Kong*.

Born on November 20, 1956 in Long Beach, California, Bo grew up the quintessential Southern California blonde, blue-eyed beach girl. Her father worked in marketing and public relations for Kawasaki Motorcycles and later Hobie Cat, while her mother was a hairdresser and make-up artist to actress Ann-Margret, Bo's godmother.

Following *Ape Man*, the Dereks shot two more film vehicles for Bo: *Bolero* (1984) and *Ghosts Can't Do It* (1989), but neither achieved the box office success of *Ape Man*. The couple lived in a 5,000-square-foot home on their 46-acre Santa Ynez ranch, where Bo pursued her love of horses and riding.

Bo sold the ranch in May 1998 after John, 71, died unexpectedly of heart complications. She continues to appear on film and television, and is politically active; one of her cherished causes is the support of wounded veterans.

Opposite top left: Miles O'Keeffe made his film debut as Tarzan.

Opposite top middle: James Parker (Richard Harris), Jane Parker (Bo Derek) and Harry Holt (John Phillip Law) seek the riches of the elephants' graveyard.

Opposite top right: The availability of trained elephants was a factor in choosing Sri Lanka as the location.

Top left: Bo Derek dressed in Gibson girl fashions for the safari.

Top middle: Jane in the grip of an uncooperative Thai python.

Top right: Jane becomes better acquainted with Tarzan after his battle with the python leaves him spent.

Bottom: Derek's struggles in the surf triggered Dandy Lion's predator reflexes, but O'Keeffe managed to ward off the nervous cat.

GREYSTOKE: THE LEGEND OF TARZAN, LORD OF THE APES *1984*

Shipwrecked in Africa, the Greystokes (Paul Geoffrey and Cheryl Campbell) bear a son, John, who, following their death, is abducted by primates and reared by the she-ape Kala (Ailsa Berk). After he grows to manhood in the jungle, John (Christopher Lambert) rescues Capitaine Phillippe D'Arnot (Ian Holm), whose scientific party is decimated by native attack. The grateful D'Arnot returns John to his grandfather, Lord Greystoke (Ralph Richardson) at the family's estate. Romance blooms between John and his grandfather's American ward Jane (Andie MacDowell), but he is unable to bear a series of tragedies, and returns to the jungle.

Tiring of the Tarzan business, producer Sy Weintraub sold his rights to National General, which did not renew them. Producer Stanley S. Canter purchased the Tarzan option in January 1973, commissioning a screenplay by Tracy Keenan Wynn and pitching it to MGM.

When MGM passed, Canter hired his friend Robert Towne to script. Enamored of the material, Towne sought to craft a faithful adaptation of Burroughs' novel *Tarzan of the Apes*. Canter signed a contract with Warner Brothers to produce the picture, with Towne attached as director. Towne's career suddenly gathered momentum as he was nominated for three consecutive Academy Awards for best screenplay, winning for *Chinatown* (1974), while the film idled in the production phase for a decade.

Despite Towne's growing industry stature, the studio was reluctant to trust the expensive project to a first-time director. Towne sought to prove himself by directing *Personal Best* (1982), but the project became mired in production difficulties and Warner Brothers hired Hugh Hudson (fresh off the 1982 Academy Award-winning success of *Chariots of Fire*) to direct the film, now titled *Greystoke: The Creation of Tarzan and His Epic Adventures*. Hudson hired Michael Austin to rework the screenplay. Upset with this development, Towne replaced his name on the script with his sheepdog's, P.H. Vazak.

Hudson initially sought Sir Laurence Olivier for the role of the elder Lord Greystoke. Hugh Grant was auditioned to play Lord Esker, but Hudson decided to hire an older actor, James Fox, who had just returned from a 10-year sabbatical doing Christian missionary work. Daniel Day Lewis, interested in playing the lead, sought a meeting with Hudson, but was declined; Viggo Mortenson did receive consideration for the role, which eventually went to an unknown, Christopher Lambert.

Principal photography for the 23-week shoot began on November 4, 1982, in Cameroon, on the West Coast of Africa, as the 13,435-foot high volcano Mount Cameroon erupted. Locations included Limbe, N'Kongsamba, and Douala and the village of Massoumba as the film's trading post, all complimented by the glass slide paintings of Albert Whitlock to add a majestic scope to the landscapes. Chosen due to its native flora and fauna and political stability, the country experienced a *coup d'état* just as the filmmakers arrived, but they managed to successfully navigate the shifting political climate.

The shoot incorporated all the difficult elements that directors dread: babies, children, animals, birds, water, uncooperative weather, and a jungle full of poisonous snakes and spiders, in a region known in colonial times as the White Man's Grave due to the disease, isolation, and hardship. African shooting wrapped on December 10.

Back in London, £1 million was spent to create a jungle on the 250' x 120' Soundstage 6 at EMI, where *Star Wars* had filmed. A controlled environment was necessary for the lighting, stunts, and animal performances required of the shoot. Crocodiles, pythons, pygmy hippos, leopards, pelicans, flamingos, bongo, a dik-dik and a black panther prowled the stage, which was dressed with £200,000-worth of live plants and took five months to construct. Faux studio smoke wouldn't

> *"From the beginning, this version of the Edgar Rice Burroughs story—which follows Tarzan to his ancestral home in Scotland—successfully re-creates the look and feel of an old-fashioned epic. It commands the big screen."*
> – Julie Salamon, *Wall Street Journal*, March 29, 1984

In 1886, following a shipwreck off the west coast of Africa, an infant child became part of a family of apes who raised and protected him.

As he grew, he learned the laws of the Jungle and eventually claimed the title, Lord of the Apes.

Yet, years later, when he was returned to civilization, he would remain uncertain as to which laws he should obey... those of man... or those of the jungle.

Now the director of "Chariots of Fire," captures this epic adventure of a man caught between two different worlds.

GREYSTOKE

—— THE LEGEND OF ——

TARZAN

LORD OF THE APES

A HUGH HUDSON FILM Starring RALPH RICHARDSON · IAN HOLM · JAMES FOX and introducing CHRISTOPHER LAMBERT
ANDIE MacDOWELL Music by JOHN SCOTT Produced by HUGH HUDSON and STANLEY S. CANTER
Screenplay by P. H. VAZAK and MICHAEL AUSTIN Based on the story "TARZAN OF THE APES" by EDGAR RICE BURROUGHS

replicate the correct effect, so the stage was plumbed for steam, which could then drift and pool realistically.

Rick Baker crafted the suits for apes that were to be intermediate between chimpanzees and gorillas, as in the Tarzan novels. The hands had six movements, and the heads 15, all operated mechanically and electronically. Twenty-two dancers and acrobats 5'5" and shorter were hired, led by Peter Elliott and schooled by primatologist Roger Fouts to depict behaviors that included communal grooming, hugging, kissing, and foraging for food. Baby chimps, supplied by trainer Mary Chipperfield, were mingled throughout the troop. Due to the heat and humidity, the ape actors could only work for 20 minutes at a time in the stifling costumes.

Floors Castle in Scotland—home of the Duke and Duchess of Roxburghe, who had cameos in the film, and the largest inhabited castle in Scotland, with floorage measured in acres—and Marlborough Castle in Kent doubled as Greystoke Manor. Interiors were filmed at Hatfield House, the Marquis of Salisbury's mansion in Hertfordshire. The production also shot at Blenheim Palace and the Natural History Museum, with exteriors at the Albert Memorial and Hyde Park. After the British shoot wrapped, the crew returned to Cameroon for pickup and long shots that the weather and conditions had previously prohibited, and to film the final scene with Lambert, Holm, and MacDowell. Two endings were filmed, including one wherein Jane joined John in the jungle.

Two-hundred-and-fifty-thousand feet of film were eventually edited to 13,000 feet. Warner Brothers cut 25 minutes from the film following test screenings. The excised scenes included mostly ape sequences and part of the trading post incident; some of the footage has been restored for DVD editions.

Greystoke was a critical and commercial success, and received three Oscar nominations: Best Supporting Actor for Richardson, Best Makeup for Baker and Paul Engelen, and Best Screenplay (adaptation) for Vazak (the only time a dog has been nominated for scripting) and Austin. The film was dedicated to Sir Ralph Richardson, who died before the picture's release.

"Greystoke *is unlike any other Tarzan movie you've ever seen. It is a wonderful original."*
– Vincent Canby, *New York Times*, March 30, 1984

CHRISTOPHER LAMBERT

Director Hugh Hudson sought a non-traditional type for his feral man, Tarzan. "He'd be slight, I decided, because he wouldn't eat a lot," he told Roderick Mann of the *Los Angeles Times*. "His height wouldn't matter, but he had to be athletic. More than anything, he had to be a man we could all identify with."

"I was looking for someone totally away from the Charles Atlas/Johnny Weissmuller mold," Hudson elaborated to Nancy Mills of *Marquee* magazine. "Weissmuller was a beautiful man, but I wanted someone you felt was a wild boy but who had a noble side. He had to look vulnerable, but he also needed a lithe body."

Hudson found his man in neophyte French actor Christopher Lambert, who had attended Paris Conservatoire, and made his screen debut as a gangster in the 1980 French film *Le Bar Du Telephone* (*The Telephone Bar*), skipping class for the shoot.

Lambert's unsettling audition consisted of sitting while allowing Hudson to stare at him for 30 minutes (Hudson said he was imitating a chimp, to see what Lambert's reaction would be). The director was impressed most with Lambert's penetrating gaze, which Lambert attributes to his extreme nearsightedness, and chose him over 300 other aspirants.

Following the initial meeting that was more observation than interview, Lambert was invited to London for a two-part screen test: he played an ape in a soundstage jungle at EMI, then dressed in costume and portrayed a lord at home in his castle.

Lambert began working out on rings and the parallel bars for two to three hours every morning to prepare for the role's gymnastic requirements. He also began studying English and chimpspeak, traveling to the U.S. to study with Dr. Roger Fouts, the famed primatologist who taught Washoe the chimp sign language, and who agreed to give a primer to the actors on how to behave around chimps. Peter Elliott (*Quest for Fire*'s technical advisor) coordinated the primates, teaching the actors to move and act like apes during three-hour daily sessions. Lambert's body was covered in prosthetic scars, which Hudson felt would result from a lifetime of jungle battles.

Hudson refused to speak to Lambert while filming in

Africa, later explaining, "Out there you were an animal. Human beings do not hold conversations with animals. But now we can talk." Lambert didn't read the Tarzan books, because he felt it might conflict with the script's vision, which he sought to portray.

Lambert's gymnastics training allowed him to perform all his jungle stunts, like vine-swinging, himself. He only used a double (due to risk of injury) for the castle scene, when he dropped from the roof to challenge Lord Esker.

After *Greystoke*, he declined numerous offers for barely-clad "hunk" roles, including Alexander the Great. He won the 1986 César Award (French Oscar) for Best Actor for his role in Luc Besson's *Subway*, and starred as Connor MacLeod in three films about the immortal Scottish Highlander.

Lambert holds dual U.S. and French citizenship. He was born Christophe Guy Denis Lambert on March 29, 1957, in Great Neck, Long Island, New York, to a French financial expert employed by the U.N. as a diplomat; his mother worked as an educational psychologist.

His father relocated to Switzerland when Lambert was two years old. There, Lambert attended boarding schools in Geneva, and, at age 12, decided to become an actor.

In addition to his roles on film and television in the U.S. and Europe, Lambert also works as a producer, on films like the hit French comedy *Nine Months* and its 1995 U.S. remake. He appeared in a recurring role as criminal mastermind Marcel Janvier on *NCIS: Los Angeles*.

Lambert was formerly married to actress Diane Lane, with whom he has a daughter, Eleanor, and to actress Jaimyse Haft.

Opposite: Apes designed by Rick Baker adopt the infant Tarzan (Tali McGregor).

Top left: Tarzan (Christopher Lambert), whose name is never spoken in the film, rises to lead the apes.

Top right: The riverboat *Lucy Fisher* was named for a Warner Brothers production executive, and was returned to England to serve as a paddlewheel tour boat.

Above: Lord Greystoke's American ward Jane (Andie MacDowell) is captivated by John (Lambert).

Left: "Ra-Zor!" John (Lambert) and D'Arnot (Ian Holm) bond over their morning ablutions.

Below: Andie MacDowell was a pitch-perfect Jane to Christopher Lambert's Tarzan, even though her voice was dubbed for the film.

Opposite left: John (Lambert) is welcomed home by his grandfather, Lord Greystoke (Sir Ralph Richardson).

Opposite right: John finds love with Jane (Andie MacDowell).

ANDIE MACDOWELL

Cover model Andie MacDowell made her feature film debut in *Greystoke*. Despite her radiant appearance, her Southern accent was deemed inappropriate for the role, and her voice was dubbed by Glenn Close. MacDowell rebounded from this setback to become a respected actress.

Hugh Hudson spotted her photo in the British edition of *Vogue*, and cast her as Jane, drawn in by her shy vulnerability. "She's a Gibson girl," Hudson told Mike Bygrave of *Los Angeles Weekly*. "She represents all those American daughters of rich families who came over and married into the British aristocracy."

Rosalie Anderson MacDowell was born in Gaffney, South Carolina, on April 21, 1958, to Marion St. Pierre MacDowell, a lumber executive, and Pauline Oswald Johnston, a music teacher. The youngest of four sisters, she was called Rosie by her family.

MacDowell graduated from Gaffney High School and enrolled at Winthrop College in Rock Hill, South Carolina. She was discovered by Wilhelmina Models on a trip to Los Angeles, and later signed with Elite Model Management in New York in 1978. She swiftly became a cover girl for *Vogue* and other magazines, and has been a long-time L'Oreal spokesmodel, earning a half-million dollars yearly for 12 days of work per year in the 1980s.

She made her Hollywood comeback in *Sex, Lies, and Videotape* (1989) as an unhappy Southern housewife. The role garnered an L.A. Film Critics Award for Best Actress, Independent Spirit Award for Best Female Lead, and a Golden Globe nomination. By 1994, her leads in *Four Weddings and a Funeral* and *Bad Girls* earned her the title of #1 female box-office draw worldwide after the films were back-to-back number one hits at the U.S. box office.

Other notable performances include *Green Card* (1990) opposite Gérard Depardieu; *Groundhog Day* (1993) with Bill Murray; *Multiplicity* (1996) with Michael Keaton; and *Michael* (1996) with John Travolta. MacDowell now appears on television as Judge Olivia Lockhart in the Hallmark Channel family series *Cedar Cove*, based on the novels by Debbie Macomber.

She has been married twice, to fellow model Paul Qualley (they met posing for Gap ads in Santa Fe, New Mexico), with whom she has two daughters and a son, and to Rhett DeCamp Hartzog, an Atlanta, Georgia, jewelry dealer and childhood friend.

MacDowell was named in *People* magazine's 50 Beautiful People twice (1991 and 2000), and was selected as one of the world's 10 most beautiful women by *Harper's Bazaar* in 1990.

TARZAN IN MANHATTAN *1989*

Wealthy industrialist Brightmore's (Jan-Michael Vincent) lackeys kill Tarzan's ape-mother Kala and chimp-nap Cheeta. Tarzan (Joe Lara) hops a plane to rescue Cheeta in the Big Apple. There, he enlists the aid of cabbie Jane Porter (Kim Crosby) and her father, crusty retired-cop-turned-detective Archie Porter (Tony Curtis), and wins the respect of street hooligan Juan Lipschitz (Jimmy Medina Taggert) and his crew. The trio must then infiltrate Brightmore's lair and expose the nefarious plot behind his illicit animal research.

Executive producers Max and Micheline Keller sought to launch a primetime network Tarzan series with the pilot *Tarzan in Manhattan*, which offered similar fish-out-of-water gags to the prior MGM entry *Tarzan's New York Adventure*. CBS aired the telefilm on April 15, 1989 as a "backdoor pilot" to see if ratings merited a season, but declined to commit to a series despite the telefilm's healthy Nielsen numbers.

Former model Joe Lara, in his first major role, portrayed Tarzan, formerly John Clayton III, son of Lord and Lady Greystoke, while actress Kim Crosby (charming in her Brooklyn accent) provided a novel interpretation of Jane Porter. Jan-Michael Vincent supplied the charm and the smarm as the devious Brightmore, a man with far more money than morals. Showbusiness veteran Tony Curtis was tasked with delivering the humor to his bantering daughter and straight man Tarzan. For Curtis, it was a chance to return to his childhood roots; a longtime fan of the ape man, he marched into a studio upon his arrival in Tinseltown and asked to read for the role. Producers told him to grow eight inches and get back to them.

Cheeta was played by Max, trained by Boone Narr of Hollywood Animal Rentals. During his trip to Oahu to film the African sequences, Max remained under provisional quarantine (able to perform, but not come into contact with other animals).

Directed by Michael Schultz, from a screenplay by Anna Sandor and William Gough, the pilot shot on Warner Brothers' New York City backlot in Burbank, California; jungle sequences were filmed on the island of Oahu, at Kapena Falls near the Nuuanu Memorial Park and Cemetery. Greystone Mansion, a popular Beverly Hills filming locale, doubled as Brightmore's manor, with Los Angeles' Griffith Park representing Central Park for the runaway horse-and-carriage scene. Some location footage was shot in New York City. The music was composed and conducted by Charles Fox, with two additional songs, Frank Zappa's *Leave My Monkey Alone* and *Pull Up to the Bumper* by Grace Jones.

Though it owed its greatest debt to the monosyllabic Tarzan of the old Weissmuller movies, the film includes a few nods to the mythology of the novels, including ape-language words, Tarzan's hereditary title and parents (who, in this version, perished in an airplane crash), and Tarzan's cry over Brightmore's prostrate body.

Tarzan film veterans Jock Mahoney, Gordon Scott and Denny Miller made a set visit in January to meet Lara and generate advance buzz for the project; after filming wrapped, Lara and Max the chimp went on a publicity tour.

Upon meeting Tarzan:

"So's whaddaya do? Circus, acting—politics?" – Jane

"I don't do anything. I just am." – Tarzan

"Philosopher!" – Jane

JOE LARA

Actor Joe Lara booked his first major part when he starred in the CBS television movie *Tarzan in Manhattan* (1989), chosen from 350 candidates. He declined to appear in the succeeding *Tarzan* television series in 1991, but returned to the franchise as the star of *Tarzan: The Epic Adventures* (1996–97).

At 6'3" and 201 pounds, he felt a bit out of place in the audition waiting room full of body builders, but he soon learned that he was just what the producers wanted. Once cast, Lara worked out six days a week for six weeks to prep for the role, gaining 20 pounds of muscle. "I wanted (Tarzan) to look like he had a sinewy, muscular body and I hope that's what comes across," he commented of his workout routine.

William Joseph Lara was born in San Diego on October 29, 1962. He enjoyed what might be considered a typical Southern California youth, which included surfing, volleyball, skateboarding, and basketball, and he worked as a gas pump attendant and grocery bagger while growing up in suburban Corona Del Mar.

Lara, 17, was working at Sergeant Pepperoni's pizzeria in Newport Beach, California, when he was discovered by a modelling scout and moved to France for nine months after high school graduation, eschewing college offers to launch his career. There, he appeared in fashion shows and print layouts for Pierre Cardin, Armani, and Gianni Versace.

Upon his return to the States, Lara signed with the Wilhelmina modeling agency, becoming a Jordache jeans model in their 1988 television campaign. He also enrolled in acting classes at Orange Coast community college. During his lean years, he lived out of his car.

Following *Manhattan*, Lara began receiving offers for parts like that of the renegade Apache Wolf in the telefilm *Gunsmoke: The Last Apache* (1990), for which he called upon his Native American heritage. He had just returned from a South African film shoot when producers Max and Micheline Keller requested a meeting for *Tarzan: The Epic Adventures*; unable to find their lead after auditioning 500 actors, they asked Lara to return. He agreed, with the stipulation that he be given a producer credit for this incarnation of the ape man, and returned to South Africa to film a season of 22 episodes.

Lara continued to appear in action films including *American Cyborg: Steel Warrior* (1993), *Steel Frontier* (1995), *Hologram Man* (1995) and *Doomsdayer* (2000). In 2009 he released his first country album, *Joe Lara: The Cry of Freedom*. Lara remains busy in his leisure time, as a licensed pilot, certified diver, licensed falconer, and marksman.

KIM CROSBY

Kim Crosby delivered a charming performance as *Tarzan in Manhattan*'s tough-talking cabbie Jane Porter, which was a departure from her usual roles in musical theater.

Born July 11, 1960 in Fort Smith, Arkansas, Crosby grew up in Springfield, Missouri. Her father was a dentist in the army, who later followed her into acting, earning his Equity card and touring with a production of *Into the Woods*.

She attended Southern Methodist University, where she studied opera and musical theater, and the Manhattan School of Music, and was named America's Junior Miss in 1978. She joined the acting union AFTRA due to her on-camera appearances as Junior Miss, and began auditioning for work.

Her first professional acting job was an Equity staging of *Something's Afoot* in Birmingham, Michigan. Television appearances on the soap operas *Guiding Light* and *All My Children* followed, along with numerous television commercials.

Crosby made her Broadway debut in *Jerry's Girls* (1985–86) before winning the career-defining role as the original Cinderella in the Tony Award-winning Stephen Sondheim-James Lapine musical *Into the Woods*, which had its tryout in the Old Globe Theatre in San Diego and then moved to Broadway.

It was during the show's two-year run that Crosby read for *Tarzan in Manhattan*. She auditioned twice on tape in New York, then was flown to Los Angeles for the final network audition. Taking her impression of Jane from the old movies, she appreciated the producers' decision to update Jane in *Manhattan*. "Stephen Sondheim got a kick out of it," she recalled of her leave of absence after winning the television role. It wasn't all champagne and roses, however—she was soiled by a baby chimp on her first night on set—perhaps a sort of baptism, albeit not one of fire.

Following her role in *Manhattan*, she returned to the Broadway stage in *Guys and Dolls*. Crosby fell in love with her *Into the Woods* co-star, Robert Westenberg, who played Prince Charming to her Cinderella. The couple married on June 19, 1991 and have three children. The family resides in Springfield, Missouri, and Crosby continues to tour and sing.

Opposite: Jane (Kim Crosby), Tarzan (Joe Lara) and Cheeta (Max).

TARZAN *1991-94*

When the networks declined to pick up the *Tarzan in Manhattan* pilot, executive producers Max and Micheline Keller retooled their concept to emulate the Johnny Weissmuller films, featuring a treehouse-dwelling monosyllabic jungle man living in harmony with nature, his chimp Cheeta by his side.

Titled simply *Tarzan*, the series was syndicated in the U.S. by Worldvision Enterprises, headed by Aaron Spelling. The program was geared to children, with little violence, and no overt romance between Tarzan and Jane in the half-hour installments. Environmental concerns like pollution and deforestation were a continued focus of the series. Three 25-episode seasons were filmed.

Wolf Larson portrayed the ape man, with an updated backstory: orphaned in a jungle plane crash, Tarzan was discovered and raised by apes. He later encountered Simon (Malick Bowens), a local who taught him to speak English. Tarzan grows to manhood, able to commune with the animals, dispense justice, and whip up herbal remedies when needed.

Lydie Denier played Jane, a modern woman and scientist pursuing environmental research in the jungle with her young protégé, Roger Taft, Jr. (Sean Roberge), son of a wealthy industry titan who provides funding for their efforts. Roger's youthful exuberance, offset by his naiveté and clumsiness, provides comic relief (and often a foil to be rescued).

Malick Bowens, who played Simon, was a Mandingo tribesman born in Mali and raised in France, and an actor with an accomplished theatrical resume. In the second season, Bowens was replaced by Errol Slue in the similar role of Jack Benton, with William S. Taylor as Dan Miller in the third season. Each episode opened from the perspective of "Simon's Journal" entries (later "Jack's Journal" and "Dan's Journal").

Archie the chimp played Cheeta, trained by David Allsberry of Hollywood Rental Animals. Among the tricks he learned for the series were paddling canoes and riding elephants. Additional animal co-stars included Tantor the elephant, Juma the African lion, and panthers, snakes, spiders, parrots, crocodiles, and non-African fauna like iguanas and pumas.

Tantor, the 13,000-pound pachyderm had to be shipped in a 20-ton truck, an eight-day journey due to poor roads and bureaucratic delays. Upon arriving, he decided the local offerings weren't up to his epicurean standards, so special hay was imported from a Mexico City racetrack.

The series filmed its first season in Palenque, in southern Mexico near the Chiapas rainforest and Yucatan peninsula, with Mayan ruins nearby. The crew found that the native Chiapas Indians spoke no English, but were familiar with Tarzan.

Transporting 100 crew members to the remote location in 25 vehicles—including 10-ton trucks, generator trucks, and catering services—proved difficult. The crew daily battled isolation, tropical storms, and the ever-present threat of disease, remaining vigilant for venomous snakes, scorpions, and insects, and working 12-hour days, six days a week. Temperatures climbed to 120 degrees, with 95 percent humidity, as jaguars and mountain lions roamed the forested areas around them.

The treehouse scenes filmed at Agua Azule, known for its beautiful turquoise waterfalls and lagoons, a two-hour commute from Palenque. The outdoor sets were dressed with banana trees, pineapple plants, and vines to add atmosphere. For the second season, production moved to Escondido; the third season filmed near Acapulco, where previous Tarzan films and the 1960s television series were based.

The series was shot on 35mm film to capture the beauty of the locations; directors included Henri Safran, Sidney Hayers, Kevin James Dobson, Gérard Hameline, and Brian Trenchard-Smith.

Though Larson did many of his own athletic feats (excepting high dives, which the insurance company nixed), he was stunt-doubled as necessary by Sonny Surowiec. Denier was doubled by Melissa R. Stubbs. Fires and explosions were among the effects used.

Among the notable guest stars were Adrian Paul (television's *Highlander*) as Jack Traverse, Jane's old boyfriend, and Ron Ely, who returned to the franchise as big game bow-hunter Gordon Shaw. In the episode, "Tarzan the Hunted", the ape man disrupts Shaw's elephant hunt, so Shaw decides to stalk the ultimate prey—Tarzan.

After the first season aired, U.S. stations declined to renew it, though it was a hit in Europe, perhaps due to the presence of a German-Canadian Tarzan and French Jane. The final 50 episodes aired domestically in 1997–98 in lieu of a second season of *Tarzan: The Epic Adventures*.

> *"I had to do a scene, deliver lines and hold a bow-and-arrow with a monkey on my back while riding an elephant in the water!"*
> – Wolf Larson, *Starlog*, November 1991

> *"I'll never be able to match this experience anywhere, anytime. Working with the animals has been great. I was able to work with the kind of animals most people only see in the zoo."* – Wolf Larson

WOLF LARSON

Wolf Larson is the only Tarzan actor who brought an MBA degree to the role, and one of the few blond actors to essay the part.

He was born Wolfgang von Wyszecki on December 22, 1959 in West Berlin to Gunther and Ingeborg von Wyszecki. The family moved to Ottawa when Wolf was an infant, where his father, who held doctorates in physics and math, worked for the National Research Council of Canada; his mother was a chemist. Larson graduated from Queen's University in

Kingston, Ontario, with a BA in Economics and Statistics, and earned an MBA at the University of Nevada, Las Vegas, where he spent two years as an instructor teaching finance.

In 1985, he moved to Los Angeles to pursue his passion from childhood, signing up for drama classes and adopting Larson, a maternal family name, as his stage name. To finance his career, he partnered with an actor friend to publish a lucrative line of swimsuit calendars. Early television credits included *Dynasty*, *Simon & Simon*, and the soap opera *Santa Barbara*.

Larson had an advantage when he read for the Tarzan role—he had taken acting classes with Lydie Denier, so they had already established a rapport. Martial artist Jeff Wincott was a runner-up for the lead, for which Aaron Spelling had final casting approval.

The 6'2" Larson capped his 12-hour shooting days with a 90-minute workout in a custom-made (albeit spartan) gym on set. "Between the heat and the intense physical activity, it was easy for me to get in shape," he noted.

One highlight of the first season was a chance to work with prior screen Tarzan Ron Ely. "[He] did all his own stunts," Larson recalled. "Lived up to what you would expect of him, playing Tarzan, in real life. In other words, it wasn't a disappointment," he told Bill Groves of *Television Chronicles*.

Larson got along well with Archie the chimp, by asserting his dominance in roughhouse play sessions. "Cheetah took a real shine to Wolf right away," commented trainer David Allsberry in the pressbook. "And after four months of working and playing with Wolf, Cheetah totally accepted him into his social structure. They became good friends." Allsberry concluded, "Wolf is the only actor I've ever worked with who could actually be an animal trainer if he decided to go that route."

Following *Tarzan*, Larson starred as Detective Chester "Chase" McDonald, opposite Steven Williams as Detective August Brooks in the syndicated buddy-cop action show, *L.A. Heat*, and returned to film work and television guest-starring roles.

"It was a once in a lifetime experience that I'll never be able to match again," he said of playing the ape man. "I felt truly at home in the jungle and secure with all the animals. If a real-life crisis happened there, I probably could have dealt with it."

LYDIE DENIER

Frenchwoman Lydie Denier played *Tarzan*'s Jane with an international flair, as a modern woman and environmental scientist doing research on endangered species in the jungle.

"It was 100 degrees every day by 9 in the morning," she recalled of the hardships on location in Mexico, in a *Los Angeles Times* interview. "One time it got up to 127. And there were these flying red ants that would come out of nowhere, bite you all over, and then go away. There was no TV, no newspapers. Even little things like chewing gum you couldn't get. The producers would fly down twice a month and bring us chocolate-chip cookies and newspapers that were three weeks old. After a while, you just lay back and let the mosquitoes bite you."

Born April 15, 1964 in Saint Nazaire, Brittany, France, Denier grew up in the country, playing in a treehouse and watching classic American films. She began modelling in *Vogue, Elle,* and other high fashion magazines at age 14, as well as walking the Parisian runways. At 16, she traveled to Africa, the Caribbean, and Germany for modelling assignments; there, she signed with Polygram to record French ballads.

Denier moved to the U.S. in 1985, and won a one-year contract with ABC, which included acting, voice, singing, and English classes. A fan of Johnny Weissmuller and Maureen O'Sullivan from childhood, she was delighted when her acting class presented her with a life-size print of Weissmuller.

She soon began appearing in videos and commercials as she learned English. Among her early recurring roles were the French nurse Danielle on *China Beach* and Yasmine Bernoudi on *General Hospital*.

After filming three seasons of *Tarzan* with Wolf Larson, Denier returned to the rebooted series in the role of French noblewoman Collette De Coude opposite Joe Lara in "Tarzan Returns", the pilot for *Tarzan: The Epic Adventures*. The character, whose flirtation with Tarzan remains unconsummated, originally appeared in the novel *The Return of Tarzan*.

Denier continues to appear in films and television guest-starring roles. In 2001, she gave a critically acclaimed turn onstage in Los Angeles as Greta Garbo in *Garbo's Cuban Lover*. In 2006, she released an online memoir, *Me, Jane . . . Not You!* based on the journals she kept during *Tarzan*'s production.

TARZAN: THE EPIC ADVENTURES *1996-97*

Tarzan (Joe Lara), having renounced his hereditary title and his claim to Jane's hand, visits a Parisian casino with his friend Phillippe D'Arnot (Dennis Christopher), befriending Countess Colette De Coude (Lydie Denier), which angers her fiancé, Nikolai Rokoff (Andrew Divoff). Swearing vengeance, Rokoff kidnaps Colette and flees to Africa, hoping to locate a lost treasure. Tarzan and Mugambi (Ralph Wilcox) pursue Rokoff into the African interior and Pellucidar to stop him before he unleashes the Mahars, a hideous reptilian race led by Mora (Cory Everson), on an unsuspecting mankind. Upon foiling the plot, Tarzan and his old friend Themba (Aaron Seville) embark on a series of adventures among the strange lands and people of Africa.

After the *Tarzan* series starring Wolf Larson ended, executive producers Max and Micheline Keller's American First Run Studio partnered with Henry and Paul Siegel's Seagull Entertainment in 1995. The newly formed Keller Siegel Entertainment announced its plan to offer a new Tarzan concept for television.

Due to the success of syndicated series like *Hercules: The Legendary Journeys*, and *Xena: Warrior Princess*, producers decided to pursue a fantasy angle for the series, initially titled *Tarzan: The Fantastic Adventures*. The hour-long fantasy-adventure series looked to Edgar Rice Burroughs' novels for inspiration, offering an intelligent, articulate Tarzan, who, disenchanted with civilization, returns to Africa.

The Siegels, who made syndication history when they revived the cancelled NBC series *Baywatch* and turned it into a global phenomenon, hoped to repeat their success with Tarzan. The production team obtained $20 million in funding by partnering with STI Entertainment Group, a Malaysian business conglomerate that was headed by HRH Prince Imran.

The two-hour pilot, *Tarzan's Return* (loosely based on Burroughs' second Tarzan novel), filmed at Disney-MGM Studios in Lake Buena Vista, Florida, using Epcot sets for scenes set in Paris and Morocco.

Orlando-based Dennis Steinmetz, former executive producer of the revived *Mickey Mouse Club*, was hired as supervising producer. Steinmetz, a creative force in Sid and Marty Kroft's *Land of the Lost* (1974–77) Saturday morning children's series, brought this aesthetic to the *Tarzan* pilot, incorporating a lost temple with gemstones that could be manipulated to open portals to other lands. The Temple of the Ancients set was planned to double as an attraction on the Disney studio tour.

The pilot shot on 16mm film in four weeks in January–February 1996, directed by Brian Yuzna, known for his horror films like *Re-Animator* (1985). Burton Armus, a retired New York City police detective-turned-screenwriter, scripted.

Practical rubber effects, including a rod puppet snake and

giant snake head, Mahar suits and rod puppets, and Sagoth facial prosthetics were provided by MAX (Make Up and Animatronic FX), headed by Kevin Brennan, who also donned a gorilla suit for the telefilm.

The series name was tweaked to *Tarzan: The Epic Adventures* to match a Trendmaster toy line, which spanned three of Burroughs' major franchises, Barsoom, Pellucidar, and Tarzan; some film designs were based on the toys.

The cost of shooting at Disney/MGM proved prohibitive, so the series moved to Sun City Kingdom, South Africa, a resort offering mountain peaks, lagoons and waterfalls, tropical jungle, and a simulated lost city's ruins. New personnel included supervising producer and showrunner Michael McGreevey, and effects wizard John Carl Buechler, who crafted a variety of creature suits and puppets for the 20 episodes. The beautiful production design of South African local Hans Nels was a highlight of the series.

Lara was the only returning member of the pilot's cast, now accompanied by Aaron Seville as Themba, an African prince returning to his homeland after 13 years of European education. Seville played the sidekick role for comic relief and as a civilized foil to the laconic Lara. Don McCleod appeared in a recurring role as Bolgani, the gorilla; he also suited up as the monsters when necessary.

In addition to Pellucidar, concepts from the novels included the Leopard Men, the Lost Empire, La of Opar, the Forbidden City, and the first screen incarnation of the Amtorians, with Anthony Guidera and Michelle Botes as Carson Napier and his love Duare.

The pilot, novelized by fantasy author R.A. Salvatore for Del Rey books, aired August 28, 1996. Dissatisfied with the series' reception, the Kellers debated a return to the Weissmuller model of Tarzan, Jane, Cheeta, and treehouse for a second season, and announced Xavier DeClie as their new ape man. The series reboot never materialized; instead, the final two seasons of Wolf Larson *Tarzan* episodes were aired domestically to fulfill contractual obligations.

LA OF OPAR

La, the High Priestess of Opar, is Jane's most consistent rival for Tarzan's affections in Edgar Rice Burroughs' stories, appearing in four of the original 24 novels.

La rules a lost city peopled by descendants of the ancient Atlantis. The men of Opar have become hairy, stunted, and crooked from years of interbreeding with apes, while the women remain strikingly beautiful, due to some strange quirk of genetics. When Tarzan is captured for offer as a human sacrifice to their sun god, La immediately falls deeply in unrequited love with the ape man, and frees him.

Jane is later captured as the sun god's intended. Tarzan's rescue of her, and avowal of his love for her, is a crushing blow for the mercurial La, who, nevertheless, continues to carry a torch for the ape man in the novels *Tarzan and the Jewels of Opar, Tarzan and the Golden Lion*, and *Tarzan the Invincible*.

La has appeared onscreen four times in the Tarzan films and television series. Lillian Worth portrayed a conventionally attractive blonde La opposite Elmo Lincoln and Louise Lorraine in *The Adventures of Tarzan*, based on the novel *The Return of Tarzan*.

Born Lillian Burgher Murphy on June 24, 1884 in Brooklyn, New York, Worth began appearing onstage in 1909, and was later contracted to Pathé, shooting films in California, New York, and Paris. With the advent of the sound era, she became a popular choice to record blood-curdling screams, a particular talent of hers. She retired from films in 1937 and died on February 23, 1952 in Los Angeles.

La's second bow was in the serial *Tarzan the Tiger*, opposite Frank Merrill and Natalie Kingston. Mademoiselle Kithnou, a French-Asian actress, portrayed the tempestuous La with an exotic flair. Kithnou was born in Pondichery, Hindustani, India, on March 24, 1904. She toured South America, Italy, Spain and Egypt with a dancing act, landing in Paris, where she debuted in the serials *Parisette* and *L'Orpheline*, by director Louis Feuillade. She made her U.S. debut for Rex Ingram in *Mare Nostrum* (1926). *Tiger* was her final known film, after which she faded from public view.

Angela Harry played La opposite Joe Lara in two episodes of *Tarzan: The Epic Adventures*, and in a flashback clip episode. Born January 1, 1963, in Fukuoka, Japan, Harry's father was a U.S. Air Force Colonel, and her mother was Korean. The family, which included a younger brother and sister, eventually moved to Southern California.

Though she was bullied as an interracial child, Harry grew up to become a supermodel, with a six-figure income and clients including Shiseido, Diet Coke, L'Eggs, Clairol, and Olga. Harry started working in high school and eventually became one of Nina Blanchard's top models. In 1995, she began appearing in television guest spots. *Star Wars* fans know her from voicing Jan Ors in the video game *Dark Forces II*.

La's fourth incarnation came in Disney's *The Legend of Tarzan* television series, with Diahann Carroll voicing the role. Born Carol Diahann Johnson in the Bronx, New York, on July 17, 1935, Carroll began modelling and dancing professionally in her teens and made her film debut in *Carmen Jones* (1954) as a friend of Dorothy Dandridge's eponymous character. She made her Broadway debut starring in *House of Flowers* (1954) and won a Tony Award for Best Actress for *No Strings* (1962), the first black woman to do so. She was also the first black woman to star in her own television series portraying a non-domestic, *Julia* (1968–71). She has been nominated for an Academy Award (for *Claudine*, in 1975), four Emmy Awards, and three Golden Globes, winning Best Television Star in 1969 for *Julia*. *The Legend of Tarzan* was her animation debut.

Opposite: La of Opar (Angela Harry) is unable to perform her priestly duties and sacrifice Tarzan (Joe Lara) on Opar's blood-stained altar.

Top left: Joe Lara (*Tarzan in Manhattan*) reprised his role as the ape man in *Tarzan: The Epic Adventures*.

Bottom left: Annika Bullus appeared as Kali, the Leopard Goddess, another temptress with a fixation on Tarzan.

Right: Angela Harry's elaborate La of Opar wardrobe was hand-crafted by South African locals.

TARZAN AND THE LOST CITY *1998*

Tarzan (Casper Van Dien), having finished his education at Oxford, celebrates his impending marriage to Jane (Jane March) when he receives a psychic summons from jungle shaman Mugambi (Winston Ntshona) to return to Africa. A band of mercenaries led by Nigel Ravens (Steve Waddington) is plundering the local tribes, capturing animals, shooting apes, and creating all sorts of jungle havoc in its quest to acquire the treasure of the lost city of Opar. Tarzan returns, with Jane following. When Jane is abducted by Ravens' band of renegades, Tarzan springs into action, with the story culminating with a mystical battle in the lost city.

Tarzan and the Lost City is the only film in the series photographed entirely in Africa, with a storyline that spans rivers, jungles, savannahs, and mountains and presents an array of African landscapes, all beautifully shot.

The film was conceived as a follow-up to *Greystoke*, shepherded by tenacious producer Stanley S. Canter, who commissioned the first script in 1985, while Warner Brothers retained sequel rights. When the studio declined to renew the option, Canter re-purchased it in 1991 and continued to foster the project.

The initial screenplay, by Hal Harris, was titled *Greystoke II: The Quest for Jane*. The story begins four years after *Greystoke*, as World War I breaks out in Europe. Jane travels to Africa to work as a nurse, where she is captured by Germans and handed over to their Arab allies. Tarzan (who has lived in the jungle with his ape tribe since his return at the end of *Greystoke*) and his friend D'Arnot come to her rescue in the action-packed tale.

Canter's aim was to emulate the successful formula of the *Indiana Jones* films. A 1991 rewrite by J. Anderson Black, titled *Greystoke II: Tarzan and Jane*, is also set in the early days of World War I. A multi-national band of hunters, led by a German, provides the conflict, shooting Tarzan's ape friends and kidnapping Jane (who is working as a nurse with Dr. Albert Schweitzer). Tarzan and D'Arnot again come to her aid. In 1994, Bayard Johnson (*The Second Jungle Book*), a fan of the Tarzan novels from childhood, was hired to rewrite, and included more plot elements from the character's literary tradition.

Twentieth Century Fox picked up the option, with George Cosmatos slated to direct. Chuck Pogue, who had written the first *Princess of Mars* draft during Walt Disney's initial round with that project, was recruited to script, but declined, citing the short turnaround time. Graham Yost and other scripters also tried a hand at the screenplay. When Fox declined to renew the option, their partner Village Roadshow retained its interest, and Canter secured German financing via Dieter Geissler's Filmproduktion company.

Sean Bean and Edward Atterton were considered for the part of Tarzan, which eventually went to Casper Van Dien, who had just filmed the high-profile role of Johnny Rico for Paul Verhoeven's *Starship Troopers*. Jane March was cast as Jane Porter.

After 14 years of development, the *Greystoke* connection became tenuous; the film is set in September 1913, nine years after D'Arnot brought a 17-year-old Tarzan to England from the jungle. The plot incorporates numerous Tarzan tropes, including plentiful wildlife. "I worked with elephants, lions, snakes, monkeys, ostriches, porcupines, zebras; it's pretty incredible, the amount of animals on the shoot," recalled Van Dien in a personal interview.

Directed by Carl Schenkel, the film shot from March through June 1997, outside Bethlehem in the mountains six hours from Johannesburg, at 6,000-foot altitude. The budget was $16 million with $2–3 million in deferments, about half of *Greystoke*'s $31 million budget of 14 years earlier.

Production designer Harold Pinter, experienced in African period pieces (such as Bruce Bereford's *Mister Johnson*, set in 1923) didn't want to rely on stereotyped Hollywood interpretations, but sought to use indigenous materials in construction and design. Five construction crews built 17 sets including the Mbiko and Chiromo Villages, a riverfront hotel and trading post, Tarzan's treehouse, and the lost city of Opar, with 30 giant statues and a colossal staircase. Opar was more than 100 feet high and used 180 tons of steel in construction, as one of the largest sets ever built in South Africa. Construction and shooting were halted during electrical storms so that the giant temple wouldn't act as a lightning rod.

Body paint for the 200 native extras was based on that of Nuba tribesmen, using river clay rather than ash for the white paint. Ape sequences in the script were minimized onscreen, since the costumes weren't on par with Rick Baker's *Greystoke* creations.

The shoot proved challenging. Filming rolled during the rainy season, the usual production timeframe in South Africa, but the unusually wet year produced swarms of mosquitoes and other biting insects. Many on the crew got tickbite fever, but Van Dien did not, despite his abbreviated wardrobe and lack of tick repellant (which had to be sprayed onto clothing, rather than skin, due to its virulent nature).

In a bid to make the storyline more family-friendly, violent scenes were excised, resulting in a brisk 83-minute running time. The film debuted April 24, 1998.

CASPER VAN DIEN

Casper Van Dien won the Tarzan role without an audition, based on a personal referral. *Tarzan and the Lost City* producer Greg Coote saw the actor's profile in a magazine, and called his friend Alan Marshall, producer of *Starship Troopers*; after a three-hour conversation and a glowing recommendation, the job was Van Dien's, based on his work ethic and dedication.

Offered the role on a Wednesday, Van Dien had to leave a Vancouver shoot for Africa immediately to begin shooting the following Monday; on his layover in Los Angeles, he stopped by Edgar Rice Burroughs, Inc. in Tarzana to get some advice from Danton Burroughs, and began re-reading the original Tarzan novels.

He also watched Jane Goodall videos and learned a little Zulu. Producers initially wanted an English accent, but Van Dien didn't feel this fit the multilingual ape man, so he used a mid-Atlantic accent.

Fortunately, Van Dien was already in top condition when he accepted the role. He worked out for two hours a day before filming—from 3 to 5 a.m.—to stay in shape. Van Dien performed his own vine-swinging, and most of his stunts (a South African stuntman performed the high dives) and also crafted his own ape growl, based on his Goodall research.

There were the usual trials on location. He was charged by a young elephant, nearly strangled by Tarzan's pet snake, and bitten on the chin by Jebba the chimp. Nonetheless, Van Dien earned the nicknames *amandla* ("strength") and *sipho* ("a gift") by the South African tribal extras, honored that he learned their language.

A believer in coincidence (he filmed *Starship Troopers* in Casper, Wyoming), he purchased a house in Tarzana upon his return from Africa, later selling the house to *Tarzan* paperback cover model Fabio.

Casper Robert Van Dien, Jr. was born December 18, 1968, the only son of Casper Robert, a former navy fighter pilot and Korea and Vietnam Wars veteran, and Diane, a retired nursery school teacher and ordained minister. He and his three sisters grew up in Ridgewood, New Jersey, on Van Dien Avenue, named for his great-great-great grandfather.

He attended military school at Admiral Farragut Academy in St. Petersburg, enrolling at Florida State upon graduation to study pre-med. He moved to Hollywood to pursue an acting career after being cast in an airline commercial on his first audition. After guest-starring on popular TV series like *Married With Children* and *Beverly Hills, 90210*, he came to fame as lead Johnny Rico in *Starship Troopers*.

Van Dien was formerly married to actresses Carrie Mitchum and Catherine Oxenberg, and has a son and four daughters. Following family tradition, his son is the seventh Casper in the family lineage.

"Tarzan is not a big, strong dumb guy . . . the appeal has always been that Tarzan shows how the human race could survive because of our intellect."
– Casper Van Dien, *Los Angeles Times*, April 23, 1998

JANE MARCH

Jane March brought a feisty spirit to the role of Jane Porter, as a woman who follows her fiancé to Africa and fights at his side to preserve the sanctity of his wilderness home.

Jane March Horwood was born on March 20, 1973 in Edgware, London, to Bernard and Jean Horwood. Her father taught design and technology in secondary school; the family included one older brother, a landscape gardener.

March launched her career when she won a "Become a Model" contest at 14 and signed with Storm Model Management as a 5'2" petite model. She began working under the name Jane March, and soon moved into her own flat with friends.

She made her feature film debut as the teenage lead in *The Lover* (1992), based on Marguerite Duras' semi-autobiographical novel of a young woman coming of age in French Colonial Vietnam. French director Jean-Jacques Annaud discovered her on the cover of *Just Seventeen*, and called her in to read on her seventeenth birthday. After several auditions, the part was hers.

In 1994, March co-starred with Bruce Willis in *The Color of Night*, and began dating his close friend, co-producer Carmine Zozzora. They married in Lake Tahoe on June 1993, with Bruce Willis and Demi Moore as best man and maid of honor. The couple divorced in 2001.

According to the *Lost City* production notes, March's motivation in accepting the Jane role was to "be able to play a really fresh character and make an adventure film. This gave me the opportunity to do both at once."

"Jane March brought a lot of femininity to Jane without sacrificing great strength, an essential part of this woman who sets out into Africa alone to find her fiancé." – producer Stan Canter

Opposite left: Casper Van Dien as Tarzan.

Opposite right: A vintage loincloth made of leopard hide proved impractical.

Top right: Jane March played Jane to Van Dien's Tarzan.

Top left: Jane (March) follows Tarzan into the jungle.

Bottom: Mugambi (Winston Ntshona), Jane (Jane March) and Tarzan (Casper Van Dien) battle to save Africa.

TARZAN *1999*

The gorilla Kala (Glenn Close) adopts a human foundling, but her mate Kerchak (Lance Henriksen), the tribe's silverback leader, is skeptical about the child's place in their family group. Young Tarzan (Alex D. Linz) grows to manhood in the jungle, alongside best friends Terk the ape (Rosie O'Donnell) and Tantor the elephant (Wayne Knight). When the adult Tarzan (Tony Goldwyn) meets Jane Porter (Minnie Driver), who is searching for gorillas to study with her scientist father, Professor Porter (Nigel Hawthorne) and their duplicitous guide Clayton (Brian Blessed), the ape man must decide whether he belongs with his family, the apes, or in civilization with his own kind.

Animation's only limit is the imagination, so Walt Disney Studios' *Tarzan* elevated the ape man's saga to a new plateau of visual wonder. With Disney Studios at the peak of their creative powers in filming 2D animation, the jungle, the creatures within it, and Tarzan's physical feats were visualized as never before.

Kevin Lima (*A Goofy Movie*) and Chris Buck were chosen to co-direct the film, under the supervision of Bonnie Arnold (*Toy Story*). A staff of 1,100 artists and craftspeople contributed to the film, which took four years to complete.

Tarzan's childhood is usually overlooked onscreen, but the production team became fascinated by Tarzan's relationship with his gorilla family, which could be portrayed in a convincing manner through the medium of animation. They identified the story's recurrent theme as "What makes a family?" The adult Tarzan is torn between two worlds, ape and human, savage and civilized.

Tab Murphy, who had received an Academy Award nomination for co-writing *Gorillas in the Mist* (1988) was hired to script, with the husband-and-wife team of Bob Tzudiker and Noni White rewriting and polishing the screenplay.

Eight members of the production team went on African safari to observe gorillas in their natural habitat. To aid their ape animation, the artists attended primate lectures, watched nature documentaries, visited zoos, and viewed a gorilla dissection at a veterinary college. Unlike previous Disney films, there was no single designer; the individual animators were responsible for ensuring their designs meshed into the overall look of the picture, assisted by cleanup artists, responsible for checking that figures drawn by different animators had consistency between scenes and matched the models.

Glen Keane, who joined the studio in 1974 and had worked as the lead animator on seven Disney features, animated Tarzan from Disney's Paris campus. It was the first time that a lead character had been drawn outside the home studio in Burbank, California.

Animating Tarzan proved a challenge, since his nearly naked body had to move and flex realistically and he is onscreen for most of the film—he is the central motivating character in every scene but the "Trashing the Camp" sequence. The ape man's actions were based on those of extreme-sports athletes and animals like gazelles, chameleons, gorillas, and jungle cats. His body language and gestures mimicked those of gorillas, rather than humans.

The film's visual appeal is enhanced by early adoption of the Deep Canvas technique to give the backgrounds a three-dimensional effect of depth. The gorillas' jungle home is characterized by cool, soothing colors, shadows and muted light, while scenes of conflict have bright light, red tones and angular landscapes. The story remains true to Tarzan's cinema history, with homages to previous films, including an elephant stampede and an ape call reminiscent of Johnny Weissmuller's.

Phil Collins was selected to compose the songs; his experience with rhythms and percussion was seen as a perfect fit for a jungle film. He also sang four of the tunes, in a departure from Disney tradition, which usually had the characters breaking into song as the story unfolded. The songs included "Son of Man", "Strangers Like Me", "Trashing the Camp" (a scat by Rosie O'Donnell), and the film's anthem, "Two Worlds". Working from his home in Switzerland, Collins' vocal demos were so well crafted that they were released as the final version. He won an Academy Award and Golden Globe for Best Song for "You'll Be in My Heart". Mark Mancina (*The Lion King*) composed the film's score for the Grammy-winning double platinum album.

The film was a creative and commercial success, and inspired two animated sequels, a television series, a Broadway musical, Disney on Ice shows, and the remodeled "Tarzan's Treehouse" at Disney theme parks.

"The cartoon must be good. It must approximate Disney excellence."
– *Edgar Rice Burroughs, 1936*

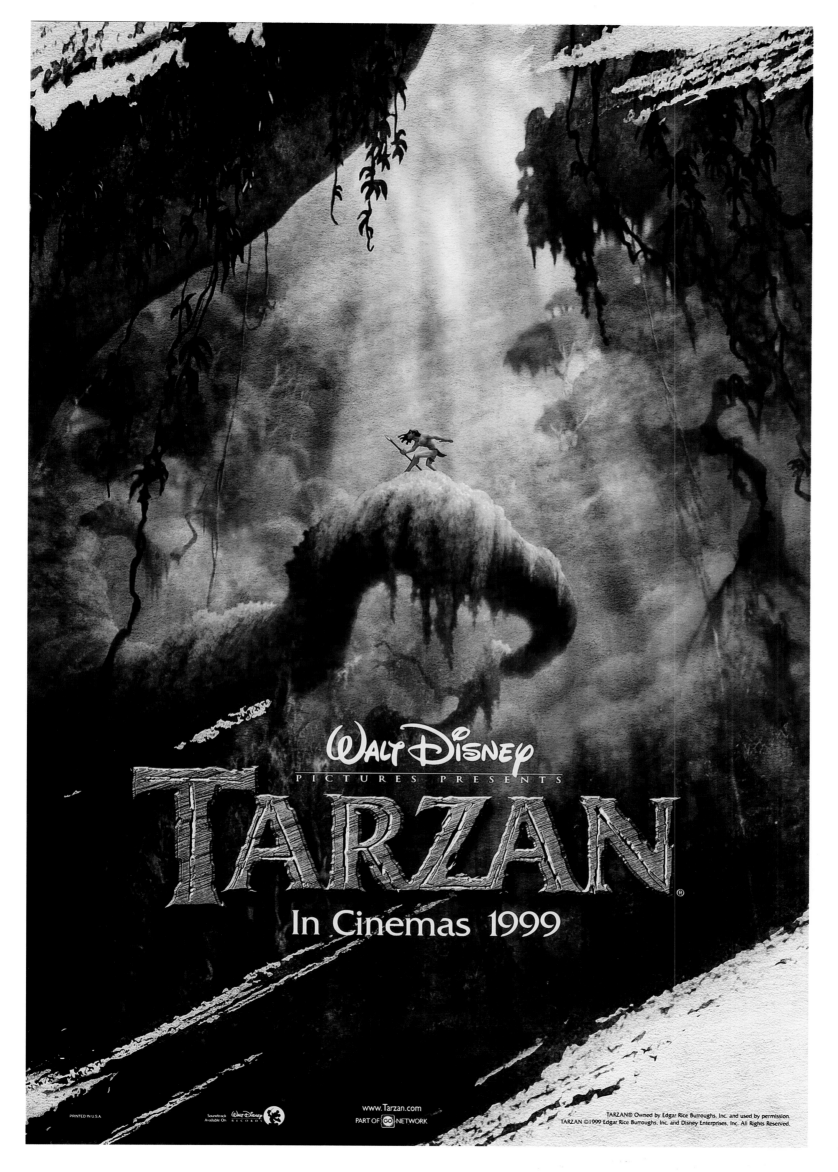

TONY GOLDWYN

Disney's *Tarzan* offered actor Tony Goldwyn the opportunity to revisit the film franchise pioneered by his grandfather, studio mogul Samuel Goldwyn, who in 1920 re-titled *The Return of Tarzan* and distributed it as *The Revenge of Tarzan*.

Born Anthony Howard Goldwyn to Samuel Goldwyn, Jr. and actress Jennifer Howard on May 20, 1960, the future Tarzan attended prep school in Colorado Springs, and received a BFA from Brandeis University in Boston

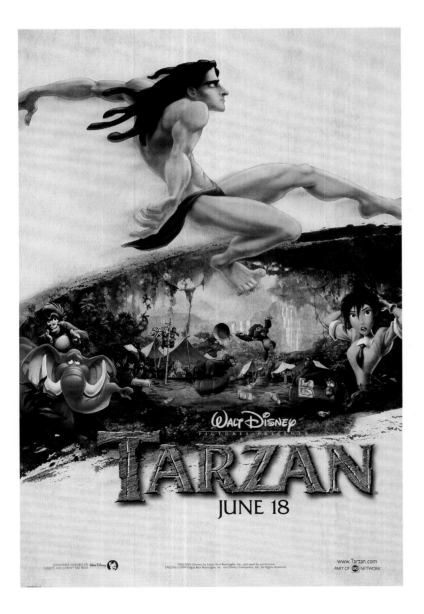

with highest honors. A stint at the London Academy of Music and Dramatic Art followed. In 1987, he married production designer Jane Michelle Musky; the pair met while working at the Williamstown Theater Festival and have two daughters.

Goldwyn was already a familiar face to viewers when he was cast as Carl Bruner, the antagonist in the blockbuster film *Ghost* (1990), starring Patrick Swayze and Demi Moore. The role took Goldwyn's career to a new level, and he began producing and directing feature films and television episodes in addition to his on-camera work.

In 1995, while appearing in a Broadway revival of the comedy *Holiday*, Goldwyn and his fellow performer Laura Linney auditioned for the leads in *Tarzan*. Linney did not win the role of Jane, but co-producers Kevin Lima and Chris Buck knew immediately that their search for Tarzan had ended. Goldwyn recorded Tarzan's dialogue in a dozen studio sessions over the next three years.

He met lead animator Glen Keane only once, but the talented artist managed to imbue Tarzan with some of Goldwyn's physical mannerisms, in the expression of Tarzan's eyes and face.

"Tony's voice has real depth," noted Keane in *The Tarzan Chronicles*. "There's a low register quality that has almost an animal sound to it. It works really well for the character. Tarzan doesn't have a lot of dialogue, so whatever he does say becomes extremely important. It has to have a visceral sense; a texture to it where the sound almost has a feeling you can touch. When I listen to his voice, I recognize it as a great blend for Tarzan."

Goldwyn's career in front of and behind the camera remains busy. His role as U.S. President Fitzgerald Grant III on the ABC TV series *Scandal* has been supplemented by directorial assignments on that show and others. He also portrays the father of lead Shailene Woodley's character Tris in the films based on the *Divergent* young adult novel trilogy by Veronica Roth.

MINNIE DRIVER

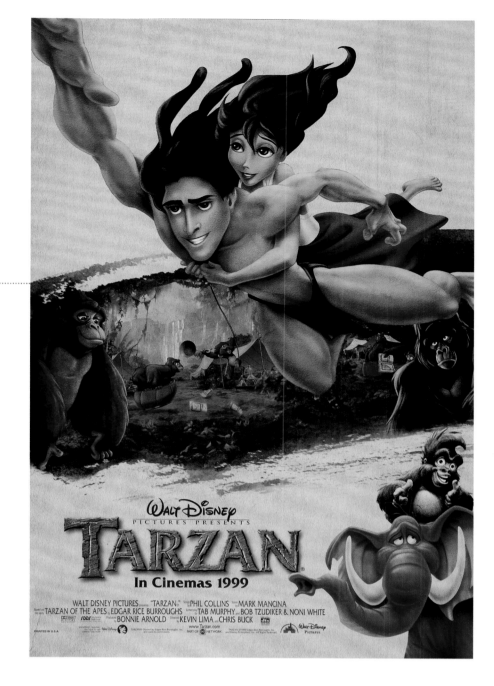

Tarzan's Jane is a lively, enthusiastic, irresistible heroine, qualities which Minnie Driver delivered in her uninhibited performance. The scene where Jane tells her father about meeting Tarzan (while energetically pantomiming the encounter) was largely ad-libbed by the actress; the animators incorporated her physical mannerisms into the scene, which was the first she recorded. The sequence ran 73 feet, one of the longest animated scenes ever accomplished by Disney, and took seven weeks to animate.

"Minnie's expressions are very broad," commented lead Jane animator Ken Duncan in *The Tarzan Chronicles*. "She would extend her neck out and use her hands to gesture. We took all of these elements and exaggerated them. We made her less dainty and played up her over-the-top attitude. Watching Minnie was a great inspiration. She puts a lot of energy into her performance and is a wonderful improviser. She was able to add humor to lines in the script that didn't come off quite as funny on the printed page. It was a joy animating to her brilliant performance." Driver's turn as Jane received an Annie Award nomination for Outstanding Individual Achievement for Voice Acting in an Animated Feature Production.

Amelia Finoa J. Driver was born in London to financier Ronnie Driver and Gaynor Churchward, a designer and former model. She was dubbed Minnie at the hospital by her two-year-old sister Kate, after Minnie Mouse, perhaps a hint of things to come.

As a child, she attended Bedales School, then earned a drama degree from the Webber Douglas Academy of Dramatic Art in London. Driver's breakout role came with her feature film debut as Benny Hogan in *Circle of Friends* (1995). In 1997, her role as Skylar, lead Matt Damon's girlfriend in *Good Will Hunting*, earned an Academy Award nomination for Best Supporting Actress. She has been nominated for an Emmy and a Golden Globe as Best Lead Actress in a Drama for her role as Dahlia Malloy in FX Network's *The Riches*.

Driver is also a talented jazz singer and guitarist, and has released three albums. She has one son, Henry Story Driver.

"I knew how I wanted Jane to be from the start. She was never going to be a boring Victorian heroine. She had to be something original. The directors really let me improvise and create. Jane is not the sort of 'damsel in distress' that we've seen in other Tarzan films. She's very adventurous, funny, and clever and I like those qualities in women." – Minnie Driver, *The Tarzan Chronicles*

THE LEGEND OF TARZAN *2001-2003*

Tarzan (Michael T. Weiss) and Jane (Olivia d'Abo), now husband and wife, make their home in the jungle treehouse of Tarzan's late parents, but their domestic bliss is continually interrupted by adventures, often instigated by their friends Terk (April Winchell) and Tantor (Jim Cummings), or Jane's father Professor Porter (Jeff Bennett), who has established a research camp nearby.

Set immediately after the events of the feature film, Disney's *The Legend of Tarzan* animated television series continued the adventures of Tarzan and Jane. An abbreviated version of Phil Collins' "Two Worlds" served as the opening theme song, with further scoring by Mark Mancina.

The series was executive-produced by Bill Motz and Bob Roth, who had previously collaborated on the *Aladdin* sequel *The Return of Jafar* (1994) and *Lion King 2: Simba's Pride* (1998). Steve Loter, who had just wrapped the series *Buzz Lightyear of Star Command*, served as producer and supervising director.

Thirty-nine episodes were produced for syndication; it was originally to debut on the Toon Disney digital channel, but was sold to UPN for Saturday morning and weekday afternoon broadcast. It was the first completely digital series at Disney TV.

The series' producers looked to the novels of Edgar Rice Burroughs for inspiration, and included storylines focused on Samuel T. Philander (Craig Ferguson), now a rival of Professor Porter; the travails of filmmakers Tom Orman (Thomas Lennon), Stanley Obroski (Diedrich Bader) and Naomi Madison (Kerry Kenney) while shooting the silent epic *Savage Man* on location; heavyweight boxing champion One-Punch Mullargan (Jon Favreau); the lost world of Pellucidar; Count Nicholas Rokoff (Ron Perlman); Basuli (Phil La Marr) and the Waziri tribe; and Queen La (Diahann Carroll) and the Leopard Men, now serving as her lackeys.

A supporting cast of original characters included Renard Dumont (Rene Auberjonois), the profit-obsessed proprietor of the local trading post, and Hugo and Hooft (Joe Flaherty and Dave Thomas), a pair of bumblers styled after Bob Hope and Bing Crosby in their "Road" movies. New apes and elephants moved into the neighborhood, and Tarzan's jungle was even visited by Theodore Roosevelt (Stephen Root), and a mysterious writer named Ed (Steven Weber), gathering material for a novel.

Conservation is a theme of the series, but the presentation isn't heavy-handed. The dangers of Tarzan's domain are amplified with the addition of a wide range of wildlife, including black panthers, rhinos, giant beetles, velociraptors, wild boar, a giant python, and the rogue elephant Mabaya. Environmental perils abound in the form of earthquakes, tidal waves, volcanoes, flash floods, hurricanes, forest fires, and tar pits.

The series contains numerous inside jokes for canny viewers, like when actor Stanley Obroski strikes a pose that matches publicity photos of Elmo Lincoln (he also wears an Elmo-style wig), or the continued exploits of the teapot styled after Mrs. Potts in *Beauty and the Beast*. It's given as a gift to La and shattered in episode 16; in episode 23, Jane and the Professor are repairing it; and Zutho breaks it again in episode 32. Jane also serves Bobby Canler and her British girlfriends "jungle tea" (dried figs, banana leaves, and a hint of dirt) with the teapot.

Producers planned a three-part finale, taking Tarzan to New York, Chicago, and Hollywood, reclaiming his Greystoke heritage along the way, before deciding that Tarzan belongs in the jungle. The final three episodes were combined into a direct-to-video movie, *Tarzan & Jane*.

The series was nominated for a 2002 Daytime Emmy for "Outstanding Special Class Animated Program", and for Golden Reel awards for Best Sound Editing in Television, Music, Episodic Animation, and Best Sound Editing in Television, Animation for the "Leopardmen Rebellion" episode.

> **"We wanted to bring Tarzan more into the Burroughs Universe— basically, to take the spirit of the novels and bring that back into the series. We've moved into more of the fantasy arena."**
>
> – Producer Bob Roth, *Starlog*, October 2001

MICHAEL T. WEISS

Michael T. Weiss's deep, resonant tones keep him in demand for voiceover work, and made him an excellent choice as Tarzan in Disney's *The Legend of Tarzan* television series and the film *Tarzan & Jane*.

"[It's] the best job," he told *Starlog* scribe Dan Yakir about being cast as the ape man. "I love it! Tarzan is both innocent and strong, a magical character. He was one of the first super heroes, and to play him for Disney is exciting . . . I voice Tarzan very soulfully and simply—after all, he isn't a man of many words. He uses few words, but wisely. In the theater, you work with your body. In film, with your eyes. And (in animation) with your voice. It's fun. There are no costumes or anything, and you don't even have to take a shower afterwards."

Weiss began acting during his childhood in Chicago. He was born February 2, 1962 to a steel-industry executive father and homemaker mother. He appeared in local television commercials and studied at Second City during high school. Weiss moved to Los Angeles in 1980 to attend USC, where his classmates included actors Ally Sheedy, Eric Stoltz, Anthony Edwards, and Forrest Whitaker. Among Weiss's day jobs while he learned his craft were stints in an electronics store and a zipper factory, and as a personal trainer to celebrities including James Brolin and Pierce Brosnan. Shortly after earning his BFA in acting, he was cast as Dr. Michael Horton on the soap opera *Days of Our Lives* and began his career.

His stints as a regular on two primetime series—the 1991 relaunch of *Dark Shadows* and *2000 Malibu Road* (1992)— were shortened by cancellation, but Weiss found longer-term success on *The Pretender* (1996–2000) as Jarod Russell, a child prodigy abducted and raised at a think tank called The Centre. After escaping the program, Jarod uses his genius to assume identities ranging from doctor to lawyer to airline pilot to help others while on the run from his former handlers. The series, which allowed Weiss to assume 80 different roles, ran for four seasons and spawned two 2001 telefilms. Weiss also made an in-character crossover appearance on three episodes of the television crime drama *Profiler*.

Weiss also works onstage—his role as Herb in *Scarcity* (2007) was nominated for a Drama Desk Award for Outstanding Featured Actor in a Play. He made his Broadway debut in *Impressionism* (2009), starring Jeremy Irons and Joan Allen.

Weiss is an ardent conservationist, active in environmental causes as befits a Tarzan. He splits his time between acting assignments on both coasts.

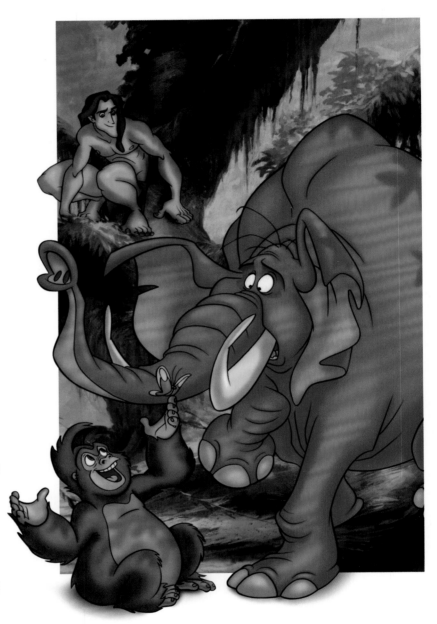

Above: Terk (April Winchell) and Tantor (Jim Cummings) continue to cause chaos in Tarzan's (Michael T. Weiss) jungle.

Opposite: Terk (Winchell) joins Jane (Olivia d'Abo) and her British friends Greenley (Grey DeLisle), Eleanor (Nicolette Sheridan), and Hazel (Tara Strong) for a spot of "Jungle Tea".

"They find something in the jungle, they just have to sacrifice it!" - Queen La, on her beastmen

TARZAN AND JANE *2002*

As Jane (Olivia d'Abo) *prepares for her first wedding anniversary with Tarzan (Michael T. Weiss), she reminisces with Terk (April Winchell), Tantor (Jim Cummings), and her father Professor Porter (Jeff Bennett) about their adventures, including the time her girlfriends tried to convince her to return to England; the time a pair of rogues tried to dupe Tarzan into guiding them to diamonds; and the time Jane's childhood friend, aviator Bobby Canler (Jeff Bennett), arrived with a secret.*

Three episodes of Disney's animated series *The Legend of Tarzan* were combined to create the direct-to-video movie *Tarzan & Jane*, tied together with a storyline that had Jane pondering how to celebrate her wedding anniversary. Two of the episodes had sequels that aired during the television show's run.

In "Tarzan and the British Invasion", Jane's haughty friends Hazel (Tara Strong), Eleanor (Nicolette Sheridan) and Greenley (Grey DeLisle) arrive to rescue her from the wildman. Jane decides to show them the beauty of the wilderness, but they become lost and face a series of hazards when their picnic goes awry. In the television sequel, "Tarzan and the New Wave", the girls bring Greenley's oboe-playing geologist boyfriend, Henry (Alex Denisof) to the jungle, hoping that he will learn Tarzan's manly ways, but Henry has some surprises—and survival skills—of his own.

"Tarzan and the Volcanic Diamond Mine" brings two treasure hunters, the smooth-talking Johannes Niels (John O'Hurley) and his less tactful partner Merkus (Jim Cummings) to the jungle, in search of diamonds. When they trap Tarzan, Jane and Professor Porter in an erupting volcano, it's up to the ape man to get everyone to safety. Niels and Merkus return for the diamonds, and find an even greater treasure in the television sequel "Tarzan and the Caged Fury".

In "Tarzan and the Flying Ace", the ape man wrestles with his jealousy and distrust of Jane's old friend, whose larger-than-life persona seems too good to be true. The character is named after an unwelcome suitor of Jane's in the novel *Tarzan of the Apes*, but the literary Canler was not a flying ace (nor nearly so charismatic as Bobby).

Tarzan & Jane featured two new songs by Phil Collins, and one by Mandy Moore, "Singing to the Song of Life".

OLIVIA D'ABO

Londoner Olivia d'Abo voiced Jane in the Disney series *The Legend of Tarzan* and the film *Tarzan & Jane*. She won the role through her portrayal of British exchange teacher (and soccer fan) Miss Anna Montgomery in Disney sports comedy *The Big Green* (1995).

She was born in Paddington to Mike d'Abo, singer and member of 1960s band Manfred Mann, and Maggie London, an actress and model. Entertainment runs in her family; in addition to her parents' careers, her cousin Maryam d'Abo is an actress, and played a Bond girl in the film *The Living Daylights* (1987).

As a child, d'Abo studied at the Royal Ballet School and attended the Lycée Français in London. Her childhood ambition was to be a ballerina and, later, an archaeologist, after her family moved to Taos, New Mexico. There, she began appearing in community theater productions with her father; following her parents' divorce, he returned to England to work in radio, and her mother moved with the children to Los

Angeles, where Olivia attended Los Feliz High School.

D'Abo made her film debut as Princess Jehnna of Shadizar in *Conan the Destroyer* (1984). A guest-starring appearance on the sitcom *Growing Pains* led to the role of Karen Arnold, Kevin Arnold's (Fred Savage) teenage hippie sister on the Emmy Award-winning comedy series *The Wonder Years* (1988–93). Her role as "Garthette" in *Wayne's World 2* (1993) generated an offer to join the cast of *Saturday Night Live*, but she declined, unwilling to be tied to a five-year contract.

A singer-songwriter and musician, she released her first album *Not TV* in 2008. She is also a skilled stage actress, debuting on Broadway as Gwendolyn Pigeon in the 2005–6 revival of *The Odd Couple*, starring Matthew Broderick and Nathan Lane. Her 2011 role in *Entertaining Mr. Sloane* won a StageSceneLA Award and a Broadway World Los Angeles Award. D'Abo remains active in onscreen and voiceover roles. She has one son, Patrick.

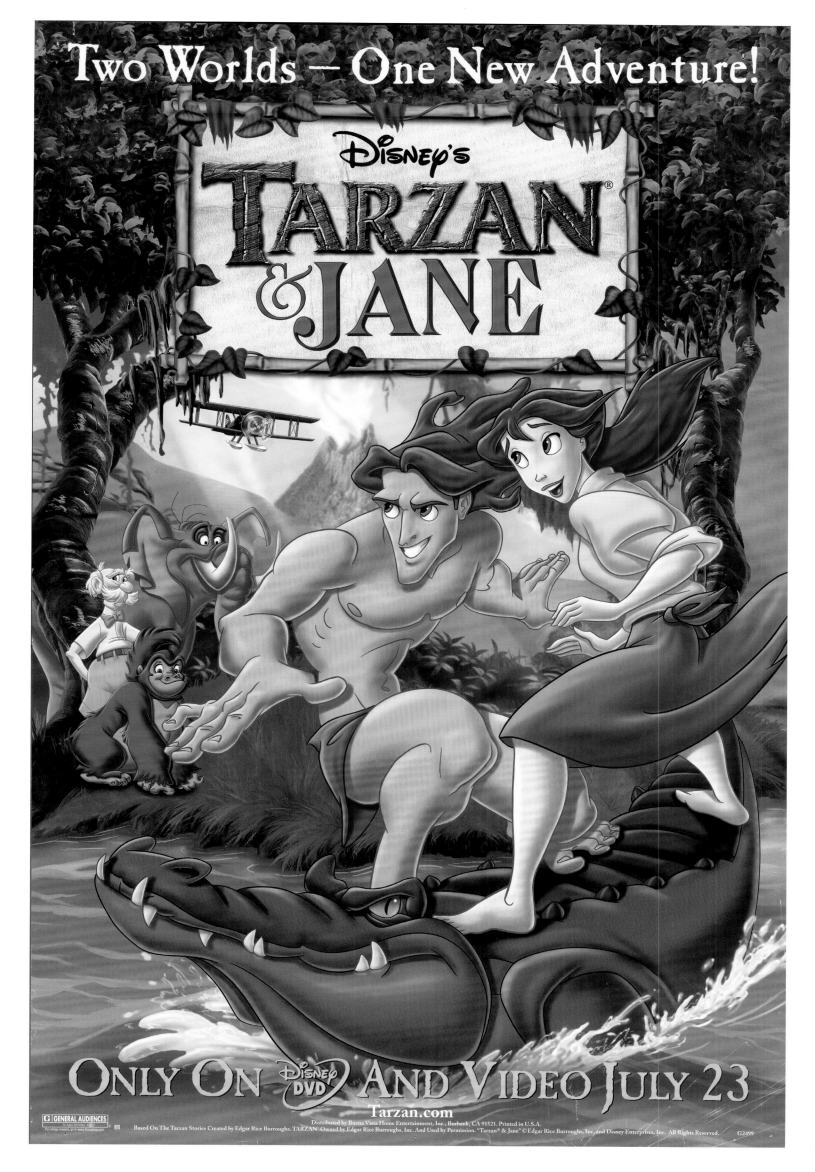

TARZAN *2003*

"The opening minutes, as the half-seen jungle king makes his first escape from urban captivity, are fantastically well executed and gripping as, for that matter, are all the action sequences. And it's sexy enough—he's the least-dressed character in modern fiction after all, and we get a good look at Jane's navel as well."
– Robert Lloyd, *Los Angeles Times*, October 3, 2003

In the fall of 2003, the WB network re-imagined the Tarzan myth as an urban drama in a bid to recreate the successful formula of the hit series *Smallville*, which focused on Superman Clark Kent's youth.

Tarzan's initial concept, "The New Adventures of Tarzan", dated December 11, 2001 and scripted by Mike Werb and Michael Colleary, had the former jungle waif enrolled in Manhattan's Stuyvesant High School with Jane Portrero, a tattooed, belly-button-pierced Latina PETA activist (and Central Park Zoo-keeper's daughter). Tarzan lived with his aunt, Tori Rutherford, and cousin, William Cecil, a hip-hop-lingo-spouting, skateboarding computer hacker who provided comic relief; the plot centered on a jewelry heist foiled by the teens.

When the network gave the initial premise a chilly reception, the series was reworked by writer-producer Eric Kripke as a cop show, experienced through police detective Jane Porter's viewpoint. The final product had no loincloth, knife, apes, yell, or jungle. The "fish-out-of-water" premise remained, with Tarzan on the run from his sinister billionaire uncle (Mitch Pileggi), using his heightened senses to help Jane solve crime as he wandered the streets of New York City.

Model Travis Fimmel was cast as John Clayton after executive producer Laura Ziskin's adolescent daughter selected his picture in one of her teen magazines as a young girl's prototypical crush. "This is what I wanted my Tarzan to look like—a dreamy young man," Ziskin said of her choice. Chad Michael Murray, also a candidate for the role, received the lead on that fall's WB series *One Tree Hill*.

Newcomer Sarah Wayne Callies played Jane. "Jane was hugely difficult to cast," recalled pilot director David Nutter in *Starlog* magazine. "The bottom line was that we needed to find someone whom people would believe in and respect as a New York City detective, which has a whole new meaning after 9/11. It was important to find someone with intelligence and maturity. I was looking for someone with Linda Hamilton's sensibility from *Beauty & the Beast*. This is

not teenager time. These are adults in adult situations, and this is an adult love story."

To give the series some marquee firepower, Lucy Lawless was introduced as Tarzan's sympathetic aunt, Kathleen Clayton, and charged with battling her enigmatic brother Richard for control of John's welfare and their media company's destiny.

Supporting characters included Miguel A. Núñez, Jr. as Jane's partner, Detective Sam Sullivan, and Johnny Messner as her possessive boyfriend, Detective Michael Foster. Leighton Meester played Jane's younger sister and ward, Nicki Porter (replacing Sarah-Jane Potts, who played the role in the pilot).

The pilot, helmed by David Nutter, a top director of genre launches, had high production values and well-crafted action sequences. Fimmel's athleticism, choreographed by movement coach Terry Notary (Tim Burton's *Planet of the Apes*) won praise. The pilot shot in Vancouver, with exterior location sequences in New York; the resulting series was based in Toronto, where the network had a prior production deal. As the retooling continued, the original pilot was recut to remove a kiss between Tarzan and Jane (the network thought it was too much, too soon), and to lighten up the dark tone. Kripke likened the show, originally titled *Tarzan and Jane*, to "a long, drawn-out, tortured, anguished love story."

The show debuted Sunday October 5, 2003, to modest ratings with 5.5 million viewers. After eight episodes the initial story arc was completed and the show went on hiatus; it was not renewed, spoiling producers' plans to introduce Tarzan's Rottweiler sidekick, Cheeta.

"It could use a chimpanzee."
– Robert Lloyd, *Los Angeles Times*, October 3, 2003

TRAVIS FIMMEL

Travis Fimmel was modelling underwear for an international Calvin Klein campaign when he was cast in his first role, the lead in WB's *Tarzan*. He was only the second model after Kate Moss to hold an exclusive, six-figure contract with Klein.

Born on July 15, 1979, to Chris and Jennie Fimmel, television's sixth Tarzan grew up on a beef and dairy farm 40 kilometers outside Echuca, Victoria, Australia, with 1,500 cows, 11 dogs, and two older brothers for company. He worked as a bartender and bricklayer while he attended RMIT University in Melbourne. In 1998, Fimmel was discovered in a Melbourne gym by a Chadwick Model Management talent booker.

Fimmel spent two years living in London, bartending and touring Europe. On his return to Australia, he stopped off in Los Angeles in 2002 with just $60 in his pocket. Broke and barefoot, he walked into LA Models agency, which put him to work immediately. He appeared in campaigns for L'Oreal, Motorola and Skechers and began studying with noted acting coach Ivana Chubbuck.

After wrapping *Tarzan* in 2003, Fimmel continued to study his craft and reemerged in 2009, as FBI agent Ellis Dove, co-starring opposite Patrick Swayze in the A&E drama *The Beast*. The series focused on a veteran FBI agent who is assigned a new partner, unaware that the young colleague has been directed to investigate his actions. Though the series was well received critically, Swayze's terminal pancreatic cancer precluded a renewal after a 13-episode season.

In 2013, Fimmel landed the role of Ragnar Lothbrok on the History Channel series *Vikings*. Loosely based on the Viking sagas, the series recounts the adventures of Lothbrok, a farmer who rose to become King of Denmark, siring sons who would terrorize England and France. During hiatus from *Vikings*, he filmed *Warcraft* (2016), a fantasy film based on the popular video game, portraying the knight Anduin Lothar, leader of the humans in their conflict with the Orcs.

> *"It's funny; as a kid, my nickname was Tarzan for a while because I never wore shoes, I fished, I camped out, and was just a grub"*
> – Travis Fimmel

SARAH WAYNE CALLIES

Sarah Wayne Callies starred as police detective Jane Porter opposite Travis Fimmel's ape man in the WB's *Tarzan*, her first leading screen role.

Callies was born on June 1, 1977, in La Grange, Illinois, to Valerie Wayne and David E. Callies, and reared in Honolulu, Hawaii, where her parents were English and law professors at the University of Hawaii, Manoa. She graduated from Punahou School (Buster Crabbe's alma mater) in 1995.

She began acting in her youth, landing her first stage lead in a high school production of Shakespeare's *As You Like It*. After graduating from Dartmouth College in 1999, with an undergraduate emphasis in Feminist Studies and a Senior Fellowship in Indigenous Theology, she attended Denver's National Theatre Conservatory to complete her Masters of Fine Arts.

Callies moved to New York City in 2002 and secured her first on-camera acting job, a recurring role opposite Oliver Platt in *Queens Supreme*. She began guest-starring on popular television series including *Law and Order: SVU*, *Numb3rs*, *Dragnet*, and *House M.D.* During this time, she was also chosen as one of the new faces of L'Oréal, and was featured in an advertising campaign.

After starring in *Tarzan*, Callies won two more high-profile series leads. She played Dr. Sara Tancredi, the love interest of lead Wentworth Miller on the Fox hit *Prison Break* (2005–9), and Lori Grimes, wife of lead Andrew Lincoln's Rick Grimes in AMC's *The Walking Dead* (2010–13). She was nominated for Saturn and Scream Awards for Best Actress, and won a Satellite Award for her part in the *Walking Dead* series. Feature film credits include *Whisper* (2006), *The Celestine Prophecy* (2007) and *Into the Storm* (2014).

On June 21, 2002, Callies married martial arts teacher Josh Winterhalt, whom she met at Dartmouth. Their daughter Keala was born in July, 2007.

TARZAN II *2005*

As young Tarzan (Harrison Chad) struggles with his identity and his place in the gorilla tribe, he runs away to Dark Mountain, where he meets the outcast apes Mama Gunda (Estelle Harris) and her sons dim Uto (Brad Garrett) and violent Kago (Ron Perlman), and investigates the mystery of the Zugor (George Carlin)—meanwhile Terk (Brenda Grate) and Tantor (Harrison Fahn) plan a rescue.

With the television show *The Legend of Tarzan* mining the ape man's adult life for material, DisneyToon Studios returned to Tarzan's childhood for an original direct-to-video sequel, *Tarzan II*.

Disney's *Tarzan* skipped the ape boy's formative years, as he quickly matured from a small child to adult via a montage set to the tune of Phil Collins' song "Son of Man". Just as Burroughs had revisited Tarzan's youth in the sixth novel, *Jungle Tales of Tarzan*—which takes place within the continuity of the original novel, *Tarzan of the Apes*—DisneyToon expanded Tarzan's boyhood with this coming-of-age tale.

Since the previous child actors had outgrown the roles, new leads were cast. Harrison Chad, a New York native with Broadway experience as Chip in Disney's *Beauty and the Beast* (2000–2001), won the title role. Brenda Grate was nominated for a Young Artist Award in the category of Best Performance in a Voice-Over Role – Young Actress for her part as Tarzan's ape pal Terk; she had previously won in the category of Best Performance in a TV Movie or Special – Supporting Young Actress for her role in the Disney telefilm *'Twas the Night* (2001). Harrison Fahn voiced young Tantor in a distinctive fashion. Glenn Close and Lance Henriksen returned as the voices of Kala and Kerchak.

Estelle Harris voiced Mama Gunda, the matriarch of an anti-social ape trio, with Brad Garrett and Ron Perlman as her sons. Comedian George Carlin proved a creative casting choice as the cranky elder Zugor, who has much to teach Tarzan—and a bit to learn from the ape boy, too. Carlin's classic comedy bits provide grist for his performance here. The name Zugor is drawn from Edgar Rice Burroughs' original novels—it means "big growl" or "mighty roar" in ape language.

Phil Collins provided two new songs, "Leaving Home (Find My Way)" and "Who Am I?" His song "Son of Man" is included in the soundtrack, which boasts a score composed by Mark Mancina and Dave Metzger. Young Tiffany Evans sings a second version of "Who Am I?" over the end credits, with a music video included in the DVD extras.

The film was helmed by Brian Smith (who directed animated sequels to *101 Dalmatians* and *The Little Mermaid*) and produced by Carolyn Bates, Jim Kammerud and Leslie Hough. Kammerud and Smith scripted, along with *Tarzan* scribes Bob Tzudiker and Noni White; additional story material was provided by Evan Spiliotopoulos and Rhett Reese.

Released on June 14, 2005, the film includes the behind-the-scenes featurette, "Bringing the Legend to Life".

"It was very hard for me, the first time I tried to do this without another actor, because for me, acting is reflection, and I respond to and listen to and reflect off whoever it is that I'm acting with. It was very difficult and all, you feel incredibly exposed . . . 20 people watching you trying to make ape sounds is mortifying!"
– Glenn Close, *Bringing the Legend to Life*

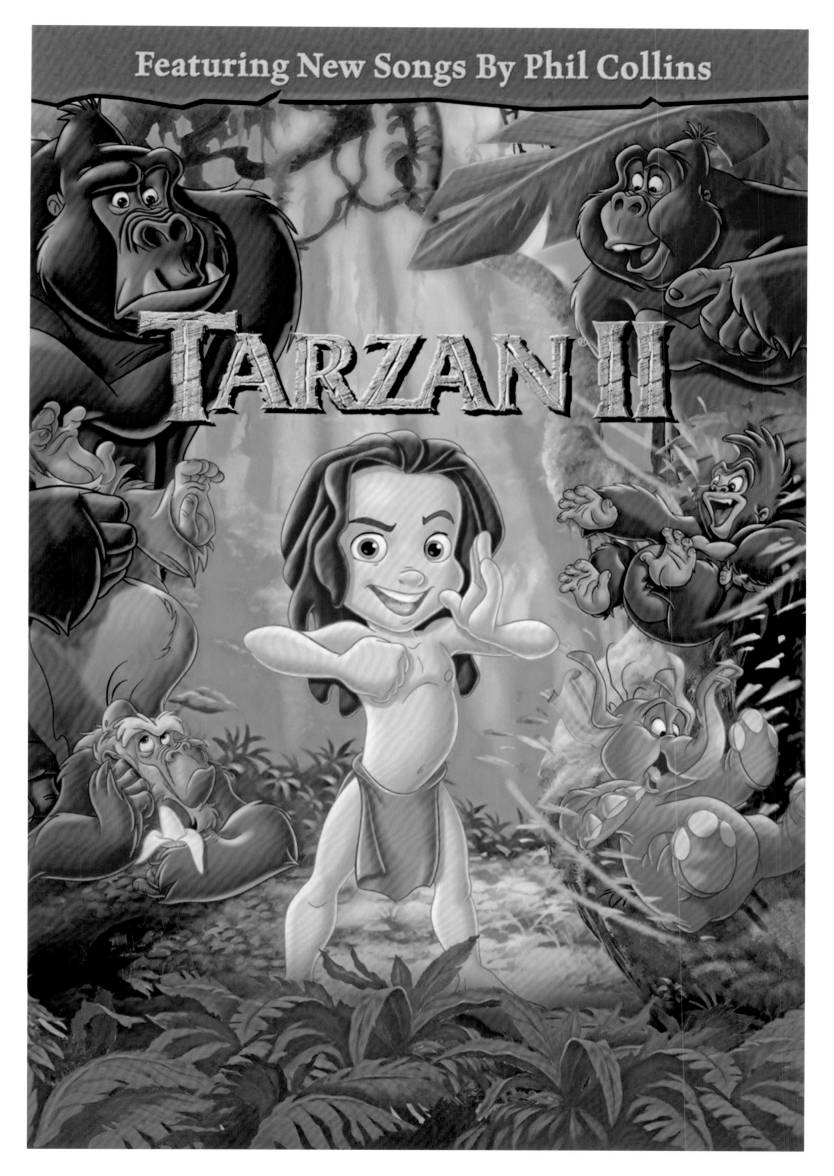

TARZAN *2013*

Young J.J. Greystoke (Craig Garner) is orphaned in the jungle and raised to adulthood by mountain gorillas, calling himself Tarzan. Fifteen years later, Clayton (Joe Cappelletti), the CEO of Greystoke Energies, tricks environmentalists Jane Porter (Spencer Locke) and her father Jim (Les Bubb) into guiding him into the jungle to find the meteor J.J.'s parents sought—an energy source with great profit potential. Tarzan (Kellan Lutz) must protect his world and his ape family from the civilized invaders, aided by his new ally, Jane.

The crew of the animated *Tarzan* 3D took full advantage of advances in motion-capture technology to portray the ape man as a supreme athlete, running, jumping, and climbing about his jungle environment, and battling silverback gorillas. The film also offered expansive scenic vistas as only computer animation can.

The film was executive produced by Martin Moszkowicz of Munich-based Constantin Film. Reinhard Klooss served as producer, director, and writer.

Tarzan was portrayed at ages four, 14, and 19, played by Craig Garner, Anton Zetterholm, and Kellan Lutz, while Spencer Locke voiced Jane at ages 14 and 19. Zetterholm was a Tarzan veteran, having portrayed the jungle lord in the

Hamburg staging of the hit Disney musical *Tarzan*. Born in Växjö, Sweden, Zetterholm won the role on the casting show *Ich Tarzan, du Jane* (2008), where he was picked in a vote by the German public and composer Phil Collins; his stage role served as excellent training in portraying the ape man's movements.

Filmmakers researched gorilla habitat in Uganda, Rwanda, and the Congo to accurately portray their natural environment in the film, which is set in the modern day. Peter Elliott (*Greystoke*) choreographed the ape actors, teaching them movement, facial expressions, breathing, and vocalizations. His technique? "Think like an ape."

Tarzan 3D was shot at Bavaria Film Studios in Munich (one of the biggest soundstages in Europe), on one of the largest motion capture sets ever built worldwide, and the biggest one in Europe at that point. Parkour artists scrambled over frameworks that doubled as rocks, trees, vines, and other jungle elements, as computers recorded their movement. Animation studios in Hanover and Munich completed the rendering of the work, which was captured by 56 motion capture cameras.

David Newman provided the musical score, with additional songs by Ellie Goulding, will.i.am, Coldplay, and Placebo. Newman was nominated for an IFMCA Award for Best Original Score for an Animated Feature Film.

The film received limited theatrical release in the U.S. before DVD release in 2014. DVD extras include the featurettes *Becoming Gorillas*, *The Making of Tarzan*, and *Behind the Scenes with Kellan Lutz and Spencer Locke*. The movie's second theatrical trailer was nominated for a Golden Trailer Award for Best Foreign Animation/Family Trailer.

> **"I also wanted to have nearly photorealistic sets to achieve a magic realism of the jungle."**
> – Reinhard Klooss, *The Making of Tarzan*

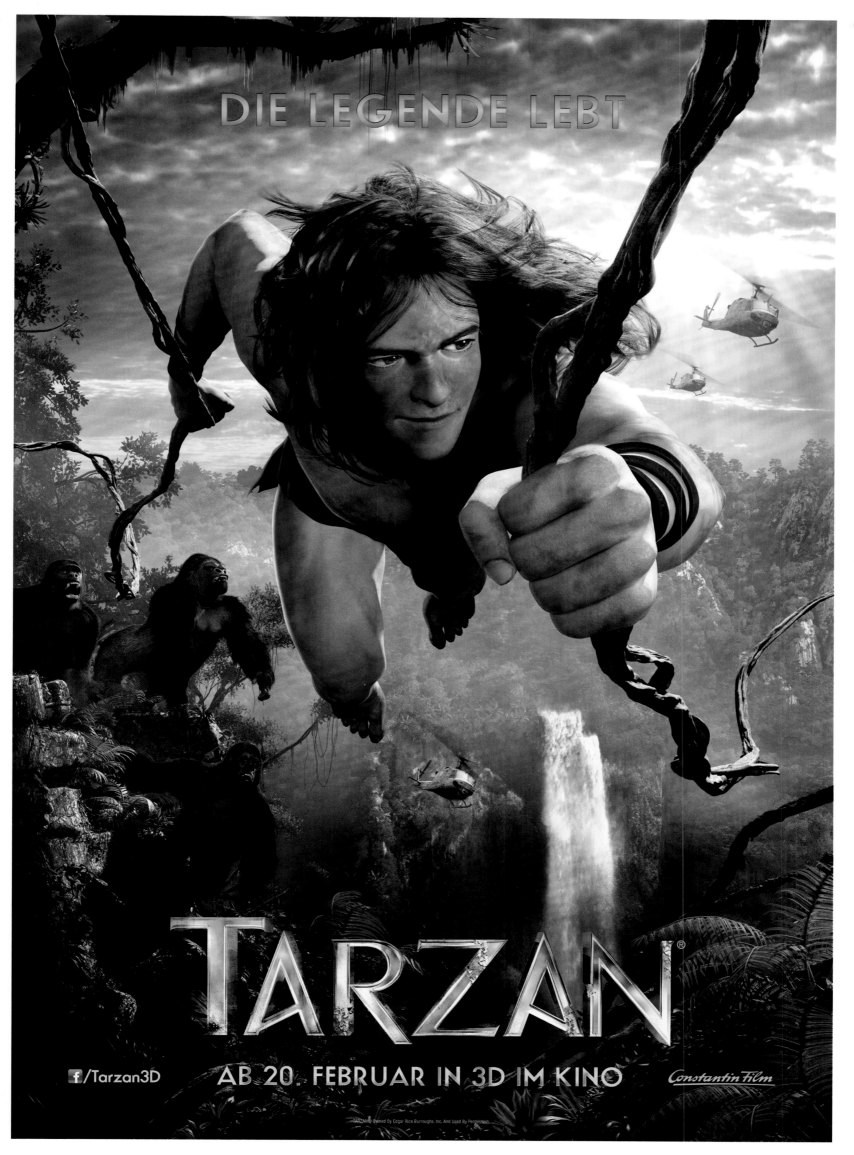

KELLAN LUTZ

Kellan Lutz has played gods (Poseidon) and demi-gods (Hercules), but his brawn wasn't seen onscreen in *Tarzan* 3D, which required his voice and movement for motion-capture animation as the Tarzan film franchise achieved another milestone in cinematic media.

Kellan Christopher Lutz was born March 15, 1985 in Dickinson, North Dakota, to Bradley and Karla Theesfeld Lutz, a middle child of six brothers and one sister. The family relocated to Arizona when he was 14, where he graduated from Scottsdale's Horizon High School. Summers were spent working on his grandparents' Iowa farm.

Lutz moved to Los Angeles to study chemical engineering at Chapman University, enrolled in acting classes, and worked as a shirtless greeter at Abercrombie & Fitch. He was soon on the cover of an Abercrombie & Fitch catalog, photographed by Bruce Weber. Lutz made his television debut in a small role on the soap opera *The Bold and the Beautiful* in 2004, and was cast as a series regular in the HBO series *The Comeback* (2005), starring Lisa Kudrow.

He was in Africa filming the HBO Iraq War mini-series *Generation Kill* (2008) (which starred fellow future screen Tarzan, Alexander Skarsgård) when he received a request to audition for the role of lead Edward Cullen in the film *Twilight* (2008), based on the best-selling books by Stephenie Meyer. Unable to make the appointment, he was instead cast as Edward's older vampire brother Emmett Cullen in the blockbuster film series, a career-making role.

Lutz has since appeared in varied fare including the horror remakes *Prom Night* (2008) and *A Nightmare on Elm Street* (2010), heroic fantasies *The Immortals* (2011) and *The Legend of Hercules* (2014), and *The Expendables 3* (2014) with Sylvester Stallone.

The 6'1" Lutz retains representation by Ford Models, and has appeared in high-profile campaigns for Levi's Jeans and Calvin Klein, making him the second Calvin Klein model (after Travis Fimmel) to play Tarzan. He teamed with designer Danny Guez of Dylan George to launch his own clothing line, Abbot + Main (named for the intersection of streets near his Venice, California, home), and also tinkers with inventions, two of which he has patented.

SPENCER LOCKE

Spencer Locke was already an experienced motion capture actor when she was cast in *Tarzan* 3D, having played lead in the children's animated horror movie *Monster House* (2004), for which she earned an Annie Award nomination.

Born September 20, 1991, in Winter Park, Florida, Locke dreamed of a showbusiness career from early childhood. She enrolled in acting classes, and began booking commercials in Orlando. By age 11, her budding career inspired her family's move to Los Angeles, where she began auditioning for film and television roles.

Locke made her film debut in James L. Brooks' romantic comedy *Spanglish* (2004), and booked recurring roles on *Ned's Declassified School Survival Guide* (2005) and *Phil of the Future* (2005). She played K-Mart in the *Resident Evil* films, based on the popular video game and produced by Constantin. Additional credits include roles on television shows, among which are *Without a Trace*, *Cold Case*, *NCIS*, and *Hawaii-Five-O*, and a recurrent role as Travis's girlfriend Kylie on *Cougar Town*.

Opposite top: While visiting her father, Jane gets lost in the jungle, finding strange perils.

Opposite bottom: Kellan Lutz's actions were captured by 56 cameras.

Top right: Fragments of an ancient meteor hidden in Tarzan's jungle prove an irresistible lure to outsiders hoping to tap it as a source of energy.

Bottom left: Spencer Locke and Anton Zetterholm enact Tarzan and Jane's first meeting at age 14.

Bottom right: Ape actors trained in primate movement portrayed the gorillas that live with—and battle—Tarzan.

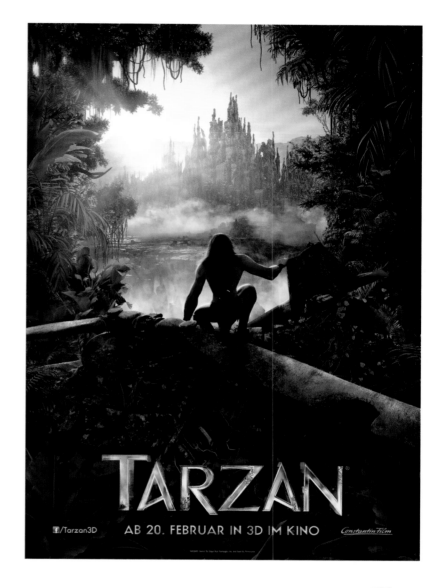

THE LEGEND OF TARZAN *2016*

After a decade in England living as John Clayton III, Lord Greystoke, with his wife Jane (Margot Robbie), Tarzan (Alexander Skarsgård) is asked to return to the Congo as a trade emissary of Parliament—as part of a plot by sinister Belgian Captain Leon Rom (Christoph Waltz).

Producer Jerry Weintraub was the driving force behind restoring Tarzan to the big screen in 2016. Weintraub began his entertainment career as a talent manager and concert promoter before transitioning into film and television. He won three Emmy Awards in seven nominations, and shepherded several big-budget film franchises (including *Karate Kid* and the *Oceans 11* trilogy) into a series of hits.

In June 2003, Jerry Weintraub Productions and Warner Brothers retained John August to script a new interpretation of the ape man's legend. December 2006 brought the news that Guillermo Del Toro was attached to direct, with John Collee now scripting. By September 2008, Stephen Sommers was slated to helm and co-script with Collee—the picture was compared to the *Pirates of the Caribbean* film franchise.

Sommers left the project, and Craig Brewer and Adam Cozad were hired to write separate scripts in May 2011; by June, Brewer was attached to direct the film from his script. In late 2012, David Yates, director of the final four Harry Potter films, was contracted, and remained in the director's chair with Alexander Skarsgård as his—and Weintraub's—choice for Tarzan. "Tarzan needs muscles, but it's more a leaner, longer, more vertical modern man than the square-jawed stereotype we're used to," commented Yates of his choice.

Christina Hendricks, Jessica Chastain, and Emma Stone were all considered for the role of Jane Porter, which was eventually awarded to Margot Robbie, following her breakout performance in *The Wolf of Wall Street* (2013). Yates' summary of the character in *USA Today* was that: "She's a really strong, assertive, beautifully knowledgeable, very sexy modern woman who can more than look after herself."

Warner Brothers postponed the film in early 2013, striving to lower the proposed budget, before resuming pre-production by the year's end. Principal photography began June 3, 2014 at Warner Brothers Leavesden Studios in the United Kingdom and other locations, and wrapped October 3, 2014. Two shuttered hangars at an airplane factory were dressed as jungles, with real running water, trees, and foliage in the 200-yard long soundstages. Yates and crew relied on computer-generated imagery to give the setting an unprecedented scope, and provide animals that posed no danger of running amok on set.

The storyline transposes the dynamic of the typical Tarzan tale. "It's almost the opposite of the classic tale, where it's about taming the beast," Skarsgård told Brian Truitt of *USA Today*. "This is about a man who's holding back and slowly as you peel off the layers, he reverts back to a more animalistic state and lets that side of his personality out."

The cast is heavy with Academy Award-nominated actors: Samuel L. Jackson (nominee, *Pulp Fiction*) and Christoph Waltz (winner, *Inglourious Basterds, Django Unchained*) joined the cast as historical figures—human-rights activist George Washington Williams and Belgian military Captain Leon Rom; Djimon Hounsou (nominee, *In America, Blood Diamond*) plays Chief Mbonga; John Hurt (nominee, *Midnight Express, The Elephant Man*) and Jim Broadbent (winner, *Iris*) also co-star.

Warner Brothers, Village Roadshow Pictures, and Jerry Weintraub Productions co-produce with Dark Horse Entertainment and Riche Productions. Sadly, Weintraub died on July 6, 2015, at his Santa Barbara home, before seeing the final product of his 12-year quest. The film is dedicated to his memory.

"This is a massive film but with so much integrity and so much character. It was an unbelievable experience."
– Alexander Skarsgård, *The Herald*, August 7, 2015

ALEXANDER SKARSGÅRD

As the son of an award-winning actor, Alexander Skarsgård's drama career might seem pre-ordained, but after early childhood success, he withdrew from acting to focus on other pursuits and reassess his life path, before returning to the profession as an adult.

Alexander Johan Hjalmar Skarsgård was born August 25, 1976 in Stockholm, Sweden, the oldest son of actor Stellan Skarsgård and his wife My, a medical doctor. He made his film debut at age seven, as Kalle Nubb in *Åke och hans värld* (*Åke and His World*). At 13, he played the lead in *Hunden som log* (*The Dog That Smiled*). Afterward, he took a sabbatical from acting to focus on his education and compulsory military service.

In 1996, Skarsgård enrolled in Leeds Metropolitan University in England for a semester (for which he was later awarded an honorary degree), and followed this with a semester studying theater at Marymount Manhattan College in New York. He resumed acting upon his return to Sweden.

Vacationing in Los Angeles, he secured a U.S. talent agent and the role of Meekus with Ben Stiller in *Zoolander* (2001). Skarsgård continued working in Sweden and auditioning in the U.S. until his breakthrough as Sergeant Brad "Iceman" Colbert in the HBO mini-series *Generation Kill* (2008), based on Evan Wright's book about a U.S. Marine Corps battalion in the Iraq War, for which he mastered an American accent.

His next big role was the vampire Eric Northman in HBO's *True Blood* (2008–14). Skarsgård appeared in *Battleship* (2012) as the older brother of Taylor Kitsch, who portrayed Edgar Rice Burroughs' second-most-famous character in Walt Disney's *John Carter* (2012). In 2013, Skarsgård participated in the Walking With the Wounded fundraising challenge, trekking to the South Pole with England's Prince Harry, actor Dominic West (who played the *John Carter* villain, Sab Than), and wounded soldiers. The group reached the Pole on December 13.

Following the December 9, 2015 release of *The Legend of Tarzan*'s first publicity photos of Skarsgård and Robbie, and the film's trailer, Skarsgård's Internet Movie Database (IMDB) Starmeter ranking jumped from 435 to number one, with Robbie at number two, up from 34. The film ranked number five on IMDB for the week.

Left: Alexander Skarsgård's Tarzan returns to Africa after a decade living in England as Lord Greystoke.

Opposite: Tarzan and Jane (Alexander Skarsgård and Margot Robbie) face peril in the African jungle in the first live-action Tarzan film of the 21st century.

MARGOT ROBBIE

Margot Robbie's career-making turn as Naomi Lapaglia, Leonardo Dicaprio's mistress-turned-second-wife in Martin Scorsese's *The Wolf of Wall Street* (2013) skyrocketed her to the top of many producers' most-wanted list as Hollywood's reigning "It" girl. *Tarzan* producer Jerry Weintraub compared Robbie's allure and talent to his former acquaintances, Grace Kelly and Marilyn Monroe.

Margot Elise Robbie was born July 2, 1990 in Dalby, Queensland, Australia, population 12,000. She and her three siblings were raised by their mother, a physiotherapist for special-needs children; her father and grandparents were farmers on the Gold Coast.

Robbie attended Somerset College, where she participated in drama, and moved to Melbourne to pursue acting after graduation. There she made her film breakthrough in the low-budget Aash Aaron films *Vigilante* (2008) and *I.C.U.* (2009), and won the role of Donna Freedman on the popular soap opera *Neighbours* on a three-year contract (2008–11). Her performance garnered two Logie Award Nominations for Most Popular New Female Talent (2009) and Most Popular Actress (2011).

Robbie took acting classes to master an American accent while working 17-hour days on the soap. Five days after her *Neighbours* contract ended, she moved to Los Angeles. One month later, she had been cast in the period drama *Pan Am* (2011), as runaway bride and stewardess Laura Cannon.

Robbie appeared in *About Time* (2013) as Rachel McAdams' competition for Domhnall Gleeson, then submerged herself in her *Wolf of Wall Street* role by imitating the New York accent of a close friend she had known since childhood. The part earned Robbie the Breakthrough Award at the Australians in Film awards dinner in October 2014 and Britain's 2014 Empire Award as Best Female Newcomer.

Wall Street was followed by *Focus* (2015), with Robbie playing a con artist opposite Will Smith, and *Z for Zachariah* (2015) with Chiwetel Ejiofor and Chris Pine in an end-of-the-world scenario. Robbie also appears in the coveted role of DC Comics villainess and sometime Joker's girlfriend Harley Quinn in *Suicide Squad*.

"[Jane is] in no way a passive partner to Tarzan. She's a really strong, assertive, beautifully knowledgeable, very sexy modern woman who can more than look after herself."

– David Yates, *USA Today*, December 11, 2015

TARZAN AND JANE *2016*

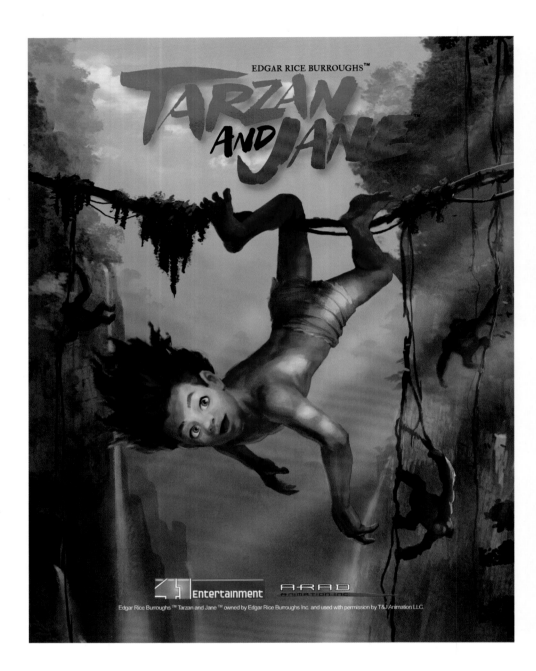

Tarzan and Jane is a Netflix computer-animated children's series that features the young Tarzan's adventures after he has been located in the African jungle and returned to contemporary England to attend boarding school.

Tarzan attempts to fit in with the ways of man, aided by his new friend Jane. They team up to solve mysteries and crimes, especially those with an environmental or conservation angle.

Executive Producer Avi Arad (Arad Entertainment), former CEO of Toy Biz, chief creative officer of Marvel Entertainment, and former founder, CEO and chairman of Marvel Studios, licensed the property for development by 41 Entertainment, with animation by ARC Productions. The initial eight-episode season debuts in 2016.

"With the Netflix Original Kids TV Series featuring Tarzan and Jane, we expect a re-emergence of Tarzan's universal appeal to kids and young adults."

\- James Sullos, President, Edgar Rice Burroughs, Inc.

THE WORKS OF EDGAR RICE BURROUGHS

NOVELS AND STORIES

Tarzan of the Apes
The Return of Tarzan
The Beasts of Tarzan
The Son of Tarzan
Tarzan and the Jewels of Opar
Jungle Tales of Tarzan
Tarzan the Untamed
Tarzan the Terrible
Tarzan and the Golden Lion
Tarzan and the Ant Men
Tarzan, Lord of the Jungle
Tarzan and the Lost Empire
Tarzan at the Earth's Core
Tarzan the Invincible
Tarzan Triumphant
Tarzan and the City of Gold
Tarzan and the Lion Man
Tarzan and the Leopard Men
Tarzan's Quest
Tarzan and the Forbidden City
Tarzan the Magnificent
Tarzan and "The Foreign Legion"
Tarzan and the Madman
Tarzan and the Castaways
Tarzan: The Lost Adventure
Tarzan and the Tarzan Twins
A Princess of Mars
The Gods of Mars
The Warlord of Mars
Thuvia, Maid of Mars
The Chessmen of Mars
The Master Mind of Mars
A Fighting Man of Mars
Swords of Mars
Synthetic Men of Mars
Llana of Gathol
John Carter of Mars
At the Earth's Core
Pellucidar
Tanar of Pellucidar
Back to the Stone Age
Land of Terror
Savage Pellucidar
Pirates of Venus
Lost on Venus
Carson of Venus
Escape on Venus
The Wizard of Venus
The Land that Time Forgot
The People that Time Forgot
Out of Time's Abyss
The Moon Maid

The Moon Men aka Under the Red Flag
The Red Hawk
The Mucker
The Return of the Mucker
The War Chief
Apache Devil
The Bandit of Hell's Bend
Beware! aka The Scientists Revolt
Beyond the Farthest Star
The Cave Girl
The Deputy Sheriff of Comanche County
The Efficiency Expert
The Eternal Lover aka The Eternal Savage
Forgotten Tales of Love and Murder
The Girl from Farris's
The Girl from Hollywood
I Am a Barbarian
Jungle Girl aka The Land of Hidden Men
The Lad and the Lion
The Lost Continent aka Beyond Thirty
The Mad King
The Man-Eater
Marcia of the Doorstep
Minidoka, 937th Earl of One Mile Series M
The Monster Men
The Oakdale Affair
The Outlaw of Torn
Pirate Blood
The Resurrection of Jimber Jaw aka Elmer
The Rider
You Lucky Girl!

TARZAN FEATURE FILMS AND SERIALS

Tarzan of the Apes (1918)
The Romance of Tarzan (1918)
The Revenge of Tarzan (1920)
The Son of Tarzan (1920)
The Adventures of Tarzan (1921)
Tarzan and the Golden Lion (1927)
Tarzan the Mighty (1928)
Tarzan the Tiger (1929)
Tarzan the Ape Man (1932)
Tarzan the Fearless (1933)
Tarzan and His Mate (1934)
The New Adventures of Tarzan (1935)
Tarzan Escapes (1936)
Tarzan and the Green Goddess (1938)
Tarzan's Revenge (1938)
Tarzan Finds a Son! (1939)
Tarzan's Secret Treasure (1941)
Tarzan's New York Adventure (1942)
Tarzan Triumphs (1943)
Tarzan's Desert Mystery (1943)

Tarzan and the Amazons (1945)
Tarzan and the Leopard Woman (1946)
Tarzan and the Huntress (1947)
Tarzan and the Mermaids (1948)
Tarzan's Magic Fountain (1949)
Tarzan and the Slave Girl (1950)
Tarzan's Peril (1951)
Tarzan's Savage Fury (1952)
Tarzan and the She-Devil (1953)
Tarzan's Hidden Jungle (1955)
Tarzan and the Lost Safari (1957)
Tarzan's Fight for Life (1958)
Tarzan's Greatest Adventure (1959)
Tarzan the Ape Man (1959)
Tarzan the Magnificent (1960)
Tarzan Goes to India (1962)
Tarzan's Three Challenges (1963)
Tarzan and the Valley of Gold (1966)
Tarzan and the Great River (1967)
Tarzan and the Jungle Boy (1968)
Tarzan's Deadly Silence (1970)
Tarzan's Jungle Rebellion (1970)
Tarzan the Ape Man (1981)
Greystoke: The Legend of Tarzan, Lord of the Apes (1983)
Tarzan and the Lost City (1998)
Disney's Tarzan (1999)
Tarzan & Jane (2002)
Disney's Tarzan II (2005)
Tarzan (2013)
The Legend of Tarzan (2016)

TARZAN TELEVISION MOVIES AND SERIES

Tarzan and the Trappers (1958 pilot)
Tarzan (1966–68)
Tarzan, Lord of the Jungle (1976–84)
Tarzan in Manhattan (1989 pilot)
Tarzan (1991–94)
Tarzan: The Epic Adventures (1996–97)
The Legend of Tarzan (2001–2003)
Tarzan (2003)
Tarzan and Jane (2016)

ADDITIONAL FILMS

The Lad and the Lion (1917)
The Oakdale Affair (1919)
Jungle Girl (1941)
The Land That Time Forgot (1975)
At the Earth's Core (1976)
The People That Time Forgot (1977)
John Carter (2012)

FURTHER READING

The 52 Tarzan features and telefilms and seven television series are this book's primary source material. The franchise's century-long history includes many thorough examinations of Edgar Rice Burroughs' work, its screen adaptations, and the men and women who contributed to the ape man's legacy, all of which were helpful in researching *Tarzan on Film*.

Two previous books on Tarzan film history are recommended for additional background on the subject. Gabe Essoe's *Tarzan of the Movies* (Citadel Press, 1968) was the first book on ape man cinema, and is a classic in the field. David Fury's *Kings of the Jungle: An Illustrated Reference to "Tarzan" on Screen and Television* (McFarland, 1994) takes a different approach and is also fascinating reading. Fury also authored two definitive biographies through his Artists Press imprint, *Johnny Weissmuller: Twice the Hero* (2000) and *Maureen O'Sullivan: "No Average Jane"* (2006).

Film historian Jerry L. Schneider has authored several works detailing the history of the franchise via ERBville Press, including *Edgar Rice Burroughs and the Silver Screen, Volume 1: The Silent Years, 1917–1929* (2002); *Volume 4: The Locations* (2003); and *Edgar Rice Burroughs Tells All* (2007). Schneider continues his research on the unpublished manuscripts for Volumes 2 and 3, which he generously shared.

For biographical information on Edgar Rice Burroughs, and his dealings with film industry personnel, see Irwin Porges' *Edgar Rice Burroughs: The Man Who Created Tarzan* (Brigham Young University Press, 1975); Robert W. Fenton's *The Big Swingers* (Prentice-Hall, Inc., 1967); and John Taliaferro's *Tarzan Forever: The Life of Edgar Rice Burroughs, Creator of Tarzan* (Scribner, 1999).

Howard E. Green's *The Tarzan Chronicles* (Hyperion, 1999) is the primary source for Walt Disney Studios' *Tarzan* feature.

There are numerous biographies and autobiographies of Tarzan film principals. Sports journalist Mike Chapman profiled Herman Brix and Glenn Morris, respectively, in his Culture House Books *Please Don't Call Me Tarzan* (2001) and *The Gold and the Glory* (2003).

Additional works include Connie J. Billips' *Maureen O'Sullivan: A Bio-bibliography* (Greenwood Press, 1990); Brian J. Bohnett's *The Remarkable Enid Markey* (Mad Kings Publishing, 2012); Gene Freese's *Jock Mahoney: The Life and Films of a Hollywood Stuntman* (McFarland, 2014); Rafer Johnson's *The Best That I Can Be* (with Philip Goldberg, Doubleday, 1998); Denny Miller's *Didn't You Used to Be What's His Name?* (To Health With You Publishers, 2004); James H. Pierce's *The Battle for Hollywood* (House of Greystoke, 1978); Marci'a Lincoln Rudolph's *My Father, Elmo Lincoln, the Original Tarzan* (Fulton County Historical Society, 1999); Woody Strode's *Goal Dust: An Autobiography* (with Sam Young, Madison, 1990); Jerry Vermilye's *Buster Crabbe: A*

Biofilmography (McFarland, 2008); Johnny Weissmuller, Jr.'s *Tarzan: My Father* (with William Reed and W. Craig Reed, ECW Press, 2002); Karl Whitezel's *Buster Crabbe: A Self-Portrait* (1997); and Henry Wilcoxon's *Lionheart in Hollywood* (with Katherine Orrison, Rowman & Littlefield, 1991).

Online resources include the websites ERBzine (Bill Hillman); ERBmania (Bruce Bozarth); The John Carter Files (Michael Sellers); Johnny Weissmuller (Geoff St. Andrews); Tarzan Movie Guide (Matt Winans); Tarzan.cc (Sky Brower); American Film Institute (AFI); Internet Broadway Database (IBDB); and Internet Movie Database (IMDB).

Two very thorough investigations of the subject include film historian Rudy Behlmer's articles in *American Cinematographer*, January and February, 1987 (MGM's *Tarzan* films), and May and June 1989 (MGM's *King Solomon's Mines*). Bill Groves covered the jungle lord franchise's history on the small screen in *Television Chronicles #8*, January 1997.

Newspaper and magazine resources include the following, in alphabetical order: *8mm Collector*; *Classic Film Collector*; *Classic Images*; *Cue*; *Exhibitor's Trade Review*; *Film Daily*; *Filmfax*; *Hollywood Citizen-News*; *Hollywood Reporter*; *Hollywood Tribune*; *Life*; *Los Angeles Herald-Examiner*; *Los Angeles Sentinel*; *Los Angeles Times*; *MGM News*; *Morgan City Daily Review*; *Motion Picture Herald*; *Motion Picture News*; *Moving Picture World*; *New York Evening Post*; *New York Times*; *New Yorker*; *Newsweek*; *OC Chronicle*; *Photoplay*; *Starlog*; *Stars and Stripes*; *Time*; *Universal Weekly*; *USA Today*, *Variety*; *Wall Street Journal*; and *Washington Post*.

Quotes from the above are cited within the text (some reviewers were uncredited); loglines that are not credited are from the films' press materials.

ACKNOWLEDGEMENTS

Thanks, foremost, to author Edgar Rice Burroughs for creating Tarzan of the Apes and bringing a century of imaginative entertainment to billions of people (by Sol Lesser's generous estimate) worldwide. The staff of Edgar Rice Burroughs, Inc., who continue to oversee the ape man's domain also have my enduring gratitude: Jim Sullos, Cathy Wilbanks, Janet Mann, Willie Jones, and Tyler Wilbanks were indispensable in making this book a reality.

To Nikki Edwards, Laura Price, Nick Landau, Alison Hau and the team at Titan Books, a hearty thanks for your patience and stamina and willingness to go on this journey with me. I am thankful to Casper Van Dien for graciously providing this book's foreword and giving us an inside glimpse into the travails of a cinema ape man. Additional Tarzan film and television principals who took the time for my interviews or to simply socialize over the years include Joanna Barnes, Eve Brent, Herman Brix, Vanessa Brown, Kim Crosby, Ron Ely, Angela Harry, Joe Lara, Denny Miller, Miles O'Keeffe, Gordon Scott, Johnny Sheffield and Woody Strode. Behind-the-camera contributors include Kevin Brennan, John Carl Buechler, Stanley Canter, Bayard Johnson, Dennis Steinmetz, and Brian Yuzna. Also of note are the past and contemporary Tarzan film researchers, whose efforts are detailed in the "Further Reading" section.

Tarzan fans are an inordinately generous lot, and I am indebted to several of them for their assistance in securing resources. Thanks to Lance Chemello, Mike Conran, John Field, Bob Garcia, Danny Proctor and Rudy Sigmund for volunteering items from their collections. "Tarzan Paul" Westman, Martin Smiddy, Rob Donkers and Ron De Laat are always willing to help with my online queries, as are too many more fans to name, so I thank you all.

I am also grateful to archives like that of the University of Louisville's Ekstrom Library Special Collections, and the Margaret Herrick Library in Beverly Hills, and for the diligent staff who provide researchers with immeasurable help on a daily basis.

Documentarians Alain d' Aix and Nathalie Barton (*Investigating Tarzan*, 1997); John Rust (*Tarzan: Silver Screen King of the Jungle*, 2004); Al Bohl and Alison Bohl DeHart (*Tarzan, Lord of the Louisiana Jungle*, 2012); and Robert de Young (*Gone With the Ape*, 2016) have all increased my understanding of the Tarzan film phenomenon, and I appreciate their hard work.

Thanks to *The Legend of Tarzan* producer Scott Cherrin; Allen Bohbot, Anna Kislevitz, and Karisa Williams of 41 Entertainment; Melanie Hahn and Gero Worstbrock of Constantin Film; Margaret Adamic and Maxine Hof of Walt

Left to right: Jim Sullos, President, and Cathy Wilbanks, Archivist, of Edgar Rice Burroughs, Inc.; and author Scott Tracy Griffin at the Edgar Rice Burroughs, Inc. convention booth.

Disney Studios; and Steven Fogelson, Mark Narmore, and Judy Ross of Warner Brothers for their help in securing images.

I am grateful to Fred Clark, the late editor of *Cinefantastique* and *Femme Fatales* magazine, who encouraged me to get the story behind the films, and provided me with some of my first professional assignments. Thanks also to my English teachers at Starkville Academy, Janet Wasson, Sharon Nobles, and Vicki Warren, and to the late Beth Jones at Millsaps College for always encouraging my writing pursuits.

Thanks to my parents, Jesse and Sarah Griffin, my late grandparents, Homer and Zetta Denson, siblings Mark and Sarah, brother-in-law Jerry, niece and nephew, Kathleen and Ryan VanBeber, and the whole Buxton clan for their contributions to my life. Longtime friends Todd Clayton, MD, Paul Wilson, USAF (ret.), and Rob Greer also deserve a shout-out, as does Don Wither, whose recollections and recommendations were of abundant help

Finally, special thanks to Southern California writer and editor Lisa Gordon Wither, without whose patience and mentoring none of this would have been possible. Love you!